WE KNOW YOU CAN PAY A MILLION

WE KNOW YOU CAN PAY A MILLION

INSIDE THE DARK ECONOMY OF HACKING AND RANSOMWARE

ANJA SHORTLAND

Profile Books

First published in Great Britain in 2026 by
Profile Books Ltd
29 Cloth Fair
London
EC1A 7JQ

www.profilebooks.com

Copyright © Anja Shortland, 2026

1 3 5 7 9 10 8 6 4 2

Typeset in Sabon by MacGuru Ltd
Printed and bound in Great Britain by
CPI Group (UK) Ltd, Croydon CR0 4YY

The moral right of the author has been asserted.

All rights reserved. Without limiting the rights under copyright reserved above, no part of this publication may be reproduced, stored or introduced into a retrieval system, or transmitted, in any form or by any means (electronic, mechanical, photocopying, recording or otherwise), without the prior written permission of both the copyright owner and the publisher of this book.

Profile Books takes seriously the responsibility of defending our authors' copyright. No part of this book may be used or reproduced in any manner for the purpose of training artificial intelligence technologies or systems (including but not limited to machine learning models and large language models (LLMs)). In accordance with Article 4(3) of the DSM Directive 2019/790, Profile Books expressly reserves this work from the text and data mining exception.

A CIP catalogue record for this book is available from the British Library.

Our product safety representative in the EU is BGC Sustainability & Compliance, 7 avenue du Général Leclerc, Paris, 75014, France https://baldwinglobalconsulting.com/

Hardback ISBN 978 1 80522 454 9
Trade Paperback ISBN 978 1 80522 455 6
eISBN 978 1 80522 456 3

To Henry, Ellie and Cristina

CONTENTS

Introduction: The Business of Ransomware	1
1. Phreaks and Hackers	13
2. The World's First Ransomware Attempt	23
3. Idealists vs Mischief-makers	35
4. Operation Flyhook	51
5. The Missing Puzzle Pieces	63
6. CryptoLocker	81
7. A Masterpiece of Criminality	95
8. The Ransomware Ecosystem	105
9. Ransomwar	119
10. No More Ransoms?	137
11. Big Game Hunting	151
12. A Matter of National Security	167
13. In One Fell Swoop	185
14. Conti 'at War' with Costa Rica	197
15. The Lockbit Takedown	209
Conclusion: Big Money – Minimal Risk?	223
Acknowledgements	237
Image Credits	239
Notes	240
Index	281

INTRODUCTION

The Business of Ransomware

You know it will happen someday. The day your computer freezes. At first you hope it is a glitch or an enforced software update, but as you sigh with frustration and look up, one monitor after another blinks out around the office. Blank, blank, blank, blank, blank ... Restarting the computer returns you to the same dismal screen. And again. IT support is not picking up the phone. You wonder when you last backed up your spreadsheets. A colleague arrives late and breathless saying they had to hurdle over the access gate and computers across the company are down. *Please not us*, you think. *Please not today. Please don't let it be ransomware.*

This fragile hope quickly turns to despair when a ransomware gang claims responsibility for the outage.

Having computers and data files held for ransom is an existential threat for most organisations. Even in the best-case scenario the road to recovery runs through a tense phase of negotiation and months of stress, improvisation and overlong working hours to maintain essential services while IT specialists try to rebuild or recover the system, one file at a time.

If this hasn't happened to your organisation already, it's likely that it soon will. Ransomware has become a huge global business. According to a global expert survey in 2024, more than half of enterprises in the Americas, Europe and Asia

Pacific with a turnover exceeding $10 million experienced a ransomware attack in the previous twelve months. Sixty-three per cent of them faced ransom demands exceeding a million dollars. The median ransom payment made was $2 million.[1] Ransomware gangs have jointly raked in around a billion dollars in revenues a year since 2020.[2] But the true cost to the global economy – which includes the cost of responding to attacks and reconstruction afterwards, regardless of whether a ransom is paid – was estimated at around $57 billion for 2025 and is predicted to rise to over $200 billion by 2030.[3]

Attacks often have far-reaching consequences. When software, manufacturing, utilities or public services companies are disrupted, it's not only their own clients who suffer but everyone up and down their supply chains. Certain types of attack deliberately put lives at risk to heighten the probability of a quick and generous payout. Since the catastrophic 2020 attack on the Irish Health Service, which paralysed hospital care over a four-month period during the critical phase of the Covid-19 pandemic, healthcare has become a veritable hackers' playground.[4] Medical care has been severely compromised in hundreds of hospitals and health centres around the world as ransomware temporarily or permanently blocked access to medical records and diagnostic services. In-hospital mortality rates for Medicare patients in the US rose by around 35–41 per cent during ransomware attacks.[5] When criminals steal and leak sensitive information, the affected clients, staff, patients or students are exposed to the risk of further financial fraud and extortion. And however difficult data recovery might be, rebuilding a company's public image poses an even greater challenge.

So, when computers at Royal Mail's Worldwide Distribution Centre near Heathrow airport went down on 10 January 2023, everyone in the company held their breath. A 'cyber incident' was swiftly declared and post offices around the UK were told not to process any international packages.[6] As frustrated postal workers apologised to waiting customers, IT officers tried to get back into the system – to no avail. Eventually, panicked news arrived from a sorting office near Belfast in Northern Ireland. Their printers were out of control, ceaselessly spewing out notes with the message 'Lockbit Black Ransomware. Your data are stolen and encrypted …'[7] If true, Royal Mail – like countless companies before them – would be in for a long, rough ride. The timing was terrible: managers were already on the edge of despair. The company's revenues had collapsed when families reeling from the cost-of-living crisis cut back on sending letters and parcels in 2022. The workforce was tired and resentful after enduring successive waves of job cuts, aggressive restructuring and falling real wages. Customer relations were strained by a service that was getting slower and patchier, even as prices were rising. The trade union had called several strikes over the previous year, culminating in an unprecedented seven days of walkouts during the peak Christmas season. Mountains of undelivered cards and parcels stacked in sorting offices around the country seemed emblematic of a company hell-bent on self-destruction. A ransomware attack that further disrupted services would be the final straw for many small businesses, who might take their custom elsewhere or go under themselves.

LockBit Black – the criminal enterprise behind the Royal Mail attack – is just one of many well-known ransomware gangs. Developed by malicious coders and placed by dedicated infection teams, ransomware rapidly spreads through the victims' computer networks. Data files are either made illegible by an encryption program or transmitted to remote storage controlled by the criminals – or both. If victims choose to pay the ransom, the criminals may or may not help them to decrypt their data. If victims refuse to cooperate, they not only have to laboriously restore the encrypted data from backups (if they exist), but they must also cope with the potential consequences of the stolen data being sold or published. In addition, the culprits could well have left themselves a back door into the system for a future attack. Paying a ransom cannot guarantee safety or fast recovery, however. One is essentially relying on an honour code of thieves, trusting that they will deliver on their promises.

Royal Mail's management was advised that LockBit was a formidable adversary. The gang had been prolific in its attacks; by 2023 victims could draw on the experiences of hundreds of unlucky predecessors. There was no point in hiring external IT specialists to decipher the affected files. The LockBit encryption could not be cracked by outsiders, but the gang's decryption keys were deemed reasonably reliable. LockBit had consistently published the hijacked data of victims who refused to pay and had deliberately fed the juiciest data to journalists. LockBit operatives also applied pressure by contacting customers or suppliers listed on the stolen databases to tell them about the data leak. On the other hand, LockBit had built a reputation among victims for keeping its word regarding not publishing or selling ransomed data. With most of LockBit's operatives working from Russia, there was nothing that law enforcement could do to get the victim off the hook. Royal Mail faced a potent threat actor with a track record of delivering on their promises – both positive and negative.

But was Royal Mail really held hostage by the dreaded LockBit Black group, as the web address on the printouts from Northern Ireland suggested? Confusingly, the leader of the gang, who went by the alias LockBitSupp, initially denied all knowledge of the attack. It took several days before

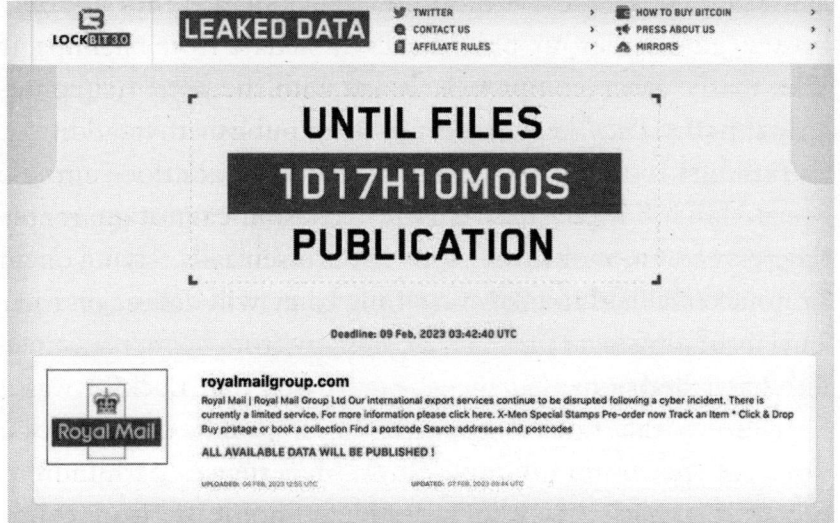

LockBit 3.0 leak site – Royal Mail web post, 7 February 2023

LockBitSupp tracked down the source of the infection and claimed responsibility. Then a Royal Mail representative tentatively began an online chat on LockBit's darknet website.[8] An operative named 'Lockbit 3.0' quickly responded and cut to the chase, posting a list of all the files taken from the company's servers and their first threat: 'Yes, don't delay. time is not playing in your favor. so far we have not reported the attack on our blog'. But making the attack public was an empty threat. The entire nation already knew that Royal Mail's parcel service had been paralysed by a Russian-linked cyberattack.[9]

Since Royal Mail forms part of the UK's critical national infrastructure, one might conclude that the crisis needed to be resolved as quickly as possible at whatever cost. However, paying large ransoms to criminals sheltered by hostile states is politically problematic and likely to encourage future attacks. Large companies that draw on public resources for financial assistance or practical help are therefore strongly encouraged by the authorities to play hardball with the extortionists. Like many other companies, Royal Mail decided to pursue a dual path. They kept the ransom option open while trying everything to contain and reverse the damage behind the scenes. Royal Mail followed a tried-and-tested tactic for hostage crises: the person communicating with the criminals was not a decision-maker so had to take everything back to the management. This insulating layer prevents a company from being pressured into hasty decisions.

Despite the LockBit operatives' frequent exhortations ('our patience is not infinite'), Royal Mail appeared to stall the process for nearly two weeks, fumbling the routine decryption process by which ransomware groups allow victims to upload a handful of encrypted files to test their restoration. Growing suspicious, Lockbit 3.0 wrote: 'Something tells me that you are bluffing and you are doing system recovery and want to get free decryption of critical files needed for recovery ... just pay for my work and get a decryptor within 5 minutes. You are making multi-billion-dollar profits from your business ... It's your greed that makes the people who are waiting for their packages suffer.'

In response, Royal Mail presented themselves as a loss-making company that could ill afford a sizeable payment: the attacker could easily Google recent newspaper reports. But LockBit 3.0 was neither convinced nor interested. On 25 January, the ransom demand was finally on the table: 'We want ... 0.5% of your revenue.' An hour later – after some pained squealing from the Royal Mail negotiator – LockBit 3.0 reiterated that they were not interested in the company's (lack of) profitability and pulled out a trump card: '0.5% of annual global turnover is much less than a 4% fine from your government', referring to the punitive fines that some governments levy on companies that neglect to protect sensitive staff, customer, student, supplier or patient data. Lockbit 3.0 spelled it out: '$80 million is 0.5% of your revenue, $640 million is 4% of your revenue. We are asking 8 times less than your state. In addition to this price you get a decrypt of your data.'

Lockbit 3.0 had based their demand on the global turnover of Royal Mail, though the damage related only to a much smaller, independently administered sub-group, Royal Mail International, with a turnover of $800 million. Applying LockBit's ransom rule would bring the price down to $4 million. For the next four days the exchange centred on who was trying to deceive whom over what was reasonable and affordable in the circumstances. LockBit reduced the demand to $70 million, but Royal Mail still stalled. The LockBit operative was truly perplexed: 'I always ask for a fair and adequate amount from each company, I do not ask for what the company cannot pay.'

But for Royal Mail, the negotiation was finished. Customers, suppliers and staff had been notified of the data breach and remedial action had been taken. A workaround had been found to move newly consigned parcels to their overseas destinations. The Worldwide Distribution Centre would eventually clear the backlog and a week or two more would not make a major difference to already disappointed customers. Preventing the publication of the stolen data was not deemed mission-critical: unlike other ransomware victims, Royal Mail did not hold super-sensitive personal or medical data.[10] They therefore did not respond to LockBit's escalating threats and demands. On 9 February, a final plaintive message arrived: 'Do you have any offer for me?' LockBit's operative wrote. Royal Mail maintained their silence.

Royal Mail took a principled stance in refusing to pay a

ransom, but it came at a huge cost to their business, staff and customers. The remediation bill for new hardware and software and for external expertise to recover data and harden the centre at Heathrow against future attacks came to £10 million. Overseas parcel deliveries were crippled for around six weeks and year-on-year business volume dropped by 5 per cent.[11] While this fall cannot entirely be blamed on the ransomware attack, it suggests that 0.5 per cent of turnover (if applied at the right level) is not an egregious amount to ask for a decryption key and the promise of data privacy. In late February 2023, LockBit duly carried out its threat of leaking technical, supplier and staff data, highlighting the most sensitive information – such as Royal Mail's disciplinary records.[12] So, once again, the organisation had to notify, reassure and protect those affected according to a complex legal protocol. Meanwhile, post office staff toiled to restore customer relationships, and the company eventually had to compensate postmasters for this additional effort and lost revenue.[13]

If the malware had spread further into Royal Mail or if LockBit 3.0 had started with a more realistic ransom demand, perhaps a deal would have been made. Every day around the world, governments, companies, critical infrastructure, NGOs, private individuals and charities are held to ransom by sophisticated malicious foreign actors in the same way: either pay up or suffer losses that are – normally – many times larger than the ransom demand.[14] This problem has taken on epidemic proportions since the early 2020s.

This book addresses four interlinked questions by telling the stories of the people, organisations and innovations that have created, fuelled and impeded the ransomware epidemic.

First, how did ransomware develop from a curiosity to a

minor nuisance, and then to a major national security threat? The first attempt to use malware to extract a ransom, in 1989, failed spectacularly. We will meet the many innovators who prepared the ground for cyberextortion to become a profitable business – as well as their adversaries working to enhance computer security, who tried everything to stop them in their tracks. The early history of ransomware is a fascinating arms race between these well-matched sides. However, digital threat extortion also spawned numerous businesses that limit the economic impact of attacks on victims. This powerful private safety net probably generated a false sense of security in the early days of ransomware's development: if organisations had felt the full effects of ransomware earlier, they might have been less content with decades of laissez-faire government policy.

Second, what are the implications of normalising ransom negotiations and payments? Many deals with foreign organised crime syndicates look surprisingly similar to standard business transactions. Victims receive prompt and helpful customer service from criminals. It's all 'please' and 'thank you' and 'BTW, the site you guys made is beautiful. Better support than normal companies :)'.[15] Ransomware has created its own ecosystem, where legal companies compete to provide help and advice to smooth the ransomware settlement process. Yet, every ransom that is paid entrenches the problem more deeply. Every victim that throws money at extortionists to solve their personal problem creates incentives for online criminals to further develop their capabilities and threaten deeper and broader harm to society. Do we need a fundamental legal reform outlawing ransom payments or the services facilitating them? The stories in this book explore how such a policy would impact on both victims and perpetrators and explain why governments have been reluctant to take this drastic step.

Third, what else can be done to deter ransomware gangs from their callous business? Law enforcement has tried to police the internet for nearly its entire history. There are exciting stories of 'hackers and gendarmes' – where the marauders eventually ended up behind bars – but many more where prolific criminals went scot-free. Great innovation, experimentation and coalition-building have gone into designing ever more spectacular strikes against criminals and their virtual infrastructures, yet international political tensions have created a geography of cybercrime that makes it extremely difficult to identify and hold the criminals to account. What's more, as we delve deeper into the cybercrime underworld to meet the perpetrators, the good versus evil narrative becomes more difficult to sustain. Those who become cybercriminals are often constrained in their life choices by nationality, location, poverty, youthful naivety and/or a neurodiverse personality type that may make a more conventional, legal path unattractive or impossible to pursue. The threat of imprisonment does not reduce crime if it traps great coding talents in the criminal underworld.

Fourth, how can we make computer users less vulnerable to security breaches and cyberextortion? Instinctively, most of us wish to outsource cybersecurity to computer experts and law enforcement. However, this strategy fails all too often. Ransomware gangs make no secret of the fact that they deliberately target system users to get into their victims' networks. As the Akira ransomware gang put it: 'The most vulnerable point is the human factor and the irresponsibility of your employees, system administrators, etc ...'[16] In the following chapters, you will learn about the manifold ways in which ransomware gangs exploit the trust, collegiality or curiosity of telephone and computer users. Cybercrime thrives on the fundamental tension between the excitement, convenience and efficiency of open communication and the vulnerability this creates. Ransomware will continue to be extremely profitable until individuals, organisations and governments make safer choices. In examining the options and difficult trade-offs involved in balancing risk and security, this book aims to empower you to choose a stance that seems right for you.

Threat extortion and the economic and moral grey zone between the legal economy and the criminal underworld have been the focus of my academic research since 2010. Studying the resolution of piracy, kidnapping and art theft I discovered a truly fascinating group of intermediaries who specialise in making trades with the underworld to save lives and recover lost treasures.[17] Several of the entrepreneurs, experts, advisors and military and police officers dealing with these crimes became friends and collaborators over the years as formal research interviews turned into long-running two-way conversations. Together we watched and analysed the astonishing rise of ransomware since 2013. We observed and discussed how companies adapted to this ever-evolving crime and quizzed rising entrepreneurs about their novel ideas for containing it. We came to realise that some business practices and laws (inadvertently) helped ransomware thrive, and raised these concerns in industry conferences, research papers and in the 2021 Ransomware Task Force that sought to shape policies and galvanise governments into long-delayed action.

This book therefore tells the history of ransomware from the unique vantage point of an independent observer inside its ecosystem. It focuses on the human experience of malware producers, victims, law enforcers, politicians and the many innovators and service providers who – deliberately or unwittingly – became actors in the ransomware business. Chapters one through five cover the period from 1989 to 2012 with its various precursors to proper ransomware. Attempts at digital threat extortion were risky and barely profitable until certain technological and social preconditions were met. In chapters six through eleven – starting in 2013 – ransomware is unleashed. It mutates in a constant cat-and-mouse game with private sector responders and becomes ever more sophisticated. When rogue governments employ ransomware as a weapon of war, risks to lives and livelihoods escalate beyond what the private sector can absorb or manage. In chapters twelve through fifteen – from 2020 onwards – governments become involved in the fight against what is now a full-blown ransomware epidemic, and the promising beginnings of a concerted fightback can be seen.

On your journey through this history of ransomware, you will meet a few surprisingly relatable villains, some rather fishy superheroes and everything in between. Both the legal and criminal parts of the ransomware world are inhabited by clever, passionate and hopeful individuals pursuing their dreams and ambitions in challenging circumstances – though often with astonishingly little regard for the welfare of others. So come and meet the intriguing cast of characters who shaped this world. And where better to start than with the dreaded 'hackers'?

1

Phreaks and Hackers: The Magic of Exploration

For most people, the word 'hacker' immediately conjures up an image of a hooded figure silhouetted against the blue light of their computer screen: anonymous, dangerous, malicious. But what does cyberspace look like from their point of view? When we get to know hackers as individuals and see how society promotes or blocks their hopes, talents and ambitions, we may be surprised.

The first hackers saw themselves as playful explorers, inventors and co-creators of an exciting anarchic space. To them, hacking did not have negative connotations but was a term of praise; it simply referred to the skill of finding ways into networks without permission. The term 'hacker' in the context of computing first appeared in an MIT university magazine in 1963 to describe a range of capers, where students used MIT computers to make free telephone calls.[1] People on the edges of society – those with health conditions and physical disabilities, the neurodiverse and the lonely, the troubled and the poor – had been the first to discover telephone networks as social spaces in the 1960s.

Analogue telephone systems used audio signals to indicate the status of phone lines and send commands to establish and break connections. Each button on a phone's dial or touchpad produced a sound of a specific frequency, and this signal was used by the phone company to place the call. Some of the first hackers in the telephone networks were blind children who had sought entertainment in the clicks, hums and whistles of their home telephones. The brightest realised that there was a whole world to explore. By trial and error, they found that if they produced the correct frequencies without using the dial or touchpad, the operator was oblivious that a connection had been made and therefore did not bill for the call. Long-distance call charges could be avoided by initially calling a toll-free (800) line, interrupting that call with a 2,600Hz signal, and then playing the audio signals for the desired connection, leaving the operator unaware of the sneaky substitution.[2] Those who learned to do this kind of 'magic' with their phone became known as 'phreaks' – a blend of the words phone, free and freak.[3]

One such was Josef Engressia (aka Joybubbles), who had perfect pitch and taught himself to whistle any access code. His ability to place free telephone calls completely changed his life.[4] Cassette players with sound recordings of the correct frequencies, or electric organs, enabled the less musically gifted to access the telephone systems too. A little plastic bosun's whistle that came as a gift with Cap'n Crunch breakfast cereal became famous for emitting the key 2,600Hz frequency that controlled the long-distance trunk lines in the system.[5] Phreaks also discovered that some lines could be used for improvised conference calls. Isolated youngsters roaming the wires hung out there to meet like-minded oddballs who did not mind shouting their greetings over taped announcements or high-pitched notes.[6] Seeking to enlarge their community, a group of blind adolescents approached the ham radio enthusiast and telephone engineer John Draper to build them multi-tone devices that became known as 'little blue boxes'. Draper accepted the challenge and became hacking royalty under the handle 'Captain Crunch'.

Making free long-distance phone calls at a time when this was a luxury for a privileged few was an obvious objective – even if it was just for the joy of hearing a recorded voice message in a foreign language. But hackers with greater know-how could sow confusion and have much more fun – especially if they knew how to make their calls and activities untraceable. The most skilled phreaks would show off by attaching expensive phone bills to rivals' numbers, switching the connections between, say, an off-licence and a temperance society to snigger over the confused or heated conversations that developed, or disconnecting some lines altogether.[7] All this was too enjoyable to leave to blind kids and social misfits – suddenly everyone wanted a little blue box.

For the technically minded, building blue boxes was an interesting challenge. The Apple Computer Company founders' first business venture is a wonderful illustration of the fun, craft and obsessiveness that techy kids brought to overcoming the engineering problems of cheating the telephone system. In 1971, an article in *Esquire* magazine alerted the young Steve Wozniak to the possibility of using high-frequency audio signals to tap into phone companies' long-distance operating systems.[8] It sounded unbelievable at first – but utterly thrilling. Wozniak's high-school friend Steve Jobs got fired up at once and rushed to join in. Wozniak had already worked out how to sneak into the technical research library at Stanford University's Linear Accelerator Center. There, nestled in the reference collection, Wozniak and Jobs found a book on international telephone technical standards. It not only confirmed the set-up but listed all the relevant frequencies. The elation is still palpable in Wozniak's retelling of the story:

> I froze and grabbed Steve and nearly screamed in excitement that I'd found it. We stared at the list, rushing with adrenaline. We kept saying things like 'Oh, shit!' and 'Wow, this thing is for real!' I was practically shaking, with goose bumps and everything. It was such a Eureka moment. We couldn't stop talking all the way home. We were so excited. We knew we could build this thing. We now had the formula we needed![9]

Their first attempt at hijacking the telephone system failed, however. Their analogue tone generators were too imprecise to hit the narrow frequency range recognised by the system. It was back to the drawing board for Wozniak. As he progressed through his degree at Berkeley, however, he learned to build a digital circuit that gave them the necessary stability and accuracy. Allegedly, it worked perfectly the first time the irrepressible young developer tried it: 'I swear to this day,' says the man who would one day design the revolutionary Apple I and Apple II computers, 'I have never designed a circuit I was prouder of.'[10]

Or in Steve Jobs's words:

> [It was] illegal I have to tell, but in spite of that we were so fascinated ... It was the magic of the fact that two teenagers could build this box for a hundred dollars' worth of parts that could control hundreds of billions of dollars' worth of infrastructure in the entire telephone network in the whole world ... That's a powerful thing![11]

Jobs and Wozniak's little blue box

Interestingly, with that superpower feeling came a sense of responsibility. The phone phreaking and later the computer hacking communities developed their own social norms. A true 'hacker' was an intellectually curious person who wanted to explore, play with and learn how phones, computers and connectivity worked. This was a noble pursuit. Phreaks felt that pilfering airtime did not significantly harm the huge telephone monopolies. For hackers, making a copy of a manual, a top-secret piece of code or a database to analyse at leisure was the aim of the game. Having a specific piece of information was a trophy, the proof that a hack had succeeded. But anyone selling such a trophy was considered a criminal – not a hacker. Downloading thousands of credit card numbers – just because you could – was fine. Using them to make purchases was not. Discovering a clever way to guarantee winning a radio phone-in contest for a Porsche was a blast – but it was not OK to repeat the trick until one ran out of friends to pick up the prizes.

While the 'little blue boxes' were ingenious and occasionally admirable pieces of engineering, selling user-friendly gadgets to moneyed outsiders so that they could surf the telephone networks without intellectual effort destroyed the secretive community of phreaking enthusiasts. A moral panic ensued about the phone lines being thrown wide open to thieves, fraudsters, vandals and organised crime.[12] With public opinion on their side, the telephone companies started to hit back. Mere possession of a blue box was made a criminal offence and could land its owner in prison for up to two years in the United States, where the base penalty for criminally negligent manslaughter is twelve months in prison.[13] Wozniak and Jobs narrowly avoided arrest when they managed to convince two police officers that their little blue box (which they had clearly just used in a nearby payphone) was a badly out-of-tune music synthesiser. As phreaking became riskier, a new avenue opened up for technical wizards to pursue the wild pleasure of exploration: electronic circuit boards, personal computers and networked systems.

The forerunner of the internet was the Advanced Research Projects Agency Network (ARPANET), started in the 1960s with funding from the US defence budget. Its initial purpose was to link computers at the Pentagon to their research centres via dedicated phone lines. However, the fear of a Soviet missile attack during and after the Cuban Missile Crisis made it advisable to build a decentralised network for exchanging data that could not be taken out by tactical strikes on key nodes. From the late 1960s, university departments across the US scrambled to join and enhance the network. Researchers puzzled out how to share data between computers using different operating systems without overwhelming the existing telephone infrastructure. They invented email communication and virtual discussion groups.[14] Built on open principles to facilitate the exchange of information, early internet and computer innovation thrived on total information sharing. Anyone who could (somehow) access a university computer or build their own terminal to communicate with the ARPANET could be part of this buzzing community.

In 1975, a group of Californian technology enthusiasts founded the Homebrew Computer Club. They were proud to call themselves hackers. They met to trade parts and discuss protocols, code and design ideas for new soft- and hardware. As their first newsletter reported, 'questions, comments, reports, info on supply sources etc, poured forth in a spontaneous spirit of sharing'.[15] No wonder that Steve Wozniak first presented the Apple I prototype to this peer group – complete with an open-source code that everyone was free to explore and improve upon.[16] Through the 1980s, however, the world of information technology became increasingly commercialised. Code and blueprints for building hardware that had once been freely shared became private property and were turned into user-friendly products for those who could afford them. By the time the Homebrew Computer Club broke up in 1986, its members had founded twenty-three computer companies – including Apple. Hackers were no longer welcome, although in 1997 Steve Jobs still traced Apple's success back to his hacking origins:

> If it hadn't been for the blue boxes, there would have been no Apple. I'm 100% sure of that. Woz and I learned how to work together, and we gained the confidence that we could solve technical problems and actually put something into production.[17]

Such leniency would no longer be afforded to others. The rising computer aristocracy engaged the press and lawmakers in an increasingly bitter fight against trespassers. The public was already worried about the new technology and could easily be led to take umbrage at the inexplicable pranks of boisterous and socially awkward outsiders. The media, law enforcement and the political establishment came to view hackers with suspicion and sometimes outright alarm.[18] The 1983 film *WarGames* – with a plot about a teen hacker who almost starts World War III by accidentally triggering a switch in a military supercomputer – is a great illustration of rising anxieties about runaway technology.

The Computer Fraud and Abuse Act of 1986 adopted a very broad definition of computer crime and gave the US authorities sweeping punitive powers to pursue the newly defined trespassers on what had previously been common land. This stance was underlined by the aggressive pursuit of computer-related 'theft' and 'intrusion' by FBI agents, who took it personally when their organisation was made to look stupid by teenage pranksters. Many of the tools that today's cybercriminals use to gain access to our computer systems were developed in the subsequent cat-and-mouse game between computer systems administrators, security engineers, law enforcement and the various kinds of outlaws who either did not feel they needed permission to explore and use computer systems for their own ends, or simply had nowhere else to go.

Unfortunately, many first-generation computer enthusiasts did not get a free choice about which side of the law they would be on. First, although the early internet economy rewarded talent, it was far from a true meritocracy. University education – especially in maths, physics, engineering and computer science – was the domain of the privileged. Alumni had social networks to give them a head start to found companies and sell their products – and a safety net if their enterprises went belly up. Outsiders had to be exceptionally talented, socially skilled and committed to be accepted into their groups and to raise funds to start their own businesses.

Second, law enforcement was subject to its own (class and ethnic) biases. Wozniak and Jobs smooth-talked themselves out of an arrest and a possible prison term. Their blue box adventure became an amusing anecdote, a footnote in the foundation story of Apple. Working-class hackers and people of colour often had to make a detour through courts and prisons after a brush with the law.[19]

Third, many gifted hackers simply did not respect the restrictive laws that favoured the interests of the privileged over the freewheeling norms of a community of sometimes awkward social outsiders. Computer technology attracts many neurodivergent people who can experience strong emotional responses to unfairness and tend to push back hard when anyone seeks to exclude them for opaque, nefarious or self-serving reasons.[20] Some of these people ended up trapped in the underworld, unable to feel at home in corporate environments.

In addition to these factors, it was sometimes unclear what exactly constituted a crime and how lawyers would interpret a clever provocation. In the next chapter we meet someone who got very creative in exploring that question. The AIDS Trojan, coded by Joseph L. Popp, Jr, was the world's first attempt to hijack data for ransom. However, Popp's scheme is probably better understood in the context of the robust pranks of the hacking community than as a profit-motivated crime.

2

The World's First Ransomware Attempt: The 1989 AIDS Trojan

Billed as the grandfather of ransomware, Joseph L. Popp, Jr, was a Harvard-educated evolutionary biologist who studied the reproductive behaviour of baboons.[1] He had been hired by the African Medical and Research Foundation and as a consultant to the World Health Organization (WHO) to advise on the biggest public health crisis of the day: the AIDS epidemic. But Popp was unhappy with his organisations' AIDS education programmes. Public discourse and pedagogy mostly presented AIDS as a disease of social minorities: homosexuals, haemophiliacs and people of colour. What about white heterosexual males as vectors of transmission? Outspoken and occasionally abrasive, Popp was not particularly well liked at the WHO, and when his application for a permanent post was turned down, he hatched an audacious plot to embarrass his WHO peers, teach a parable on sexual behaviour and raise money for alternative AIDS education programmes all at the same time.[2]

Since the mid-1980s, there had been fascinating parallel discourses in the worlds of computing and AIDS research.[3] The nascent internet brought both opportunity and danger: every connection to an unknown computer presented a risk. Computer scientists therefore commonly used HIV/AIDS as a metaphor to illustrate issues of trust and uncertainty in a world where people freely exchanged digital information with others. The term 'computer virus' was coined precisely because it helped naive new PC users to understand a complex problem and its solutions.[4] When exchanging electronic data we need to trust not only the organisations to which we connect, but also everyone else that the partner organisation has ever connected with.[5] As the British software developer Karl Feilder graphically put it: 'We are exchanging digital fluids with each other every day as we experience the bump and grind of unlimited Internet access. We're hooked on our daily cyber orgasms. But are we practising safe computing? Are we wearing virtual condoms?'[6]

In 1989, Popp turned this idea around: he would use computer software as a vehicle for AIDS education. His campaign would deliver a sharp wake-up call to people who considered themselves invulnerable and acted against clear advice. He wanted to shock his victims, but he had no intention to destroy them. When his victims received the message that their computer had been 'infected', he wanted to render their PCs unusable and their saved work inaccessible until they paid him a fee. But on receipt of payment, he would restore their computers to perfect working order. Popp thereby invented ransomware: malware that seizes the victim's computer hard drive until the originator of the malware is paid to unlock it.

Popp needed a payment mechanism that was accessible to victims but made it difficult for the police to track him. He followed the lead of countless other rogues who hide their dealings behind shell companies in Panama. In early December 1989, he incorporated PC Cyborg Corporation with a few untraceable foreign-sounding names as company directors.[7] Popp's sham company then hired a Panamanian PO box, where his victims could send their bankers' drafts, cashiers' cheques or international money orders.

With these basics covered, the next hurdle was to install the malicious code in the targets' computers. Popp wanted to maximise the impact of his campaign and planned to infect thousands of computers. At this time, the internet was still in its infancy and its main users were computer experts based in research, educational and military establishments. Many were on the lookout for emerging threats and therefore far from ideal victims for software-based mischief. Communication by 'electronic mail' was just beginning to be marketed to a wider public, but network subscribers could only send plain text messages to each other using slow, noisy and expensive dial-up connections. Businesses and families communicated by telephone, letter or fax. The best way to smuggle code into other peoples' computers was for the users to voluntarily install and run the malicious program. Popp therefore had to copy his code on to floppy disks and place them directly into the hands of his intended victims.

But why would someone insert an unsolicited floppy disk from an unknown source into their machine – the computer equivalent of casual sex? Popp had to rouse the recipients' curiosity with some legitimate-sounding cover story to smuggle the hidden destructive payload into their computers. Computer scientists call this double-layered program a 'Trojan Horse' or 'Trojan' after the mythical Greek hero Odysseus' wily strategy to enter and destroy the city of Troy by hiding his crack troop of soldiers inside a gift horse. Popp hoped that his victims would find it difficult to resist taking a sneaky peek at an interactive questionnaire promising to assess their personal risk of exposure to the HIV/AIDS virus and advise them how they might minimise the risk. HIV/AIDS was a hot topic in the late 1980s; deaths and new infections were rising rapidly, and the newspapers were full of AIDS-related celebrity obituaries. Users who answered his thirty-eight questions would receive plain-speaking advice like 'Buy condoms today when you leave your office' or 'Danger: reduce the number of your sex partners now.'[8]

How could Popp anonymously give away thousands of floppy disks to targets likely to be responsive and sufficiently affluent to pay his fee? He decided to post them. Anticipating a significant failure rate, he produced 20,000 disks and printed an accompanying letter and licence agreement for each. He had two main target groups in mind: colleagues at the WHO, the organisation that had dismissed his work and ideas; and the arrogant 'masters of the universe' of the business world, whom he found socially irresponsible and voracious in their appetites. Popp used the name of one of the (untraceable) directors of PC Cyborg Corporation to buy several business mailing lists – including that of *PC Business World* – as well as the mailing list of delegates to the 1988 Fourth International AIDS Conference in Stockholm.[9] Next, his 20,000 envelopes needed stamps. He couldn't use the more convenient franking machines because these were registered by the Post Office. The packages would then have to be taken in batches to individual postboxes – preferably some distance away from his home address.

Popp's targets would receive and start using the disks at different times. Ideally, they would also follow his exhortation to 'share this program diskette with other people so that they can benefit from it too'.[10] It was therefore important that the alarm was not raised too quickly. Popp decided that the malicious code needed to lie dormant for a considerable period, just as an HIV infection takes time to develop into full-blown AIDS. The program therefore included a counter, registering each reboot of the computer. The encryption stage was only activated when the counter reached its maximum at 90, buying Popp valuable time to maximise his haul.

And finally, Popp relied on his victims' curiosity, inattention and opportunism to further push the parallel with AIDS. Every floppy disk was mailed out with a letter containing installation instructions warning that the software on the disk was proprietary: 'If you use this diskette you will have to pay the mandatory licence fee.'[11] The small-print licence agreement on the back of the letter explicitly warned users that installing the AIDS Information program without payment would 'adversely affect other programs' and their PC 'would stop functioning normally'.[12] On installation, the computers displayed and printed out an invoice for $189 to be sent to PC Cyborg Corporation. But just like the fever following the initial HIV infection, this slightly unusual symptom looked like it could be safely ignored. Popp's counter lulled his victims into a false sense of security. Ninety reboots later, the program was activated. The screen locked and affected users were once again asked to pay their licence fee of $189 for 365 individual user applications or $378 for lifetime use of the program. In return they would receive a 'renewal' of their subscription and an automatic, 'self-installing diskette' to return their computer to full working order 'within minutes'.

Hiding the extortionary nature of his software in plain sight made Popp's scheme arguably legal. Yet Popp suspected that US courts would take a dim view of his money-spinning AIDS education campaign. However, the UK (a) did not have a law to explicitly forbid this kind of software and (b) lots of bright and argumentative barristers would happily (if expensively) discuss the matter at length in a court of law. After all, the users were told what to expect and were expressly agreeing to a bad deal by pressing enter at the installation stage. Popp covered his backside by pruning all US addresses from his mailing lists, leaving the UK as the primary target. He flew to London to post his floppy disks, hoping to obscure his trail and save on postage.

When Popp was ready to launch his *AIDS Information – Introductory Diskette* on 11 December 1989, he was thousands of dollars in the red from funding their production and distribution. He had completed a mammoth intellectual and logistical task in taking his novel idea from conception to launch. He would send a vital message to the world, and to break even, he only needed a small percentage of his targets to pay.

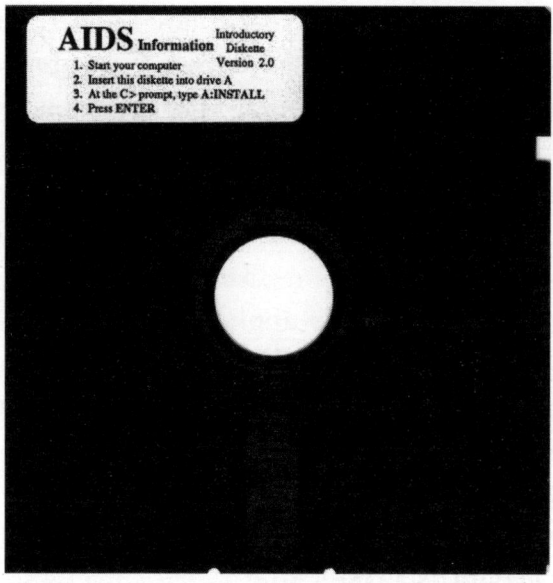

A floppy disk carrying the first ransom malware

With the benefit of hindsight, including subscribers to *PC Business World* among his mailing list of targets for the dodgy disks was not the most brilliant aspect of his plan. Computer experts had already created multiple online discussion forums to collect and disseminate information about emerging threats and opportunities. In the UK, the Compulink Information eXchange (CIX) connected 3,000 technically savvy specialists: engineers, software authors and journalists. The first message describing the AIDS questionnaire as a 'Trojan' appeared on CIX on the evening of 12 December. A cautious recipient had suspected mischief, analysed the code and found the hidden malware. His warning was confirmed by another CIX user half an hour later.

The UK's computer elite thus knew within thirty hours of their posting that the AIDS disks should not be used under any circumstances, negating Popp's time delay idea. Over the next week around forty new messages a day relating to the AIDS Trojan were placed on CIX, as more users reported receiving disks. However, the CIX message board was only available to subscribers. Lacking an early warning system, the AIDS research community did not weather the crisis nearly as well. Hundreds of recipients installed Popp's program, chucked away the printed invoice for $189 and grumbled about the banal and predictable results of their AIDS questionnaires. But after a few days, lurid rumours started to circulate about an AIDS Trojan carrying a potentially fatal computer virus that would render PCs unusable. Some researchers overreacted to the news and took drastic remedial action: they wiped their hard drives clean. One Italian AIDs organisation lost ten years' worth of irreplaceable data as a result.[13]

Meanwhile, CIX community members calmly analysed the code and debated the legality of the scheme under UK law. As the experts dug deeper into the program, they noticed – and admired – its striking similarity to the AIDS virus. Here was an opportunistic bug that insidiously infected the host's system and then lay dormant to encourage further infections before finally revealing its true nature.[14] The WHO researchers who had destroyed their own files and databases failed to see the irony, however. They reported the attempted blackmail and data losses to the police. The idea that the boot might be on the other foot – i.e. that they had tried to cheat Popp out of his licence fee – never occurred to them, or indeed the police. Eager to prove themselves, Scotland Yard's tiny new Computer Crime Unit – established in 1985 – jumped on this high-profile opportunity. They threw everything they had at what they saw as a clear-cut case of extortion and criminal damages. It would be the biggest investigation of its kind for many years to come. There was an early breakthrough when the normally uncooperative Panamanian authorities swiftly revealed everything they knew about PC Cyborg Corporation. This was highly advisable: the US government had tired of Panama's dictator General Noriega and decided to depose him in mid-December 1989. After a lightning-quick military operation, American troops were on patrol in Panama City and could personally knock on the door of any bureaucrat who dragged their feet.

As his plot unravelled, Popp went to pieces. The US invasion of Panama had destroyed his business model by severing all communication with his victims. Popp had not intended to paralyse global AIDS research. Yet his entire community was fretting about the AIDS Trojan: everyone knew someone who had lost precious data and had taken to staring forlornly at their blank file directory. And to top it all, the British police were on a manhunt. Popp started to behave strangely. On Christmas Eve 1989, he was arrested at Schiphol Airport in Amsterdam after writing a bizarre message on a fellow passenger's suitcase.[15] When the Dutch police searched him, they found paperwork connecting him to PC Cyborg Corporation in Panama and called the Computer Crime Unit in London. The delighted detectives rushed in. Although the muddled

THE WORLD'S FIRST RANSOMWARE ATTEMPT

Popp was released to his parents in Ohio, the FBI kept him under surveillance. When detectives searched his home, they found incontrovertible evidence that Popp was the originator of both the code and the AIDS diskettes. Scotland Yard had their man and prosecutors in Cleveland decided to extradite him to the UK to stand trial.

And yet, Popp had actually done very little harm. Help was soon at hand for around a thousand people who had installed the program – except of course for those who had rashly taken matters into their own hands and wiped their hard drives clean. An editorial advisor of the periodical *Virus Bulletin*, Jim Bates, became briefly famous when he published a detailed technical report dissecting Popp's Trojan on 1 January 1990. Bates poured scorn on Popp's code – albeit with typical British understatement. While he praised the conception as 'cunning and extremely devious', the code itself was 'quite untidy'. Clearly, the programmer had been 'unfamiliar' with basic programming tools and 'not particularly well schooled' in writing programs. The encryption was 'simple': Popp's program only changed the filenames on the PC's root directory and made them invisible to a non-expert. This was easy to reverse.[16] The only thing that took Bates serious amounts of time was scouring the disk for the incurable virus that the AIDS connection suggested. Bates had to prove a negative. It took him hundreds of hours of painstaking forensic investigation before he was ready to stand up and state categorically that 'there is definitely no virus present in the code.'[17] Unlike the real AIDS virus, Popp's puzzle had been solved and Bates would freely share the remedy. *Virus Bulletin* provided two addresses to which every affected reader could call, write or fax their address for a free floppy disk containing Bates' AIDSOUT and CLEARAIDS code, which removed the Trojan and restored all encrypted files.[18]

Remanded in Brixton prison, Popp's mental health deteriorated. His US defence team argued against the charge of attempted blackmail, since Popp's software licence had correctly spelled out the terms and conditions of the deal. There was no criminal damage, because the files in the root directory were only encrypted, not corrupted. Popp's friends went on the record saying that he had always wanted to donate any profits to AIDS education. But Popp's UK defence team's main line of argument was that he should be released on account of diminished responsibility. As if to prove his poor mental state, Popp's behaviour became ever more erratic. British newspapers reported with fake concern that the crazy culprit had taken to wearing a cardboard box on his head or a condom on his nose.[19] He also tried to protect himself from 'radiation' and 'microorganisms' by putting curlers in his beard.[20] Eventually he was moved to a psychiatric unit and, much to the disappointment of the diligent detectives who had assembled reams of evidence against Popp, the judge declared him mentally unfit to stand trial.[21] The intriguing legal question underlying Popp's scheme – whether he was an extortionist or whether his supposed 'victims' had tried to cheat him out of his intellectual property right – was never examined. Popp was returned to the US, where he faded into relative obscurity. Unfortunately, he never published his own version of events. His life was sadly cut short by a car crash in 2006.

Joseph Popp left a triple legacy. The first – and most treasured – was a bird and butterfly sanctuary in Oneonta, NY, that he founded with his partner, and which was lovingly (if somewhat eccentrically) managed by her in his memory after his untimely death.[22] Second, Popp's antics exposed that the British legal system was far behind the curve when it came to defining crime in an era of expanding computer use and increasing connectivity; the UK's Computer Misuse Act of 1990 was rushed through Parliament to plug a wide range of legal gaps and loopholes. Popp's third legacy was the blueprint for ransomware he bequeathed to later generations of hackers. Initially, however, the spectacular failure of Popp's attempt to take data hostage and extract a payment served as a cautionary tale to anyone interested in computer-based extortion. Many further innovations were still required to make ransomware a profitable criminal business model and help aspiring extortionists to operate untraceably from the shadows.

3

Idealists vs Mischief-makers: Insecurity by Design

Joseph Popp's ransomware escapade would have run much more efficiently if he had been able to send his malware straight to his victims' computers, rather than laboriously printing and mailing out thousands of letters and floppy disks. If he had waited another five or ten years, Popp would probably have tempted curious computer users to install and run his rogue program with a carefully crafted email instead. Through the 1990s, more and more firms, governments, educational establishments, media corporations and research institutes saw the power and possibilities of networked information technology and rushed to connect their organisations to the internet. Many found that the flipside of the convenience and commercial potential of connectivity was a vulnerability to hackers' pranks and cybercrime. Every internet-facing computer terminal and email address is an entry point into a network. How did we get ourselves into this precarious situation? What trade-offs between connectivity and security were considered when designing the internet?

In this chapter we delve into a small social bubble of scientists working on computer networks who were obsessed with frictionless communication – to the exclusion of everything else. They succeeded spectacularly in their objective but were horrified when the real world intruded into their utopia. By the time the world of commerce and state bureaucracies had adopted their fabulous invention, the opportunity for secure design had been well and truly missed. All that could be done was to retrofit some basic security measures, patrol the perimeters and recruit law enforcement to punish trespassers.

When reading the research papers of the 1970s and 1980s and talking to people involved in the development of the early internet, it quickly becomes clear that its founders were primarily technological problem solvers. Academic researchers hardly looked outside their cosy peer group as they built their very own 'nerds' paradise'.[1] Their work was undertaken in a spirit of exploration, competition and collegiality. For most, the objective was to supercharge their academic research by sharing data and ideas with like-minded enthusiasts anywhere in the world, to enhance the educational experience of their students, and to minimise boring admin tasks. Most looked for peer recognition and career advancement, although a few saw novel commercial opportunities and sought to monetise their inventions. Ultimately, they all participated in a red-in-tooth-and-claw global competition between ideas and protocols, in which there could only be one winner. The history of the internet is not just the story of the winning protocol but of the thousands of dreams, ideas and systems that were sacrificed to make room for ever better solutions. It is easy to see how in the headlong rush for the elusive top prize in efficient communication, other design considerations fell by the wayside.

'I never saw the point of computer security ...' said Roland Rosner, the former principal scientific officer at the Rutherford Laboratories as we delved back into his work of the 1970s. His attitude was typical of the researchers who created the early 'ethernets' and brought the World Wide Web into being. Rosner's calling and mission in life was to create a seamless global computer communication network.[2] When he started his career in information technology, government departments, companies and academic researchers were still punching information on to cards or loading it on to magnetic tapes. These were carried or posted to their colleagues or a central storage facility. Yet, the success of telephony and radio suggested that if the data could be converted into an appropriate format, it could be sent by cable between computers – and over long distances using unoccupied bandwidths on the telephone and radio networks. Those at the technology frontier designed themselves modulator-demodulators (quickly shortened to 'modems') that converted digital information to signals that could be transmitted through the existing communication infrastructure.

The next set of problems concerned packaging, addressing and delivering the data to its intended destination (and only there), and unpacking it at the receiver's end.[3] First, one needed a reversible protocol to encode the data for transfer. Second, given the limitations of the ropey infrastructure, data had to be chopped into manageable chunks for transfer (called packets). Third, network operators needed clear and comprehensive information to ensure that each packet reached the correct address – even if they took different routes to their destination. Some packets would get lost altogether – a problem that would need to be recognised, communicated and rectified by resending. Finally, the recipients had to make sense of a potentially huge pile of packets from various senders as they came helter-skelter through their digital front doors. Imagine receiving thousands of puzzle pieces, with no idea of how many puzzles they belong to or whether they are complete, and having to assemble them all as fast as possible for an impatiently waiting boss.

This was truly revolutionary, cutting-edge research. University laboratories, major corporations and forward-thinking government departments all wanted a slice of the action. Research funding poured into groups all over the world to create small experimental networks. As a result, many organisations ended up with multiple incompatible and inefficient systems: one for the library, another for HR and payroll, further ones for teaching, research data collection and analysis.[4] To reap the full benefits of information technology, different networks needed to freely exchange data with each other – ideally using a common, non-proprietary protocol. This was not just a technological challenge but primarily a social one. Individual professors, ministers and business leaders had huge personal and economic stakes in their own systems. The very idea of a common standard (other than their own) made group leaders gloomy and anxious. As IT enthusiasts they got very excited about dialling into phone lines and viewing, downloading or sharing data with far-flung colleagues, but giving up a personal vanity project, grant income and way of life was often too steep a price. Moreover, commercial enterprises wanted to sell their software and services, not give them away for free.

The alternative to adopting a common protocol was to write code that would render files from one system legible in another. If one knew what system a partner's ethernet used to encode the information, it was possible to decrypt the gibberish that arrived in one's own modem. Over time, more and more conversion codes were written and made widely available. However, given the slow speed of transmission and limited computing power, endlessly translating information back and forth left academic collaboration in the UK far behind the US universities that had developed their network protocols collaboratively ever since connecting to the Pentagon-initiated ARPANET. Hoping

A man's world: the Minister for Industry Kenneth Baker visiting the Rutherford Appleton Laboratory in 1981

to emulate the freewheeling cooperative spirit that ultimately resulted in the development of the InterNet protocol, Rosner invited the key IT people in British universities and research councils to two- or three-day 'Network' meetings. He would win their hearts and minds over wine, canapés and the latest research. As Britain's IT elite forged closer connections with like-minded, generous people engaged in similar academic endeavours, they too realised that adopting a joint protocol would lead to a step-change in academic productivity.

On April Fool's Day 1984, Rosner's team launched JANET, the UK's Joint Academic Network. The acronym had been chivalrously retrofitted to flatter the Network's secretary, who had helped Rosner jolly (or bully) even the most reluctant bigwigs towards cooperation. As Rosner had envisaged, JANET used a common protocol to connect sixty British universities and research councils at what now seems an astonishingly lame transmission rate of 9.6kbits/sec.[5] It was seen as a triumph of its time.

Yet, Rosner himself had already resigned from his post. His ultimate goal was global communication – and unfortunately the JANET protocol was incompatible with and well behind the cutting-edge technology used by universities in the US and international commerce.[6] Returning from a trip to the United States in 1989, Rosner astonished his former collaborators in the Network by proposing to bin his (and their) work of the previous decade and switch JANET to the InterNet protocol. Unable to convince most of his shocked colleagues to take this drastic action, Rosner once more created a coalition of the willing. His Bloomsbury Computing Consortium raised significant funding for workstations that communicated directly with the American university network.[7] Soon the technology did the talking for him. Staff and students queued to use the Consortium's brand-new InterNet workstations, excitedly clutching handwritten lists of URLs that had been urgently recommended by their peers. They felt as if they had been sucked through wormholes into the most fascinating parallel worlds. Never mind the snail's pace at which the grainy pictures materialised on their screens – many became instant converts and advocates for the InterNet protocol.

In October 1993, JANET became a casualty of what computer engineers have termed the 'Protocol Wars': new computers at British universities adopted the InterNet protocol as their default setting.[8] This started a long transition period. Given the paucity of British university funding, it took almost a decade to flush the outmoded protocols and equipment out of the system.[9] For those working at the technology frontier, however, the single protocol for the World Wide Web transformed academic research and teaching: fuelling innovation, solving mission-critical problems and spreading ideas. However, it did not take long for universities to realise that there was a flaw in their utopian vision of an open, accessible network: people, or more specifically, inquisitive students. University computer officers like Robert Clark – Rosner's colleague in the Network meetings – were soon fully occupied with guarding their IT systems. It did not come as a shock to them that their fellow IT enthusiasts had highly questionable attitudes towards intellectual property, copying and generously sharing software.[10] Clark's first genuine misgivings came when he was shown what he sourly described as 'a crude pornographic animation' on a Mac 128K floppy disk that was doing the rounds. 'I was amazed – it never occurred to me that the new technology could be used for such things.'[11] More worryingly, the porn and various nonsense that university students (and some staff) downloaded from the internet often carried viruses that threatened the integrity of entire networks. Even worse, it was clear that some students had turned into hackers. Moving freely within and between university networks, they played practical jokes, slowed down legitimate processes, defaced websites and occasionally caused significant damage. As Clark bitterly complained on the letters pages of newspapers and learned journals: the godfathers of JANET had inadvertently birthed 'cybervandals' and 'cyberstalkers'.[12]

With innovation proceeding apace, governments struggled to create rules fast enough to keep up with the latest cyber-capers and crime. Universities deliberately kept their own rules vague ('... bringing the college into disrepute ...') so they could discipline culprits in their student bodies.[13] However, they struggled to get outside support from a technologically backward police and judiciary. Clark recalled an incident where multiple colleagues took umbrage at a spate of rude emails apparently sent by a group of female students. At a hastily convened disciplinary meeting the young women were cooperative but mystified; they had done nothing of the sort. After a thorough investigation Clark's team found that a single user had been in a university computer room at all the times the offending missives had been sent. In due course – with the assistance of a brawny security officer – Clark apprehended the culprit who had been impersonating the women: it was likely the UK's first citizen's arrest of a suspected cybercriminal. The police subsequently found so much incriminating material on his floppy disks that Scotland Yard's Computer Crime Unit decided to pursue the case. To their frustration, however, the puzzled elderly magistrate failed to grasp the gravity of the case and threw it out.

Sporadic and unpredictable law enforcement did little to deter would-be offenders from hacking into any network, computer or account they were interested in. The earlier disregard for security in creating the protocol was now coming back to haunt network administrators. Safety features had to be retrofitted. Someone needed to permanently keep an eye on suspicious activity and individual users had to take personal responsibility for securing their accounts. Creating pop-up screens asking for a password to log into a network or an account was a sensible first step. However, learning (and teaching users) what makes a secure password is still an ongoing process. For the longest time, 12345 was a popular choice. Other users took the idea of a password literally, choosing a memorable word or name. Hackers therefore wrote programs that used an electronic dictionary to guess such passwords; given enough attempts, they were often able to find a match. In 1991, the computer security consultant Alec Muffett decided to point out this problem by making a program called Crack freely available to download from his website.[14] Crack was presented as a tool for IT security personnel to check the safety of the accounts in their system. It worked with the central file that stored all the system users' passwords. The output was a list of user accounts with their cracked passwords, so the administrator could individually contact those who had chosen unwisely. Yet nothing stopped criminals from downloading Crack from Muffett's website and beating the computer officers to their job.

Muffett's publicity stunt triggered an incensed reaction from network administrators. Clark testily complained about the irresponsibility of so-called security consultants who handed free breaking and entering tools to cybervandals in the newspapers' letters pages.[15] One day, there was a knock on Clark's office door and a charismatic young man with wild red hair and a flamboyant floral-print shirt introduced himself: 'I'm Alec Muffett: do you hate me?' It was as if the glamour of Silicon Valley had suddenly landed in a classically drab London university back office.* Muffett pointed out that his program for testing password security was only helpful to hackers if system administrators made it possible to access the file that stored all the passwords. Wouldn't someone spot a program spending days or even weeks trying out every word in the dictionary against every stored password? And if not – why not? From exchanges like this one, network administrators around

---

* Clark cannot guarantee that he correctly recalls Alec Muffett's sartorial choices. But this was the lasting impression left by his unexpected visitor.

the world learned a hugely important lesson: safeguarding the integrity of computer systems and networks couldn't be done cheaply and on a part-time basis.

Since system administrators were mostly scientists and engineers, they perceived security primarily as a technological challenge. They made it more and more difficult to access and move through computer systems without proper authorisation and took care to hide the most sensitive data behind multiple layers of security checks. The hacking community saw this raising of barriers as an interesting challenge. Elite hackers went wholeheartedly into codebreaking. However, for most trespassers the easiest way into computer systems is to manipulate existing users to let them in – a skill called social engineering. Kevin Mitnick was a legend in this domain. Despite sometimes being derided as a 'script kiddie' – a pejorative term for hackers with limited coding skills – he often beat 'real' hackers to the punch in head-to-head contests to retrieve information from some inner sanctum.[16] To get a flavour of the single-mindedness, range of skills and sheer audacity hackers bring to their strange vocation, it is worth taking a closer look at Mitnick.

Kevin Mitnick was an extremely perceptive child. He pulled off his first social engineering feat in 1975, at the tender age of twelve. Left to babysit himself while his mother worked long hours, young Kevin observed that bus drivers punched a distinctive pattern into blank bus transfer tickets to permit free onward travel in the greater Los Angeles area. Discarded books of blanks were easy to find in the bins around terminus stations, so if Kevin could get hold of the right holepunch, the whole of LA would be his oyster. He asked a friendly bus driver where to buy one – ostensibly for a school project – and was directed to a shop that sold them.[17] Exploring the LA bus network without paying was Kevin's first taste of freedom and adventure. Next, thanks to another chatty bus driver who liked to talk about his hobbies, Kevin discovered ham radio. He rushed to find out everything about it and soon got a licence to make free calls to amateur radio operators across the world.[18] His all-time favourite hack became wreaking havoc at the local McDonald's Drive Thru by disconnecting the server at the order window from the speaker system and impersonating them instead. Even in middle age, riling the poor duty manager remained one of Mitnick's happiest childhood memories.[19]

When a high-school friend taught Mitnick the basics of phone phreaking, a door to an even grander and more fascinating network opened – and once again he barrelled through. Kevin started his foray into his local telephone company Pacific Bell by listening and observing. Soon he set himself challenges that far exceeded the imagination of his classmates. While their ambition ended with making free calls or finding out the time in Melbourne, Mitnick dreamed of controlling the switchboard. For this he had to know the network inside out and learn the idiosyncrasies of its corporate hierarchies and language. Getting the tone right is paramount to gaining someone's trust. Mitnick undoubtedly had a talent for imitation, a pleasant voice and good manners, and these turned out to be enough to wheedle or trick information out of unsuspecting telecoms staff.[20] In 1978 – aged fifteen – Mitnick had learned to sound convincingly like a technician seeking a specific piece of information, an engineer who needed access to a particular line, or even an angry supervisor. If he failed to get his way with one employee, he could always dial someone else. By reflecting on hundreds of these low-stakes encounters – both successful and unproductive – Mitnick worked out the basics of social engineering: sound like an insider (and ideally route the call through an inside line), don't ask for too much at a time, and build relationships through positive interactions. An encounter only needs to yield a tiny piece of information or build some goodwill to be worthwhile.

In the early 1980s, having already attracted the attention of the law and a year's probationary sentence for his mischievous phone-phreaking antics, Mitnick moved on to computing, hanging out at branches of the computer retailer RadioShack to learn on their demonstration machines. Obtaining the source code of various computer systems and popular electronic devices became his next obsession. As before, the thrill was in the chase: he had no intention of doing more than downloading the sensitive information just to prove that he could.[21]

Mitnick's passion for illicit exploring and tinkering with software was unstoppable. He was repeatedly busted, and in 1982 he was sentenced to six months in jail. Afterwards, Mitnick lost out on several promising job opportunities when potential employers saw his criminal record and – correctly – concluded that his character had not been reformed. Even after getting married, he sneaked off to spend long nights in cheap motels, prospecting for the latest virtual treasure or playing pranks on peers.[22] Unable to afford a powerful computer, he stashed his trophies on an account he had created in the University of California's network. Administrators eventually spotted his ever-expanding unauthorised file store and complained to the authorities. A former hacking buddy (who had failed to see the hilarious side of one of Mitnick's pranks) betrayed Mitnick to the police in 1988 and he was arrested and charged.[23] This time, his lawyer successfully pleaded that his client was an addict and not fully responsible for his actions. He was handed a relatively lenient sentence and a twelve-step programme modelled along the lines of Alcoholics Anonymous. The subsequent three-year probation period during which he was banned from using computers was perhaps well meant, but it also prevented him from taking any job that he would have been qualified for or interested in.

Mitnick often astonished elite technical hackers with the speed of his operations. As a 1989 article on him in the *Los Angeles Times* put it: '... when he got behind a computer, he became a giant.'[24] While others spent long hours analysing code for a weakness, Mitnick might just saunter into a company's headquarters and look for a hard copy of a manual or briefly commandeer an open desktop computer in an empty office. He was rarely challenged. When he was frustrated by a virtual security feature of his target network and couldn't guess the gatekeeper's password, he simply picked up the telephone to be let in. He was often surprised by how far he could push his victims without raising suspicions.[25]

After an FBI agent tempted Mitnick to break his probation conditions, Mitnick went on the run. His hacking and social engineering skills kept him one step ahead of the FBI for two and a half years. With every failed attempt at capture, the FBI and the press became more convinced that Mitnick was a dangerous criminal. And they had to make it look so, because only a serious threat to public security could justify the considerable resources spent on the chase.[26] After he was arrested by the FBI in 1995 – again, thanks to a tip-off from a rival hacker – Mitnick spent over four years in pre-trial detention while the authorities tried to work out how to deal with a world-famous 'criminal' who had never stolen money, never sold access or personal data, and never frozen or destroyed anyone's system. Until the end of his life, Mitnick remained puzzled by his notoriety as 'Cyberspace's most wanted' FBI fugitive. He was simply a man who loved to roam.[27]

Having done his time in prison (and enduring further years of stringent release conditions), Mitnick reinvented himself as a computer security expert. Trading on his reputation as the world's most famous hacker, he launched himself as an entertaining public speaker and author on social engineering. He founded Mitnick Security Consulting, offering to test companies' cybersecurity stance against a multi-pronged penetration test by the 'elusive and exclusive' Global Ghost Team.[28] If Mitnick's hand-picked hacking team failed to find an intrusion point, the master enchanter would pick up the phone, walk or smuggle himself into a building and, if necessary, crawl through the ceiling ducts to reach his goal.

Mitnick was also at the forefront of raising awareness of the latest phishing and spear-phishing techniques, and trained his customers to spot the red flags of manipulation. When he died in July 2023, aged fifty-nine, he was an upstanding, widely admired and economically successful US citizen. Overcoming or sidestepping boundaries, exploring and finding hidden treasures had remained his passion and vocation to the end. By some accounts, Mitnick's hyperfocus and tenacity are far from an exception in this field, which raises the question of the extent to which law and imprisonment can be truly effective in deterring and reforming cybercriminals like him.

This chapter leaves us with four important takeaways. First, every time a computer connects to the internet it automatically and unavoidably opens a potential entry point for curious or malicious outsiders. Second, preventing unauthorised access is largely up to users, but the cards are stacked against them. Although some hackers exploit weaknesses in software or operating systems, humans are generally the most insecure part of any computer network. When we arm ourselves against potential intruders, we should bear in mind that our opponents are often very determined, extremely well prepared and have a wide range of tried-and-tested tactics at their disposal to convince us to lower our guard. Social engineers exploit what they perceive as flaws in our own mental hardwiring – for example, our instincts towards collegiality, obedience or compassion. In the real world, social norms restrict the exploitation of such desirable traits. When operating anonymously online, however, these rules can be broken with impunity – and for profit. Third, cybercrime often has an offline dimension. The unfamiliar colleague or helpful officer on the phone, the likeable jester smoking by the back door, the sweet lady who brings cookies on Thursdays or the heavy-laden delivery person – invisible under their helmet – could well intend to use you as a convenient stepping stone into your organisation's systems.

Finally, cybercrime can be viewed as the shadow twin of the vast wealth of the tech elite and the (savvy, lucky or well-connected) shareholders who invested in their ventures. In formally granting property rights to powerful business leaders, governments split the early hacking community down the middle. IT professionals and illicit hackers are cut from the same cloth. Some are amateur sleuths passionately puzzling out how things work. Others are inventors pushing the boundaries of technology. A few are dedicated explorers, mapping the networks of universities, governments and large companies. When lawmakers drew the line between legal and criminal activities, many gifted individuals were caught on the wrong side by accident of birth, through social biases, discrimination or lack of resources. In the next chapter we will meet two young computer geeks who turned to extortive cybercrime, mainly because they were born in the wrong country.

4

Operation Flyhook:
The Risky Business of Cyberextortion

If you grew up in Russia in the 1990s, you could get an excellent education in mathematics and computer technology. If only there was something to do with it ... There were almost no IT jobs. Technology companies were few and far between, their salaries were absurdly low and it was extremely hard to find the capital to start new ones.[1] Whatever lies the statistics office had valiantly tried to maintain, the Soviet economy had stuttered and stalled. Central planning had not kept up with the complexity of a modern economy; the ageing infrastructure creaked and the political elite had run out of ideas for saving the USSR. The collapse of communism in 1990/91 only made things worse. As the state contracted, unemployment, inflation, social inequality and corruption skyrocketed, while those with political connections gained control of productive assets, promptly laying off even more workers. Anyone who tried to run even the tiniest business – like a kiosk – soon found themselves lost without protection from organised crime.[2] When Perestroika-era restrictions on the production and sale of alcohol were lifted, astonishing numbers of people simply drank themselves to death.[3] For a young computer geek like Alexey Ivanov, stuck in a crumbling grey high-rise in a provincial Russian city in the mid-1990s, the outlook was dismal in every direction.

Except Alexey's home-built computer constantly gave him tantalising glimpses of a parallel universe. Over in America, IT enthusiasts were clearly having a ball. Clever new code, fascinating products, interesting communities and brand-new infrastructures materialised at an astonishing rate. Entrepreneurs and their remarkably casual staff playfully made fortunes doing what they loved over endless inside jokes and cups of coffee. Meanwhile back in Russia, competent programmers were being forcibly recruited by the Federal Security Service (FSB), the successor of the fearsome KGB, or the Military Intelligence Services (GRU).[4] Few wanted to spend the rest of their lives in a dank basement working for an insultingly low state salary. In the mid-1990s, the contrast between sunny California and crummy Chelyabinsk, with harsh winter winds sweeping down from Siberia and the Ural Mountains, could not be starker. Teenage Alexey had a dream: '… that dream of a land in which life should be better and richer and fuller for everyone, with opportunity for each according to ability or achievement …'.[5]

But it turned out that the American dream was not accessible to those with a Russian passport – however hard they tried. In early 1999, Alexey hacked into a US job search website and wrote a program that automatically sent out his impressive CV to job listings at over 5,000 companies. Yet of the few companies that deigned to reply to the clever boy on the other side of the globe, none was willing to even start the process of getting him a coveted green card.[6] Somehow, Alexey had to keep body and soul together in Russia without showing up on the radar of the FSB. His official job – which he got by hacking into the servers of a local internet provider and convincing them to hire him as a security consultant – paid a measly $75 a month. To supplement this, Alexey joined forces with a group of local hackers. They ran a scheme stealing credit card details from banks and online vendors and using them one by one to buy a few hundred dollars' worth of toys, DVDs, CDs and computer parts.[7] To avoid leading the authorities straight to their door, the group had the goods shipped to impoverished women in neighbouring Kazakhstan. Smuggled back into dreary Siberia, the group's high-quality contraband sold like hot cakes to youngsters desperate for a small slice of Western life. Operated at scale, the scheme paid well enough, but it was not exactly glamorous. Besides, taking carloads of Western goods past heavily armed guards on the Kazakh–Russian border was bad for the nerves.

Bored and dissatisfied, Alexey and his entrepreneurial friend Vasily Gorshkov decided to upgrade their business. They split from the pedestrian card fraudsters and registered tech.net.ru as a company offering website design services. Behind this legal front, however, the two hackers and a few hired programmers experimented with automating and elevating their card fraud business and diverting victims to scam websites.[8] Alexey wrote code to steal the email addresses of PayPal users on eBay. He contacted potential victims with a $50 offer to lure them to enter their passwords on a replica site. Soon a stream of passwords flooded in. Although it wasn't clear what the group would do with their harvest of online credentials, it was a hack that Alexey was only too pleased to take credit for. Just as their American hacker-counterparts might have said: 'We mainly did it for fun.'[9] So, what next? If the hackers wanted to do greater mischief on eBay, they had to become 'reputable' customers. No one in their right mind did high-value online business with unknown buyers in the Wild East. PayPal had a $500 limit on unchecked accounts.¹⁰ Could the kids at tech.net.ru fix the 'rate the buyer' feature on eBay? Yes, they could ...

But before they could fully implement their scheme, the pair got distracted by yet another revenue stream: freelance security services. If American companies were not persuaded by the Russian lads' CVs, perhaps they could be convinced by a practical demonstration of their skills. If the tech.net.ru guys hacked into supposedly secure American company servers, system administrators should be interested in their advice on how to patch the problem. If not, things might start to go subtly wrong. And if they still weren't paying attention? Oops, some data might get destroyed or become inaccessible ... As Ivanov put it in one of his emails: 'after this you company be ruined. I don't want this, and because this i notify you about possible hack in you network, if you want you can hire me and im allways be check security in you network. What you think about this?'¹¹

Several system administrators thought this deal was worth a few thousand dollars a year – and quite a few paid it out of their own pockets to avoid telling the management about the intrusion.¹² Security consulting turned out to be intellectually stimulating, occasionally exciting and handsomely profitable. But Alexey and Vasily were still stuck in a polluted factory town in the Southern Ural Mountains, dreaming ... Maybe one day they could raise enough money to get their own technology platform off the ground.¹³

In late 1999, the FBI started to receive a string of complaints from internet service providers and e-commerce sites across the United States. Someone calling themselves 'subbsta' had hacked into their systems, stolen credit card information and made escalating threats to pressure IT managers into buying security reviews.¹⁴ The FBI had another, harsher word for this business:

cyberextortion. When forensic computing specialists examined the source of the trouble, all leads converged on computers in Russia and a server named tech.net.ru. The same servers also appeared to be implicated in creating unusually heavy traffic on Yahoo and eBay.

Eventually, somebody made a connection to Alexey Ivanov's thousand-fold applications via the job search website he had hacked into earlier in the year. Alexey's CV and photo were still on the server, and he had given his email address as subbsta@surenet.ru. Alexey lived in Chelyabinsk, Russia, and samples of his code were available for download from a server called tech.net.ru.[15] He had also provided his phone numbers in case potential employers wanted to get in touch with him at his home or office. Effectively, the FBI had been handed everything on a plate, including a reason to contact him. They proposed to invent a job offer to lure Alexey to the United States, with the twin aims of finding out more about the Russian hacking scene and hopefully putting a prolific and dangerous criminal behind bars. The Department of Justice gave the green light for the sting operation and the FBI meticulously prepared their trap. Given his wide job search, Alexey/subbsta should jump at the chance of working for a computer security start-up in the US. An ideal little company – Invita – was set up for the purpose of enticing him to an interview in Seattle.

When the FBI agent called Alexey's office about an opening at Invita, he got a surprise. The man answering Alexey's phone was beyond excited about this unique opportunity. But hang on – he was not Alexey. His name was Vasily Gorshkov, and he wanted to work in the US, too. Turning the tables on the surprised agent, Vasily suggested that Invita should give both men a chance to prove themselves. If they successfully completed a test hack, could they be interviewed together?

The FBI agreed and paid a private company to prepare a test honeypot for Alexey and Vasily. The pair passed with flying colours, taking only a few minutes to fully compromise the system.[16] Their modus operandi was consistent with what was known about subbsta's hacks. So, it was definitely worth inviting this criminal duo for an 'interview' in Seattle: visas to be arranged, flights to be paid and transport from the airport to be provided by Invita. Alexey and Vasily could not believe their luck. All the FBI needed was an office in which to interview the Russians and someone who sounded like a computer enthusiast to play the owner of the fictitious start-up. Lacking the necessary skills in-house, the FBI engaged Ray Pompon, a local data and network security analyst.

Ray was delighted to help, but he was less than impressed by the FBI agents' efforts to style the event location. Invita's suite of offices looked like an idealised police station, not an internet start-up! Where were the half-empty coffee cups and soda bottles, the overflowing rubbish bins, the tangle of cables, the broken equipment? In short, the generalised messiness of an IT business that would make a hacker feel at ease.[17] As Ray swept through the offices like a whirlwind scattering debris, the delighted Russians went on an extended city tour of Seattle with their entourage of undercover FBI agents.

Ray Pompon had steeled himself to face evil. Instead, he found two kindred spirits. Alexey was an enthusiastic, wide-eyed twenty-year old with a deep understanding of computers and programming. Vasily was fun too: a bit older and more boisterous, buoyed in equal measure by joy and a celebratory drink or two on the plane. Ray dived into the conversation: 'They were techies like me. They loved technology and enjoyed devising interesting and powerful new ways to use it.'[18] He quickly came to appreciate their predicament in Russia, their immense creativity and the skills they had developed despite – or perhaps because of – the technological limitations in their homeland. These youngsters had travelled around the world and wanted to apply their skills honestly and earn a fair salary for it.

But whatever his private feelings, Ray had a different job to do here: entrap them. Everything was prepared: more test hacks on a computer that was primed with sniffer software to record their keystrokes. To the agents' delight, the pair logged into the tech.net.ru servers to download some of their code to expedite their set tasks. Ray and the FBI agents were treated to an impressive display of hacking magic. Ray, who knew what would happen next, asked the naive duo whether they were afraid of law enforcement. 'The FBI cannot get us in Russia,' they replied.[19] If they had committed crimes (and they weren't saying that they had), they would have done so on Russian soil. Little did they realise that they had just voluntarily extradited themselves. After a most satisfactory interview, Alexey and Vasily were complimented and escorted off the premises to be driven to their lodgings. Not a hotel, alas, but a jail cell. A few minutes into their journey, their car stopped suddenly. 'FBI. Get out of the car with your hands behind your back.'[20]

Meanwhile, back at Invita's offices the rest of the team huddled over the bugged computer. Wow, these guys were so good, so cool, so cunning, surely, the FBI agents presumed, they were part of an organised crime ring – maybe even the Russian mob.[21] This was going to be BIG.

Eureka! The agents had found the passwords for Ivanov's and Gorshkov's accounts at tech.net.ru. Clearly, that's where the prosecutors would find proof of the hackers' misdeeds. So far, the FBI had mostly collected circumstantial evidence and the data from the crime-like hacking tests the agency had devised for the sting operation. Now, the agents had to act quickly. If there was a whole group of top-notch hackers out there and the terrible two disappeared without a trace, someone at the other end would likely become suspicious and change their passwords.

There were only two problems. The FBI had prepared an arrest warrant for Alexey Ivanov but not for Gorshkov, and they had no search warrant for their property. Would snooping around the tech.net.ru servers without a warrant breach the Fourth Amendment to the American Constitution, protecting citizens from 'unreasonable searches and seizures'?[22] Probably it was best to act first and ask questions later: if the agents missed their chance to download the files, the prosecution would not have much of a case. So, they decided to raid the computer, copy whatever material they could and seal the copied files until the warrant arrived.

Except, the pair's computers were physically located in Russia. Before computers made remote transborder searches possible, it would have been unthinkable for a police force to seize a suspect's property in a foreign jurisdiction without the sovereign's express permission. Yet clearly there was no time for diplomatic niceties: the Russian government was unlikely to respond promptly or positively. But what would be the political and practical implications of conducting an unauthorised remote raid on a computer in Russia – with a view to displaying the evidence in court for the world to see? There was no legal precedent for such transnational searches: the FBI was moving in uncharted territory. In taking the decision to raid the computers in Russia, the Feds turned into hackers themselves – bending if not breaking both domestic and international law.[23]

Indeed, by the time the search warrant came through, the passwords on the Russian servers had been changed. Just as well then that the agents had already downloaded 250 gigabytes of data.[24] The server's set-up indicated that tech.net.ru was used by a relatively small group. Although there were a dozen subdirectories in the home directory, the FBI were conscientious and limited their search. Or at least they only handed over the two directories that had been accessed by the suspects during the interview for forensic analysis to the prosecutors. Still, the folders and files contained therein did not disappoint; they made clear that Ivanov and Gorshkov were personally responsible for multiple cyberattacks on American firms, the bulk theft of credit card details and using these cards to make online purchases.[25] However, there was no evidence that the FBI had captured members of a major organised crime group. The assertion that Ivanov and Gorshkov were linked to the Russian mob was quietly dropped.[26]

Vasily Gorshkov was tried on twenty charges in a Seattle court. Controversially, the judge ruled that, as a foreign national, Gorshkov's rights to privacy were not protected under the Fourth Amendment.[27] The incriminating evidence found on the servers was therefore admissible and Gorshkov was swiftly convicted of all charges against him. He was sentenced to three years in prison minus time served – and hotfooted it back to Russia after his release.

Ivanov, however, faced a long trek through various US courts based on the location of each of the companies he had victimised. In his first trial, the defence counsel raised highly pertinent questions about how much US investigators had bent privacy rules, international treaties and constitutional law in the pursuit of foreign cybercriminals. Alexey could read the room: everyone ached for his conviction, but no one particularly wanted to debate these procedural questions. So, he decided to do a deal and plead guilty to all charges.[28] His crimes earned him a four-year prison sentence and a substantial fine but – most importantly – permission to work in the United States after completing his sentence.

This is a story of happy endings. The Department of Justice and the FBI were absolutely delighted with their sting operation and the substantial fines and prison sentences for the cybercriminals. 'The success of this prosecution shows that the Department of Justice and the FBI will expend whatever resources are necessary to protect the integrity of the Internet and legitimate businesses from the devastating damage that can be done by illegal hackers.'[29] Awards were given to two of the FBI agents and the media hyped up the nature of the threat that had been so cleverly neutralised by the US authorities: Ivanov was said to be 'responsible for an aggregate loss of approximately $25 million'.[30] The pair were titled 'kingpins of Russian computer crime'[31] and 'Two of the World's Most Dangerous Cyber Criminals'.[32]

Alexey Ivanov had reasons to celebrate too – after a small delay. Having served a year in prison, he landed exactly where he had always wanted: in a job in the United States.[33] He could earn real money at last, even if some of it had to be paid back to his former victims in restitution.[34] Given that doing honest work in the USA had been Alexey's express wish all along, this outcome leaves the impression that the public funds used for the FBI's elaborate sting operation, the complex preparations for the court case and the subsequent incarceration were squandered.

Looking at the geopolitics of Operation Flyhook, one could argue that its costs were incalculable. In 2002, one of the FBI agents had the questionable honour of being charged by Russian counterintelligence services with hacking into a foreign computer network and illegally seizing evidence against Russian nationals.[35] Suddenly the boot was on the other foot:

who were the cybercriminals here? Although Alexey's guilty plea had allowed the US courts to gloss over this question on his case, the legality of transborder data seizures would exercise scholars and courts for many years to come.[36] And of course, setting this precedent and ignoring Russia's justifiable objections poisoned the diplomatic relationship. A door to future cooperation on cybercrime was closed while the floodgates for international espionage were opened.[37]

Finally, for those who could see beyond the Department of Justice's self-congratulatory statements to the media, the lessons from the cases of Ivanov and Gorshkov looked extremely worrying. American companies' computer systems were absolutely riddled with security flaws. It did not take supernatural, elite intelligence or mafia powers to compromise American business networks: a couple of bright kids from nowhere could do it. Ivanov and Gorshkov were good – but they mostly exploited known vulnerabilities that companies had been too lazy to fix. Many of their victims had not even realised that their systems had been breached – even when money had gone missing from their customers' credit cards. When the hackers chose to reveal themselves, system administrators were mostly powerless to expel them, and some even paid them hush money.

Financial fraudsters and extortionists from around the world could clearly find ample low-hanging fruit in the United States – and everywhere else. Neutralising two minor figures on the Russian hacking scene (and one of them only for a short period) changed almost nothing about this ever-intensifying threat situation.[38] But it would take another ten years of innovation before cyberextortion would morph into profitable ransomware. Deep in the hidden underbelly of the internet, criminals were learning how to cash out ill-gotten gains without getting caught.

5

The Missing Puzzle Pieces: Innovations for Safe and Profitable Ransomware

A combination of three factors kept a lid on virtual extortion schemes until 2013: traceability of communications, codebreaking and the interception of ransom payments. As the stories of Popp, Mitnick, Ivanov and Gorshkov illustrate, any one of these was sufficient to deny the criminal a return or facilitate their arrest and conviction. Ransomware could only be scaled up once all three technological preconditions had been met. Although hacker forums and a potent blueprint for taking data hostage were developed in the 1980s, it took more than two decades of technological and social innovation for ransomware to become a safe and profitable business model for cybercriminals.

The first concern for an aspiring cyberextortionist was that law enforcement could pin down the location of the computers and servers used by cybercriminals from their Internet Provider (IP) addresses. Hackers whose activities were repeatedly brought to the attention of law enforcement were asking for trouble. Cybercriminals living in Western countries ran a high risk of being raided by the police – especially if the media got hold of and embellished their stories, compelling law enforcement to conduct no-expense-spared manhunts. Eastern

European, Russian and Asian cybercriminals had to take care not to end up on the FBI's most wanted list if they had travel plans outside the former Soviet Union. For ransomware to be securely operated at scale, cybercriminals needed anonymous communication channels.

Second, anyone who used the same encryption code for multiple victims could expect to collect their ransom only a few times before their decryption key would be shared among the victims. Ransomware coders had to learn how to generate complex encryption that was unique to each victim and not easily reverse-engineered – automatically and preferably at scale.

Third, taking payments was cumbersome and risky. Cash and cheque transactions could be intercepted and financial transfers traced. A few plucky cyberextortion pioneers tried to stay below the radar of law enforcement in the noughties by demanding store gift cards or forcing their victims to call premium phone lines. But these prosaic payment channels were hardly suited to making a mint. For sophisticated criminals there were better ways to benefit from their computing skills than extortion. Card fraud and electronic theft offered richer pickings.

The problem of making online communications less traceable was initially tackled by legal private enterprises, and eventually gloriously resolved by the US military. The demand for online privacy first came from large businesses that wanted to share files securely between authorised users located in different offices. Microsoft developed and released a protocol for a VPN (virtual private network) for this purpose in the late 1990s. VPNs connect their customers to the internet through private servers, concealing the users' identity and encrypting their communication. As soon as people had the option of hiding their location and communications behind VPNs, the internet became a hive of illicit activity. Computer enthusiasts used chatrooms and filesharing applications to rekindle the joyful anarchy and community spirit of their early days in cyberspace. Impecunious and rebellious film and music lovers downloaded their favourite works from filesharing sites, denying the producers the income of their labour. When record companies and bands complained, the website administrators were identified and sued. As filesharing sites in the clear web were shut down and liquidated amid much fanfare – such as Napster in 2001 – illicit sharing quietly moved into the Deep Web.

The Deep Web is the part of the internet that is invisible to search engines such as Google or Yahoo. To access a site in the Deep Web, somebody must tell you its address and login details. Instructions on how to join a website are often closely guarded and there may be multiple layers of identification and password protection. Common – and perfectly legal – examples are news and video-streaming services behind paywalls and the password-protected parts of bank websites, where customers check their balances and make transfers. The Deep Web's illegal side is known as the Dark Web and this is where images of child sexual abuse, extreme political views and instructions for building bombs are shared, and illegal and stolen goods of every ilk are advertised for sale, whether drugs, weapons or looted antiquities. State actors around the world therefore set their sights on cracking VPN protocols so they could monitor this worrying activity. By the early 2000s it was no longer safe to use VPNs to send politically sensitive communications via the internet. Ironically, to protect their own secret communications from prying foreign states, the United States developed what soon became the preferred mode of communication for cybercriminals.

The Onion Router (TOR) protocol was designed to protect the anonymity of communication between spies and dissidents in hostile states and the US Intelligence Community.

TOR conceals the content of every communication in multiple nested layers of encryption (like the layers of an onion) and then bounces the information around multiple randomly chosen anonymous relay servers before it reaches its destination. This makes it extremely difficult to trace the origin of a sensitive message, especially if the information is hidden in a torrent of unrelated communications. To create the necessary background noise, the protocol for TOR was publicly released in 2004, promising – but not quite delivering – free speech and online privacy for all.[1] Hackers, political activists, people with impolite fetishes, abusers, drug dealers, peddlers of stolen goods, and terrorists around the world were delighted. They too could use the TOR protocol to conduct their business in the Dark Web.

Using the TOR protocol, internet users conceal their identity behind a nickname of their choice (otherwise known as a 'handle'). This turns out to be a mixed blessing for conducting criminal business. On the one hand, anonymity – or rather, pseudonymity – makes the Dark Web a very safe space for trading illicit goods, services and information. Unless physical goods are sent to real-world addresses, it is extremely difficult for law enforcement to work out who is hiding behind a nickname. On the other hand, the buyers, sellers and sharers do not know their partners in crime. Are they honest and financially sound, are they crooks ready to pull a fast one, or are they perhaps undercover police officers? The flipside of anonymity is lack of trust.[2]

Especially in the business of crime, one must suspect that potential customers and colleagues are mavericks and rule-breakers. Online, crooks can easily impersonate vendors or buyers with a good reputation and can shed their own bad reputation with a few keyboard strokes. A pseudonym that has been 'burnt' can be retired and a new one chosen. If an anonymous criminal defrauds another, there is no third-party enforcement, and the cheated party cannot seek redress on their own: the fraudster is not personally known to them and could be located on the other side of the globe. As one cybercriminal put it when asked about doing online business with someone hiding behind a pseudonym: 'I don't know you from a bar of soap. So, no way.'[3]

Some of the earliest cybercriminal meeting places of the 1990s were virtual 'chatrooms' where participants posted their ideas on virtual message boards under their nicknames. These messages were permanently displayed, so that anyone looking for potential collaborators could view their entire record of outpourings. By sharing detailed information on their pranks, hacks, code and other criminal innovations, individuals could gain recognition and respect in their community. If a criminal in search of a collaborator saw someone whose online personality looked like a kindred spirit, they could start a careful private conversation about doing business together. They might test them with a small task and then cautiously progress to trusting them with ever more sensitive or lucrative assignments. However, this was tediously long-winded for those with a lot of illicit goods or information to sell.

Successful hackers often stole hundreds of thousands or even millions of credit card details or bank account data in their heists. The information then had to be cloned on to fake or blank cards to make purchases or cash withdrawals. This was a risky business that could lead to rejection, embarrassment and possible arrest if a shopkeeper or security officer grew suspicious, or the account had been deactivated in the meantime. Few crooks were willing to try cashing out at scale. Those who did probably had an expensive drug habit to feed, i.e. they were probably best avoided. In the words of the former cybercriminal Kevin Poulsen, trying to sell a major haul of financial data was 'like offering a 747 for sale at a flea market ... the online credit card market was a depressing bog of kids and small-timers ... [whose] typical deals were in the single digits, and their advice to each other was tainted by myth and idiocy.'[4] Enterprising hackers therefore embarked on a quest to improve criminal cooperation and raise productivity, despite the challenges of anonymity and police attempts to disrupt their activities.[5]

The hacker groups that ran the online cybercriminal forums in the late 1990s and early 2000s laid much of the groundwork for today's ransomware gangs. The most successful of the early financial fraud websites was CarderPlanet, where small-time crooks could buy stolen credit card data from virtual bank heists in small and larger batches. CarderPlanet's founding members solved the problem of pseudonymity by meeting in person at a now infamous 'convention' in the Ukrainian city of Odesa in 2001. Revealing their identities to each other created a measure of confidence and camaraderie between them. However, they knew that they could not trust the shadowy traders they hoped to attract to their novel venture. The administration of their marketplace was therefore multilayered and strictly hierarchical. There were several layers of checks: potential vendors were vetted by approved reviewers, whose work was supervised by moderators. These in turn reported to hand-picked administrators – called Capo in mafia fashion – each of whom was accountable to the 'Capo di Capi'. CarderPlanet also offered an escrow system for both money and goods – with the administration watching their agents like hawks. CarderPlanet was the first truly transnational virtual marketplace for profit-oriented cybercrime – but with a crucial offline dimension: the personal relationships between its founders.

As financial crime moved online, so did law enforcement. Police and intelligence officers posed as buyers or vendors on criminal forums and harvested data. The TOR protocol that many had thought conferred complete anonymity was in fact traceable, with sufficient computing power. Pseudonyms could be cracked if criminals ever linked real-world information to their nickname. Moreover, cybercriminals who had been apprehended often had few qualms about betraying their shadowy comrades to reduce their own prison terms. Law enforcement used the traitors' pre-vetted nicknames to infiltrate illicit marketplaces, map their structures and try to work out who was secretly running the show. In 2004, the FBI swooped on CarderPlanet, arresting a major vendor who was extradited to the US while another was detained in Ukraine. CarderPlanet's administrators hurriedly shut their forum down to contain the damage.[6] However, other marketplaces set up by rival sellers to tout their own wares were already waiting in the wings, and the vendors and buyers ejected from CarderPlanet quickly migrated towards them. Below the headlines, the takeaway message was that careful small-time crooks could get away scot-free even if a forum was blown up. The new forums tended not to last particularly long either, whether through infighting or betrayal.[7] Western police forces were on the ball and cleverly played the administrator criminals off against each other. One major virtual criminal marketplace – DarkMarket – even ended up being run as a sting operation by Keith Mularski, an undercover FBI agent.[8] In three years, Mularski helped to put four top-level administrators and fifty-two of the most prolific traders on DarkMarket behind bars before shuttering the marketplace.[9]

The successful infiltration and takedown of DarkMarket by the FBI in 2008 provoked a serious rethink among the financial cybercrime community. The geography of cybercrime started to shift towards countries beyond the reach of the FBI, Interpol and Europol.[10] Sophisticated hackers could safely attack lucrative Western targets from Russia and allied countries, from North Korea, Iran and China. Only their virtual infrastructures and nicknames were at risk, and both were expendable. The risky business of cashing out could be subcontracted to small-time criminals in the rest of the world, who were replaceable if rumbled. However, subcontracting the cashing out meant sharing the proceeds of crime: not just with the lowly 'money mules' and their 'herders' but also – at least occasionally – with law enforcement when their assets were seized. The most entrepreneurial cybercriminals cast around for a new business model. Rather than stealing financial information and laboriously draining one credit card or bank account after another, wouldn't it be easier to extort ransoms?

While the cybercriminals' preferred communication protocol had its origin in US military research, it was academia that provided a blueprint for digital extortion.[11] Again, this happened with the best of intentions. In the mid-1990s, the intellectually curious and far-sighted research duo Adam Young and Moti Yung started to contemplate what dystopias might unfold if someone subverted recent advances in encryption technology and used them aggressively.[12] Combining the mindset of a former hacker with the skills of a cutting-edge coder, it seemed to them that it was only a small hop from cryptography to 'kleptography'. Young and Yung were particularly worried about computer programs called 'viruses' that had first been coded in the 1970s.

Computer viruses became a significant drain on the digital economy in the 1990s. Viruses corrupt or permanently destroy files in their host computer, modifying or overwriting other programs and leaving a copy of themselves in every infected file. As computer users spent increasing amounts of time connected to an ever-speedier internet, virus transmission rates were accelerating. Yet, with reasonable cyber-hygiene, the threat could be contained. Computer security experts were constantly on the lookout for new viruses. Some specialised in antivirus software development: extracting virus code from infected files, analysing it and writing programs to remove the malware and – ideally – reverse the damage. They also learned to 'vaccinate' computers against known viruses by installing programs that would prevent viruses from establishing themselves or disable their capacity to destroy.

Young and Yung, however, saw the writing on the wall. What if a virus was programmed to create encrypted copies of itself?[13] Analysing the encrypted code would become more challenging. Such viruses would spread unimpeded for longer and infect many more hosts than their straightforward forerunners. But even worse, encryption technology could also be used to make a target computer dependent on the viruswriter. Viruses could be programmed to encrypt data files on the victim's computer in such a way that removing the virus would render them useless. Files could then only be recovered by reversing the encryption program that the hackers had used. Young and Yung warned that if critical data or resources were not backed up (or the code was easy to crack), paying the viruswriter for their decryption key would be the best way of making a recovery. They noted, however, that if the same encryption key was used for encrypting multiple computers – a technique called symmetric encryption – only one victim had to pay for a decryption key and everyone else could share it afterwards.

Young and Yung's former experience of the hacking community led them to anticipate that some bright spark might solve this problem by using 'asymmetric encryption' – a cryptographic method first proposed in the 1970s. Young and Yung's blueprint for a hypothetical criminal business plan had two parts. First, a virus code could be programmed so that the virus subtly mutated every time it spread to a new host. Second, each new infection would trigger the creation of a pair of encryption keys. Of these, only the first – the 'public key' – would be visible on the victim's computer. This public key is useless for the purpose of data recovery: its only purpose is to identify its unique counterpart that contains the decryption code. However, the recovery key – called the 'private key'– would be transmitted back to the virus-writer. They could choose whether to keep it, give it away or sell it to the desperate victims. Thanks to the mutation coded into the first step, each victim would be faced with a unique decryption puzzle to solve, so every new infection presented the extortionist with a new profit opportunity. Young and Yung surmised that unless digital housekeeping was perfect, matching individual computers to their specific private keys could become horrendously complicated in the case of a mass infection. It was likely that someone would make a mistake and lose a whole bunch of keys. Important data could be lost for ever.

Young and Yung's doomsday scenario was no mere thought experiment. Carefully isolating their machines from the rest of their network, the researchers programmed a tiny but powerful trial virus and unleashed it into one of their computers. They watched with horrified fascination as events unfolded from a different machine that took the role of the virus-writer to which the virus reported its progress, and the information needed to produce decryption keys. Young and Yung's virus took only a few seconds to establish itself in the target computer. After the next reboot, the virus searched for filenames of interest like 'payroll' and 'e-money' and encrypted them in such a devious way that a genuine victim would have had no hope of recovering the information without the virus-writer's key. The final flourish was to display a ransom note. Mission accomplished for the virus and QED for the researchers. The alarmed team rushed out to alert their community in lectures and academic papers that what they termed 'cryptovirology' would facilitate hostage-taking and extortion on a grand scale. They had proven the existence of the computer equivalent of the gory Facehuggers in the 1979 sci-fi film *Alien*: disgusting creatures that did fatal harm to their prey but could not be removed by shocked bystanders without killing the victim and causing massive damage to their surroundings.[14]

As so often happens, the voices of the lone criers in the wilderness were met with scepticism and amusement and their warnings were largely dismissed.[15] In the mid-1990s, the kind of ransomware epidemic Young and Yung imagined seemed like science fiction. Ordinary computer users were only just beginning to apply for email addresses, and used clunky dial-up connections to get briefly online. Most thought that there was nothing to steal on their computers. Those who conceded that data had value still doubted that victims would pay a ransom for it. And if someone wanted to try running this kind of extortion scheme with potentially thousands of victims, they would really struggle to find a way of being paid that could not be disrupted or would not lead the police directly to them. Hardly anyone had heard of the 'e-money' Young and Yung referenced in their papers as the likely solution to the cyberextortionist's payment predicament.

But change was afoot. After the launch of Amazon and eBay in 1995, the pioneers of e-commerce realised that banks and credit card companies created unnecessary friction in online markets. Payments by money orders, cheques and wire transfer were far too slow for this brave new world. Card payments were faster, but issuers charged hefty commissions on transactions – card fraud was rife, so these commissions had to cover the cost of many fraudulent transactions. There were several avenues of innovation. First, some pioneers saw the future for digital cash in the form of prepaid chip-cards for making online and offline purchases.[16] Second, companies like PayPal (launched in 2000) sought to increase the convenience and security of online payments by creating tamper-resistant protocols for transferring money directly between bank accounts, thereby reducing commissions.[17] And third, there were a handful of entrepreneurs who wanted to fundamentally redesign online payments to cut out the middlemen and meddling governments altogether. They wanted to invent a new money for a new age: a digital currency that kept its value, was widely accepted, and passed freely from person to person without reference to a third party.

For something to be accepted as money it must be widely trusted by users. Central banks like the Federal Reserve that had established trust as monetary guardians were not interested in issuing or regulating e-money. Everyone else had to start from scratch. Investors needed to be convinced that the new e-money supply would be restricted to grow in line with money demand. Any imbalances would cause the money's value to fluctuate. Excess supply would cause inflation and, unless corrected, the value of the money would collapse. For this reason, the e-money would have to be administered impartially, be extremely difficult to counterfeit, and be tamper-proof, so that no one could create additional money by copy-pasting their money files or double-spending their e-cash. The e-money would also need to be stored and transmitted securely so that no hacker could intercept or spirit it away. And finally, some of the people most interested in creating e-cash for the online world cared passionately about personal privacy in the context of real-world markets that made buyers' and vendors' transactions transparent to their banks, governments and anyone else who was curious.[18] Could someone come up with a secure technology to facilitate anonymous and untraceable online transactions without a central authority to regulate and enforce contracts?

These were very high standards to reach. Successful e-money depended on top-notch cryptography, and this was something that Young and Yung were watching with a beady eye. The references to e-money in their 1996 paper referred to the earliest attempts to create peer-to-peer digital payments in the 1990s, such as eCash, B-money, Bit Gold, Hashcash and DigiCash. Most of these ideas were only published as concept papers. They never saw the light of day after bruising peer reviews. A few forms of e-money made it to the proof-of-concept stage and were made available to interested users. However, they remained too small to become a viable alternative to established currencies or prepaid digital cash cards. They folded when disappointed users gave up on finding vendors willing to accept them or a hacker found a way of breaking the encryption protocol for their own gain. Yet, Young and Yung saw that it was only a matter of time before someone succeeded in creating the elusive difficult-to-trace electronic money that would be tailor-made for online extortion. The only hope of preventing their predicted horror scenario was for computer users to wake up and stay one step ahead of the opposition. In 2004, they reached out directly to potential victims with their wake-up call book *Malicious Cryptography – Exposing Cryptovirology*.[19]

Yet once again, the public response to their alarm call was muted. One unconvinced reviewer described their book as 'of little practical use'[20] while another thought that 'cryptoviral extortion didn't pose a serious threat' because it was too complex for criminals to implement.[21] A potential funder fobbed them off saying: 'We do not consider these attacks as high priority or immediate.'[22] As climate change campaigners can attest, most people need to experience an impending catastrophe before they act. Until ransomware became ubiquitous, governments, firms and individuals simply refused to worry about it.

In 2008, a white paper proposed a new form of e-money, this time named Bitcoin. Those who had previous experience of e-money initiatives knew to be cautious. Programmers and researchers had participated in failed e-money projects in the 1990s and the early adopters had lost their investments. The set-up of the Bitcoin project showed that its founder(s) had absorbed the lessons of the successes and failures of its predecessors. However, they shied away from the robust academic debate that usually probes novel ideas and propositions. They released their concept paper under the pseudonym Satoshi Nakamoto and when fingers were pointed at various potential authors, each roundly denied their involvement in the project.[23] On the one hand, Bitcoin's murky origin did not inspire confidence, but on the other, getting involved in this novel open-source project with a small group of clever and competitive programmers seemed like fun.[24]

The Bitcoin protocol is set up so that there is a hard limit for the total amount of Bitcoin that can be created, or 'mined'.[25] At the point of their creation, Bitcoin are a reward for solving a computational puzzle, which requires effort, time and energy. The puzzles started off very simple but with every puzzle solved, the complexity of the following puzzle was raised a notch. This process will continue until the puzzles become infinitely difficult to solve. Puzzle-loving computer wizards mine Bitcoin if they are paid adequately for their effort, and do something else if the reward is too low. Money supply therefore closely follows money demand: the invisible hand of the marketplace replaces the traditional central bank. No government is involved in creating or regulating Bitcoin and – perhaps more importantly – no politicians can create Bitcoin to fund additional spending.

The first Bitcoin miners had no idea whether they were mining worthless fool's gold. This did not matter though: the first Bitcoin were trivially easy to mine. As Adam Smith said: 'The real price of everything is the toil and trouble of acquiring it.'[26] When solving the computational puzzles was as easy as picking up pebbles from a beach, the price of a Bitcoin was less than a cent. In May 2010, a hungry programmer paid 10,000 Bitcoin for two large pizzas and he was jolly pleased that his hobby had earned him and his kids a real reward.[27] To make serious money from Bitcoin, people had to hold the digital assets they had created or bought until their price rose, trusting that no fraudster or hacker would steal their treasure away from them in the meantime. The Bitcoin exchange protocol safeguards investors in this respect by using an asymmetric encryption protocol. To hold or spend Bitcoin its owner needs two randomly generated sequences of letters and numbers: a public key address to identify themselves to the network and a private key that unlocks the specific Bitcoin. The all-important private key information can be held in online exchanges, in offline wallets or on a piece of paper in a locked box in a secret drawer.

To transfer Bitcoin between two accounts, the sender and recipient identify themselves to each other with their public address key. Although these keys are visible to the entire network, they provide no information about the sender's or recipient's identity or location. The sender decides on the amount to send (as well as offering a transaction fee) and transfers the right to the Bitcoin to the receiver by sending them the private key(s). The intended payment is then sent to a pool of transactions that require confirmation. This is where the Bitcoin miners do their work. The system sets digital puzzles at regular intervals; the first miner to solve a puzzle picks out a set of transactions awaiting confirmation from the pool – prioritising the payments with the most generous transaction fees, of course. The miner carefully checks the selected transactions for their validity (for example, whether the sender has spent the Bitcoin before) and combines the legitimate transactions into a block that registers the approved changes in Bitcoin ownership. Once complete, the new block is sent to several nodes in the network where its conformity with the protocol is verified again. The information is saved locally and passed on to further nodes. The additional nodes verify and pass the information on further, until all active nodes have a copy of the new status of Bitcoin ownership. Once the transactions in a new block have been accepted by a quorum of nodes, the miner gets their reward (in Bitcoin) for completing the work – and pockets the transaction fees offered by the senders.

All old and newly completed blocks are stored in the nodes of the network, and each block references the one that came immediately before it. The resulting 'blockchain' is thus a confirmed register of the current global state of Bitcoin ownership as well as a faithful record of every single transaction of every Bitcoin that was ever created. The near-random allocation of individual miners to blocks of transactions, the anonymous and decentralised nature of the verification process, the repeated checks of the completed work, and the storage of copies of the record in nodes all over the world make it extremely difficult to tamper with the blockchain.

When Bitcoin was launched in 2009, there were not many

believers in this complex and untested set-up. However, there were just enough curious individuals willing to help create this unusual digital asset. Depending on the miners' enthusiasm and spare time, merchant or investor appetite for difficult-to-trace assets, positive or negative press and social media coverage, and occasional government interventions, there were wild price fluctuations. This made the new e-money unattractive to legal businesses. They never knew what their Bitcoin wallet would be worth the next day and whether it would cover the dollar costs of running their enterprise. It was a different matter for buyers and sellers in underground markets. To them, the appeal of banking and transacting using a pseudonym (i.e. the randomly generated public key address) and without financial institutions checking larger transactions for potential money laundering was overwhelming.

Much of the initial demand for Bitcoin as a means of transaction thus came from dealers in the Dark Web.[28] But when Bitcoin reached parity with the dollar for the first time in February 2011, more people started to get interested. At first it attracted mainly those who wanted to hide assets from their enemies, law enforcement or tax authorities, and computer geeks in countries where runaway inflation made the capricious Bitcoin a worthwhile store of value. As Bitcoin's value rose, however, financially savvy investors in the Global North came on board – much to the relief of the crooks. The more popular Bitcoin became with global financial elites, the less likely that regulators would suppress it.

Cryptocurrencies truly came of age when the first Bitcoin ATMs appeared in North American cities in 2013.[29] Those who had got Bitcoin – by hook or by crook – could now convert it to cash and spend it in the legal economy. This development solved all manner of criminal finance problems. Thanks to the pseudonymity offered by TOR, years of experience in organising underground markets, tried-and-tested asymmetric encryption protocols and Bitcoin for cashing out, at last all the preconditions for large-scale, profitable ransomware campaigns were in place.

6

CryptoLocker: Ransomware Unleashed

Unbeknown to many of us, from sometime in the late 2000s until 2014, an audacious and highly successful financial crime empire was quietly syphoning tens of millions of dollars out of bank accounts across the globe via an invisible network of digital gossamer threads. Its staff were spread across Russia's eleven time zones, carefully placed to follow the business day across Asia, Australia, America and Europe. The operation was directed by just six individuals calling themselves the 'Business Club', supported by a network of around fifty assistants. Like the team in *Ocean's Eleven*, every board member was a specialist in their own field: malicious software development, phishing, technical support, banking and recruitment of temporary assistants and money mules to launder the proceeds.[1] At the top of the table in the Club's virtual boardroom sat 'Slavik' – a talented programmer who had created the most insidious malware program of its time: the Zeus Trojan.

The primary purpose of Zeus was to gather financial data, and its various descendants are still used for this purpose today.[2] Like other Trojans, Zeus relies on computer users to voluntarily download the malware, for example by opening a seemingly urgent or tempting-sounding email attachment or clicking a link to a malicious website. Once installed, Zeus captures the keystrokes of victims as they enter online login details – including one-time keycodes. When Zeus was used by the Business Club, an alert was sent to a purpose-built instant messaging app called JabberZeus every time a victim tried to access their bank from an infected computer. The criminals then took just a few seconds to hijack the victim's account. The affected users were shown a subtly modified interface of their bank's webpage, with extra boxes asking for additional details that were unnecessary for the transaction in question. Once the data was divulged, victims were diverted to a new screen saying that the desired service was temporarily unavailable and to try again later. Meanwhile the criminals used the captured login details on the genuine bank website to transfer money into accounts controlled by them. In another of the Business Club's favourite fraud schemes, the criminals added the accounts of dozens of money mules to companies' payrolls just before payday. Mostly, money mules are desperate or greedy citizens recruited through work-from-home schemes. Their 'work' consists of handing over their bank account details to their criminal employer, not asking questions about funds arriving in their accounts, and quickly transferring the money (minus their commission) into a series of further accounts given to them by their 'boss'.[3]

Zeus had a second capability: it turned infected computers into 'bots' (short for 'robots'), a very appropriate term in that it was derived from a Czech word meaning forced labour. Although the owners of the infected devices could still use their computers, unbeknown to them their machines could also be operated remotely by criminals through their command-and-control servers. Infected machines could, for example, be instructed to dispatch phishing messages or to send spam messages to overload specific target servers. The Business Club hired out their

Zeus botnet to scammers for fraud and extortion campaigns. If criminals can send hundreds of thousands of emails, it does not matter if only a low percentage of recipients respond positively. Technically savvy crime syndicates could also buy a licence for the Zeus code for a few thousand dollars as a DIY botnet construction kit, multiplying the Trojan's ill effects across the globe.

Slavik's Business Club operated their schemes on an impressive scale, transferring millions of dollars from banks, businesses and personal accounts via hundreds of money mules and to (fake) enterprises registered on the Chinese side of the Russia–China border.[4] The Club had no moral qualms about their impact on victims. Their operatives would drain whichever accounts they accessed: they just kept going until the victim or their bank grew suspicious and stopped them. Their heists included stealing a six-figure sum from a Native American Nation in Washington State and the entire operating capital of an organisation providing assisted living facilities in Pennsylvania.[5]

When law enforcement started to look for the source of this evil, they realised that several non-criminals were already monitoring the JabberZeus network. A tiny coding mistake had inadvertently given outsiders access to the instant messaging app used by the Business Club. Brian Krebs, a journalist at the *Washington Post*, had monitored the criminals' chat for several years. Much to the Club's chagrin, Krebs regularly wrote about the crime syndicate in his column. For months, his morning routine was to check the chat while drinking a morning coffee then warn companies of impending payroll scams – preventing millions of dollars' worth of fraudulent transfers.[6] FBI agents also plugged themselves into the network, closely studying the business and personal messages going back and forth between the criminals. It was the happiest of personal messages that rocked the Club's cosy existence: a key operative known as 'Tank', who organised the recruitment of money mules, proudly announced the birth of their daughter Miroslava on 22 July 2009, giving her birthweight. A search of the birth registers of Ukraine showed only one baby girl of that name and weight born on that day. Her father's name was Vyacheslav Penchukov: a young DJ in the Eastern Ukrainian town of Donetsk, known for his sweaty midnight raves and penchant for high-end sports cars.

However, arresting the flamboyant Mr Penchukov proved surprisingly difficult. He was closely connected to Eastern Ukraine's pro-Russian political and business elite. Little Miroslava's godfather was the son of the corrupt president Viktor Yanukovych, who was swept from power in a popular uprising in 2014.[7] When a group of FBI agents joined the security forces of Ukraine in 2010 to arrest Penchukov, they were treated to a suspiciously protracted vodka-fuelled stay in Kyiv. When their bibulous local hosts finally brought the group to Donetsk for the raid on Penchukov's residence, the DJ was out. Not only had the suspect shaken off the Ukrainian agents who had supposedly had him under close surveillance as he moved between his residence and various nightclubs for the previous week, but there was no sign of any incriminating evidence in his apartment either. As the disgruntled lead FBI agent recalled: 'Tank was missing and the apartment looked unnaturally clean – as though a maid had just been through ... It was quite obvious no one had been there for a few days.'[8] Penchukov's name and photo would just have to go on the FBI's most wanted list – and stay there for the foreseeable future.[9]

Even with advance warning, international arrest warrants and the possibility of police raids clearly felt uncomfortable to some Club members. Slavik announced their retirement in 2010, saying that they had sold the source code for Zeus to a fellow cybercriminal. However, in 2011 the Zeus source code was publicly released – a chance for hackers to innovate and improve this already powerful malware. A Zeus update was badly needed; law enforcement and software giants were moving forcefully against its botnets. In one such action in 2012, the digital crimes unit at Microsoft identified and disabled 800 web addresses used as command servers by criminals, thereby taking down Zeus-based botnets that between them had infected several million computers.[10]

However, it did not take long before someone developed a private and more robust version of Zeus. Proudly called 'GameOver Zeus', the new Trojan was like the original Zeus in its sophistication and effectiveness, but its botnet was hugely more resilient to disruption. Rather than being directed from a central command server, the GameOver botnet had a network architecture. Commands were sent from a central server to multiple proxy nodes. From there commands cascaded through the network, with each computer taking instructions from peers and sending back stolen banking credentials to the criminals.[11] If contact with the centre was lost, each computer would scan a regularly updated list of alternative servers until a new domain name from the list was activated by the criminals to retake control. This flexible, dynamic structure made it very challenging for law enforcement or other outside actors to step in.[12]

GameOver Zeus spread like wildfire, and its operators soon controlled between half a million and a million infected computers.[13] The criminals running GameOver primarily targeted medium-sized companies for their banking credentials, employing the botnet as a diversionary tactic. Overwhelming spam attacks were used to capture the victims' and their banks' attention while the criminals executed large-scale transfers out of their accounts.[14] There was only one problem with GameOver Zeus: it was too successful. With millions of electronic bank vaults ready to be cracked open, there was not enough reliable human capital to scoop out the loot. The various online forums in the Dark Web were already flush with stolen financial information and prices had come tumbling down. With the added risk of coming into the crosshairs of a police sting, stealing and selling login data was becoming ever less attractive.[15] Was there another way to make money from infecting computers that could be automated and operated at scale?

The mastermind in charge of the GameOver Zeus botnet thought that a new generation of ransomware might fit the bill. Millions of computers running Microsoft Windows were vulnerable to GameOver Zeus. The Trojan could be primed with encryption malware and sent to potential victims in dozens of guises via the botnet, dwarfing the scale of all previous cyberextortion attempts. Asymmetric encryption technology would make it extremely difficult for victims to recover on their own and make it impossible to share previously released decryption keys. Servers in the Deep Web would keep the criminals' communication with their victims reasonably private. And the increasingly mainstream Bitcoin offered the perfect payment mechanism: hard to trace and easy to cash out.

In September 2013, the development and experimentation phase was over and the GameOver Zeus crime syndicate unleashed their new monster: CryptoLocker ransomware. The CryptoLocker malware encrypted all Word files, spreadsheets, databases, PC games, photos and videos on the target computers as well as on any connected storage media. A red-alert ransom note then popped up to inform the victim of a successful attack. They were given a code identifying the unique private

CRYPTOLOCKER

The CryptoLocker screen explaining payment in Bitcoin

key required to recover their files and urged to pay around $100 in Bitcoin or a third-party payment method within seventy-two hours. Meanwhile, a countdown timer showed how much time was left before the private decryption key would be deleted for ever ...

CryptoLocker's infection and encryption technologies worked extremely well. However, the technological skills of their customer base left much to be desired. Seventy-two hours turned out to be too short a time frame for many shell-shocked victims to complete the transaction. They had to acknowledge and understand their problem, check for usable backups, consider their options, contact the extortionists, and work out how to make the requested payment. The cut-off time truncated many transactions that could have resulted in payments further down the line. Moreover, computer users with up-to-date antivirus software never even got to first base: CryptoLocker encrypted their files but then the antivirus program removed the virus. Their files were locked, yet the victims were not offered the option of buying the decryption key. Third, many victims who paid chose the more familiar payment option of prepaid money cards rather than the criminally convenient Bitcoin.

Ever the innovators, the criminals went back to the drawing board. To maximise their haul from CryptoLocker, the gang fine-tuned their ransom note and provided better customer education and support. The time issue was easy to fix: there was no need to delete decryption keys after three days, so deals could be completed at a more leisurely pace. The main question was how to convince victims not to drag their feet and yet keep the door open for late resolutions. The CryptoLocker crew settled upon raising the price fivefold after the deadline, creating a strong incentive to complete within seventy-two hours. Those who crawled in late did so because they were desperate for the decryption key and would pay the higher rate.

Reversing the accidental damage wrought by antivirus software was a little trickier. The victims needed to know that their troubles were due to CryptoLocker and that they had to somehow recover the code for the unique decryption key to unlock their files. The CryptoLocker team designed a different window for those caught out by the antivirus program: they were asked to deliberately reinfect their computers with Zeus malware. One might imagine this to be a hard sell, but the criminals were extremely matter-of-fact about it: 'If you need your files you have to recover CryptoLocker from the antivirus quarantine or find a copy of CryptoLocker on the internet and run it again.'[16] After a while they took pity on their victims and provided a link to a website where they could download the Trojan.

The criminals also realised that most of their victims needed support and encouragement to make what was likely their first ever Bitcoin payment. They decided to offer another financial incentive as a nudge. Bitcoin would be the cheapest way to pay, though other options remained available. The pop-up then explained briefly how to pay in Bitcoin. If the victims needed more help than this, they were encouraged to download the TOR software and start a chat with the criminals in the Deep Web. This was another hurdle for many, requiring clear guidance and some handholding. Successive generations of CryptoLocker lockscreens and pop-ups from September to November 2013 provided ever more detailed support for victims opting to make a payment. They are a fascinating case study in learning by doing.

However, the criminals were not the only people who spotted economic opportunities here. The GameOver Zeus phishing emails were primarily targeted at businesses. Some of these companies had cyberinsurance, and this included cover for business interruption. So, insurers had every interest in helping the insured to expedite the resolution of the attack. Computer security firms also offered help and advice – including many suspicious fly-by-night outfits offering resolution services online. CryptoLocker proved everyone wrong who had dismissed the threat of ransomware out of hand on the basis that surely no one would pay a ransom. Not everyone did, of course, but most victims saw no better option than spending a hundred (or a few hundred) dollars to resolve such a profound business crisis. This included a police station in Massachusetts that paid the late penalty fee of $750 to recover their investigative files and digital archive of mug shots.[17] From around a quarter of a million infected computers, the CryptoLocker crew made an estimated haul of $27 million. The criminal underworld sat up and took note. The ransomware business model was working at last – and it could readily be copied.

However, law enforcement was not just looking on passively. With mounting financial losses due to GameOver Zeus (at least $100 million in the US alone), in 2013 the FBI once again took the lead in building an international cybercrime taskforce. This time they did not waste energy on trying to get the Russian or Ukrainian security forces on board. Instead, the FBI was joined by Europol and ten national crime agencies, as well as software and computer security firms. Code-named Operation Tovar, the combined forces' brief was threefold: neutralise the Game-Over Zeus botnet, stop CryptoLocker, and unmask and arrest the hackers behind this evil enterprise.

The cyber sleuths started by investigating the botnet and intercepting its communications by deliberately infecting carefully primed computers with GameOver Zeus. They were stunned when they mapped the dense network of hundreds of thousands of computers all over the globe – with a notable absence of infections in Russia. This innovative network did not have a single command centre in a specific geographic location but many regional command nodes instead. There was no way to trace the criminal(s) to their lair or to bring down the network with a single raid. Yet, now subsumed into the GameOver botnet, the Tovar honeypot computers received the weekly list of randomly generated domain names that would be used to find the new command centre if communication with the peer nodes was lost. If law enforcement simultaneously disrupted all the regional command nodes and registered all the listed domain names, the criminals would permanently lose their power to communicate with their bots.[18] Here was the beginning of a plan to unravel the botnet. Once law enforcement gained control over the botnet, they could stop CryptoLocker from spreading further. However, to recover decryption keys potentially stored in the botnet, they first had to apply for government or judicial authorisation to hijack and search hundreds of thousands of personal and business computers for the information.

The first part of Operation Tovar in June 2014 was a great success. Once the various forces had been given the green light, they severed the criminals' control over the botnet by redirecting the hijacked computers to servers controlled by the authorities. Search warrants allowed security experts to look for and retrieve locally stored files containing stolen financial credentials and decryption keys. The keys were offered to CryptoLocker victims who had not bought them from the crime syndicate. The unwitting participants of the GameOver Zeus botnet were then given instructions on how to rid their computers of the virus.[19]

Identifying and apprehending the criminals was a different matter, however. As with Vyacheslav Penchukov and the Business Club, it was good old-fashioned human intelligence that lifted the veil on the elusive master hacker. A secret source revealed that the CryptoLocker team was directed by someone with the handle 'lucky12345'. An email address of that name turned up on the social media profile of one Evgeniy Bogachev: a resident of the Russian Black Sea resort of Anapa and the proud owner of multiple properties and – allegedly – a string of luxury cars parked in airport car parks dotted around Europe.[20] In some of his pictures Bogachev looks ready to audition as a Bond villain: shaven-headed and bare-chested behind the steering wheel of his boat or hamming it up in indoor sunglasses holding a sleek Bengal cat wearing what looks like a leopard-print onesie. Bogachev's profile also revealed that his other handle was 'Slavik'. The mastermind behind the Business Club and CryptoLocker was the same person, and the FBI could finally name one of their most wanted cybercriminals.[21] Yet the other team members remain phantoms: we are still to uncover the true identities of 'Temp Special', 'Ded', 'Chingiz911 aka Chingiz' and 'Mr Kykypyky'.[22]

Although the Operation Tovar team sent the indictment and the home address for Evgeniy Bogachev to the Russian government, they refused to arrest or extradite him. In Russia, cybercrime is only a crime if the victims are Russians on Russian soil – in which case retribution is swift and certain. Bogachev had been very careful to avoid crossing this line. Instead, he had made his GameOver botnet available to the intelligence services. Rather than hacking into computers themselves, Russia's spies had peered over Bogachev's shoulder: snooping on foreign businesses, garnering information contained in files marked 'top secret' and 'Department of Defense', and paying special attention to military intelligence from Georgia, Turkey, Ukraine and Syria.[23]

Bogachev was accordingly treated as a national hero and issued with multiple passports to facilitate incognito travel. In his hometown of Anapa, he was admiringly nicknamed 'Fantomas' after a shape-shifting evil genius – the star of a series of 1960s French crime comedies that had been hugely popular in the USSR.[24] Bogachev's lifestyle was apparently not extravagant, and his neighbours liked him and his family.[25] With anti-American sentiment running high, few locals were prepared to find fault with him.[26] Even the lure of a $3 million bounty for information leading to Bogachev's arrest and/or conviction did not tempt anyone to blow his cover.[27]

However, the FBI is patient and has a long arm. If Mr

Bogachev travels westwards, he must be careful. His former colleague Mr Penchukov (aka Tank, the Business Club's master of money mules) was arrested in Geneva in 2022. Once again, his family proved to be the careless DJ's Achilles heel. Penchukov's wife had moved to Switzerland after the Russian invasion of the Donbas, and a visit to her led to his arrest and extradition to the US in 2023. In 2024 Penchukov pleaded guilty to multiple charges of cybercrimes.[28]

We have heard very little about Mr Bogachev since 2017, which would be expected if he really works for the Russian intelligence services. However, we have certainly heard a lot about his famous innovation of 2013. His ransomware business model was about to be copied around the world.

7

A Masterpiece of Criminality: Ransomware-as-a-Service

Think of a hospital in Hollywood ... and then think again. The Hollywood Presbyterian Medical Center in Los Angeles is not a sleek glass and steel palace for intoxicated celebrities, the worried well, achy sports stars or starlets seeking cosmetic treatment. It is an 'acute care hospital serving the multicultural population in Hollywood and nearby communities.'[1] In other words, a hospital for people who probably needed urgent medical attention well before they made the decision to call for an ambulance. A place where timely intervention saves lives. One day in early February 2016, the IT helplines at the Hollywood Presbyterian started to ring off the hook. Anxious calls were coming in from multiple lines: staff who had tried to look up patient records, laboratory results, X-rays or CT scans had black and red 'death screens' on their computers and their files were locked.

The system administrators immediately raised a red alert: if this was a ransomware attack, it would spread like wildfire. Rather than watch the malware rip through their entire system, they decided to shut down all the hospital's computers and call the police. As forensic IT experts and FBI investigators converged on the hospital to examine the affected computers, hassled doctors, nurses and pharmacists struggled to provide medical care without phones, email or access to their patients' medical records, tests or scans. With the hospital unable to reach anyone by phone or email, elderly and infirm patients travelled there in person to pick up test results and medication. Behind the reassuring facade ('patient care has not been compromised in any way'[2]) there was mayhem on the wards. An 'internal emergency' was declared. Hundreds of patients were turned away or transferred to other hospitals.[3]

The tight-lipped management only told patients that the hospital had been 'hacked', so exaggerated rumours quickly spread. A hearsay claim that the criminals had demanded the astronomic sum of 9,000 Bitcoin to restore the network – around $3.6 million at the time – was announced in dramatic news bulletins: 'Right now, a hospital in Hollywood is at the mercy of hackers. The computers are down, and the hackers are demanding a huge ransom … the situation is serious, and the hospital is even turning patients away.'[4] With pressure mounting on all sides, the hospital's management weighed up the FBI's advice never to pay extortionists against the safety of their patients. The criminals' actual demand of 40 Bitcoin (US $17,000) seemed a small price to resolve the crisis, and the administrators decided to swallow the bitter pill. As the president and CEO of the hospital explained: 'The quickest and most efficient way to restore our systems and administrative functions was to pay the ransom and obtain the decryption key. In the best interest of restoring normal operations, we did this.'[5] Ten days after the attack, the incident was declared resolved. Undoubtedly the exhausted staff and their fearful patients breathed a collective sigh of relief.

Unfortunately, Hollywood Presbyterian Medical Center was only the first of many healthcare providers to be targeted by a worryingly virulent new strain of ransomware in 2016. When just a few weeks later the Methodist Hospital in Kentucky had to switch to emergency pen-and-paper mode for the sake of a measly 4 Bitcoin ($1,600) ransom, the malware program was already well known to security experts.[6] 'Locky' ransomware had surged through the world like a tidal wave. Hundreds of thousands of email accounts had been spammed with emails carefully crafted in the users' preferred languages purporting to contain crucial business information. The attached documents looked hopelessly garbled when the recipients opened them safely in 'protected view'. However, the sender had anticipated this problem and promised that the formatting could be fixed by overriding the computer's security settings and clicking on 'enable editing'. That careless click unleashed the Locky ransomware virus. Every day, tens of thousands of hoodwinked victims reported infections. IT experts swiftly concluded that the Locky ransomware campaign was a well-planned 'masterpiece of criminality'.[7]

Many of the victims were healthcare providers, whose multiple endpoint users had been deliberately targeted. The combination of poor cybersecurity – IT expenditure rarely reaches the top of the wish list of medical professionals – with critical reliance on computer systems made hospitals sitting ducks for cyberextortion.[8] This was a world away from the playful innocence of the early hackers and a departure from the 'spray-and-pray' approach of previous ransomware campaigns. Attacking healthcare was the work of hardened, cynical, business-minded criminals. Why the change – and what could explain the astonishing scale of the Locky operation?

Imagine that you have developed a product that is irresistible to most people you offer it to. You have spent a lot of time, money and effort in developing this product. You maintain an intricate infrastructure that could deliver millions of units anywhere in the world in seconds. However, processing each transaction takes time. Occasionally, a deal becomes tricky and considerable skill is required to reach a satisfactory conclusion. Every transaction that leaves a customer disappointed harms the reputation of your product. So, if you are greedy and take on more business than you can handle, your business will fail. Moreover, demand for your product could disappear overnight unless you constantly keep up with the latest fast-moving technology. There simply is not enough time in the day to get it all done. And finally, every transaction with a customer puts your own security at risk. If you scale up your operation it increases the chance that your firm will be targeted by Interpol or the FBI and (if you are within reach) you end up behind bars. Welcome to the world – and headaches – of a successful ransomware developer.

The developers of Locky ransomware decided to approach these dilemmas in a novel way, by copying an established business model in the licit economy: software-as-a-service. Locky automated the process of encrypting the data, the ransoming, and the release of the decryption keys. The group also maintained a powerful infrastructure for sending spam messages, thereby enabling criminals with relatively limited computer skills to conduct ransomware operations. If someone could compose a convincing email to get a computer user to open an attachment and enable the virus, the Locky support infrastructure largely took care of the rest of the process. When the victims' files were encrypted, a message about a successful Locky attack directed victims to a TOR-encrypted site in the Deep Web – as well as giving detailed directions for getting there. Once on the Locky website, victims identified their computer using the unique code from the 'death screen' displayed on their computer. The user-friendly Locky interface then provided them with a step-by-step guide on where and how to obtain the necessary Bitcoin and make the payment.[9] All instructions were available in a choice of languages that could be selected from a drop-down menu at the top of the page. Once the payment had been made, the decryption key was automatically released.

Locky also had other top-class features: the encryption was so effective that the FBI told victims that: 'Recovery of encrypted files is impossible without data backup or acquisition of the private key.' While law enforcement 'did not recommend that the victim pay a ransom', they admitted that many victims would have to take this step as part of their 'business continuity plan'.[10] The FBI strongly warned victims against attempting to remedy the problem in-house or using antivirus software, which could interfere with running the criminals' decryption program. But even for those who could theoretically restore from backups, with Bitcoin still trading at less than $1,000, Locky's maximum demand of 2 Bitcoin was low enough to encourage engagement with the criminals. Many victims decided it was cheaper and easier for them to pay this 'nuisance expense' to recover their data than take the hit of an extended business downtime.

Running Locky as an 'affiliate' was as easy as taking candy from a toddler. Affiliates could send millions of spam messages through the botnet created and maintained by Locky.[11] A number embedded in the code identified which affiliate had successfully breached each target. When an affiliate had hooked a new victim, the central command-and-control server sent them an alert. All the lucky affiliate had to do was to set a ransom amount between 0.5 and 2 Bitcoin for their initial demand – with the possibility of raising it later if the victim dawdled. Time to sit back and wait for the cash to roll in – or run the next campaign. The affiliate contract specified how the ransom would be split between the affiliates and the developer. Affiliates could negotiate cuts of more than 50 per cent for their work in placing the 'infections' and for taking the risk of operating at the coalface of cybercrime. However, running Locky was not particularly risky for affiliates, especially if they lived in Russia or Eastern Europe. The Deep Web locations of the Locky portal and Locky servers in Russia and Ukraine provided excellent cover for their operations. In addition, Locky set up a unique Bitcoin address for every victim on a fishy cryptocurrency exchange, making it extremely difficult for Western law enforcement to track the payments.[12]

Ransomware-as-a-service was the force multiplier that ransomware developers had been (consciously or unconsciously) looking for. The partnership model meant that developers could focus on their key business (i.e. programming) while outsourcing the criminal business of breach and extortion to others. The Locky crew did this with alacrity, pushing out one clever software update after another.[13] Meanwhile their affiliates merrily infected computers around the world. Targeting healthcare and critical public services got swift and certain payouts. The ruthless ransomware campaigns called for beefed-up security responses from the victims, which trapped the malware developers and IT engineers in an ever accelerating game of one-upmanship. But it was not just computer security professionals who watched Locky conquer the world; it was also of great interest in the criminal underworld. Locky's ransomware-as-a-service model was soon copied by others in the ransomware business. But was the affiliate model really a magic bullet?

A MASTERPIECE OF CRIMINALITY

As more and more cybercriminals jumped on to the ransomware-as-a-service bandwagon, the strain began to show. First, it turned out that one couldn't hire any random computer enthusiast as an affiliate. Although encrypting data can be automated, restoring networks to working order can be quite complicated. Antivirus software often made decryption problematic. Some victims needed detailed advice on how to prepare their computer(s) for the debugging operation. In systems with multiple affected machines, there was the danger that a computer that still harboured the malware could be reconnected to the network by mistake and start the encryption process all over again. At the ransomware operators' command-and-control centre this would look like a completely new set of infections, requiring more payments to release a new set of decryption keys – something a victim might justifiably dispute. And depending on the computing and communication skills of both victims and extortionists, one could sail around these buoys multiple times.

This requirement for advanced computer skills, forethought and commitment was not a significant problem when experienced hackers ran their own ransomware campaigns. They had a clear incentive to spend time trying to resolve their victims' problems: there was value in running a 'brand' of ransomware that was known to work. Less so for the hired hands, who had already made their money from the attack by the time their unlucky 'customers' came begging for help. Why should they be diverted away from the tasks of infecting new computers, setting their demands and spending the (not too hard-earned) cash to engage with the tedious business of aftercare? This is a classic free-rider problem. Disappointing a few awkward customers has little impact in a huge global business. However, if all affiliates routinely shirk their duty the trust problem becomes endemic. Word will eventually get round that for all but the simplest set-ups, paying for a specific brand's decryption key is a waste of time and money.

Second, the more lucrative the ransomware model became, the more cybercriminals decided to go for it. If victims paid ransoms unquestioningly, it did not matter if the criminals' coding skills were basic. Several would-be ransomware kingpins overreached and launched malware that trashed rather than encrypted the victims' data. So what? By the time victims found out that there was no workable decryption key, the Bitcoin was already safely in the criminals' wallet. Add to that the scareware programmers who didn't even attempt to encrypt anything but just popped up a ransom demand on their victims' computers – perhaps imitating the design of a well-known ransomware brand. All these guys were free-riding on the reputation of ransomware developers who had wisely chosen a small number of highly skilled staff, monitored their activities closely, and largely delivered on their side of the bargain. But on the wild new frontier of ransomware there were no trademarks, no patents and no regulator punishing substandard service providers. Somehow these problems would need to be resolved from the bottom up in the multitude of interactions between victims and their attackers.

Third, internal divisions sometimes arose within cybergangs about the ethical profile of a ransomware brand. Early cybercrime had a David vs Goliath flavour: plucky hackers against business giants, clever teens against the FBI, poor against rich with the bill paid by insurance. But attacking the weakest in society was different. Were all foreigners legitimate prey? What about ordinary hospital patients seeking urgent or surgical care – that is, any one of us?[14] What about the Syrian father who could not afford the Bitcoin to decrypt the photos of his beloved children killed in the war?[15] Affiliates who overstepped the mark in ethical terms could damage loyalty and trust in the joint enterprise.

And there was one final challenge: could criminals trust each other to pay for services rendered? At Locky and most other ransomware brands, affiliates rely on the code correctly attributing successful attacks to the right affiliates and the centre faithfully sharing the proceeds. This is probably not a problem if one is working with a few trusted friends. However, it is trickier to build trust if the staff are strangers recruited from an online forum – and even more difficult to maintain that trust if said affiliates are carelessly damaging a brand by shirking their aftercare duty. If a particularly cash-rich business is breached, the temptation to default on a commitment and retire on the proceeds might be overwhelming.

The case of Change Healthcare, hacked in 2024, illustrates this problem well. After weeks of being unable to process medical claims, the victim's parent company UnitedHealth Group caved in and paid an exorbitant $22 million ransom to a ransomware gang called ALPHV. But when an affiliate with the handle 'notchy' asked for their agreed share of the proceeds, ALPHV's administrators gave them the silent treatment. They placed a bogus statement on their website saying that the gang had been shut down by law enforcement. Unable to contact their partners in crime in any other way, the jilted affiliate started to post bitter complaints on cybercriminal forums. Pointing to a 350 Bitcoin transaction on the blockchain that proved and justified their claim, notchy urged other cybercriminals to stop dealing with ALHPV until the issue was resolved.[16] To no avail. There was no honour among these thieves; ALHPV had vanished into thin air. Notchy had fallen victim to an exit scam.

Indeed, the path of ransomware is littered with broken promises, angry posts on virtual message boards, and failed partnerships. Thanks to internal tensions and irresistible temptations, ransomware partnerships rarely last longer than a year or two. To the casual observer, the ransomware landscape looks confusing: so many nicknames, so many brands that are briefly famous and then vanish. When a brand's reputation is burnt, or the partners fall out, or law enforcement infiltrates and targets their infrastructure, the group just fades away or shuts down. Everyone has a holiday and enjoys their winnings for a while. When the GandCrab ransomware group disbanded in 2019, they posted the following grand exit message to their affiliates: 'All the good things come to an end. For the year of working with us, people have earned more than $2 billion ... earnings with us per week averaged $2,500,000. We personally earned more than 150 million dollars per year. We successfully cashed this money and legalized it ... We were glad to work with you. But ... we are leaving for a well-deserved retirement.'[17]

When the developers burn through the cash or grow bored of yachting on the Black Sea, they generally return for another round on the carousel with an updated code and under a new name. Software engineers often recognise key pieces of code that are recycled in subsequent incarnations of ransomware – like DNA running down family lines. Indeed, even before posting their boastful farewell, many of the developers behind the GandCrab group had already regrouped under the brand name REvil. When REvil was targeted by law enforcement in early 2021, the group seemingly imploded – but resurrected as BlackMatter in July 2021.[18] This morphed into ALPHV/BlackCat in December 2021 – with each new generation learning from the mistakes of the past.[19] We will see this ever accelerating game played out in later chapters. In the next chapter, however, we will look at how law enforcement, insurers and entrepreneurs reacted to the changed threat landscape created by the callous and unreliable first generation of ransomware-as-a-service.

8

The Ransomware Ecosystem: Ransomware-Settlement-as-a-Service

Being hacked is intensely unsettling. Victims of online crimes report similar symptoms to victims of violent crimes, such as increased anxiety, depression and a general loss of trust.[1] In severe cases, victims suffer physical illness, relationship breakdown or PTSD as a long-term consequence.[2] For many businesses a ransomware attack is a make-or-break moment too. Even in a best-case scenario, the company's activity is paralysed for days, as computers are switched off to prevent the spread of the infection. Everyone in management, PR and IT has to work round the clock to limit the extent of the damage and start the recovery.

In the early days of ransomware, most victims found that their back-up routines were too patchy or haphazard to facilitate a rebuild – or that it would take months to download the data from wherever it was stored. When managers decided to take the plunge and engage with their extortionists, their staff had to work out how to do a shady deal in an unfamiliar cryptocurrency. They then waited anxiously to see whether the gang would deliver on their promise and whether the decryption would proceed smoothly. The larger the organisation (and the more complicated their network), the greater the chances of wasting days getting nowhere at all or permanently damaging important files. In fact, it seemed like a very good idea to outsource the data recovery process to specialists, if it was at all affordable.

When ransomware took off in the mid-2010s, there was already a highly evolved service industry for resolving cyberattacks. It had been created to support cyberinsurers in managing the losses created by previous generations of cyberperils and crime. From the moment they connected to the internet, companies had been at risk from a wide range of pranks, computer viruses, theft, fraud, defacement of webpages, overloaded servers, power outages and software faults. Even relatively minor problems could cause lengthy business interruptions or reputational damage. Many organisations had inadvertently breached intellectual property rights laws with material posted on their websites. Companies and clubs sometimes failed to protect sensitive information about their customers, staff, suppliers, members, patients or students. Copyright infringements or theft and disclosure of personal data had left some companies embroiled in expensive lawsuits. Moreover, regulators threatened punitive fines if they deemed that companies had failed to implement adequate security measures. For all its commercial potential, an internet presence could end up endangering or even killing a company. So, from the mid-1990s cautious chief financial officers had presented these worries to their boards and insurance brokers.

Initially, most underwriters decided that these risks looked like the kinds of risks their customers had faced before: damage to property, indemnity for third-party liabilities, kidnap and extortion, media insurance and so on. All that was needed, then, were extensions to existing insurance policies. However, it did not take long before the first companies asked their insurers to cover surprisingly large 'cyber' losses through their traditional insurance policies. Many insurers had not correctly budgeted for this eventuality in the rush for a toehold in what had seemed like a promising new market. When a few insurers decided to deny the claims, puzzled elderly judges struggled to settle the tricky question of whether, for example, lost programming information was the kind of 'physical damage' that was covered by property insurance.[3] As a result of the legal uncertainty, insurance lawyers became ever more cautious in crafting policies that precisely defined and limited the various cyber-risks insured. Getting insurance for all the manifold and diverse risks posed by e-commerce thus became a tedious job – and one that had to be repeated annually when the various insurance policies came up for renewal.

Soon companies started to demand 'cyberinsurance' – a single product to cover their online risks.[4] Predictably, such a product looked very risky to underwriters. Budding cyber-insurers initially agreed that their insurance premium should depend on customers' efforts to make their IT systems secure against potential intruders. However, their meticulous multi-day fact-finding missions and offers of security advice fell on stony ground with potential customers. Companies sought insurance precisely because they wanted to take risks online. To them, security measures were a barrier to productivity and a source of exasperation for their employees. Bosses just wanted cover in case things went wrong.[5] Yet, having learned about the risks that their customers faced, cyberinsurers' appetite for selling insurance with fulsome compensation promises was strictly limited. A stand-off ensued. Realistic pricing and tight underwriting practices sapped demand for cyberinsurance until 2002, when the US Insurance Services Office formally stated that data was not 'tangible property' and needed to be insured separately.[6] From this point, tech and media companies and financial institutions had to buy cyber cover.

A second source of demand for cyberinsurance came from tightening data privacy regulations. Organisations were increasingly concerned about incurring heavy regulatory fines, being pilloried in the press and becoming embroiled in class action lawsuits. Yet companies and their IT officers still resisted any form of security micro-management by outsiders. Insurers read the market correctly and relaxed their underwriting standards. Unable to control the number of incidents, they decided to focus on reducing the size of each claim instead.[7] When underwriters had first offered cyberinsurance in the 1990s and early 2000s, they had left their clients to their own devices when resolving hacker attacks. Insurers just settled the final claim when all the costs had been added up. Soon, however, observant claims adjusters realised that most companies compounded the original damage and dragged out their recoveries with avoidable mistakes. They could soon catalogue a whole list of expensive pitfalls in the resolution process. Insurers realised that they could add immense value to their product by helping their clients recover from cyber losses in a calm, informed and cost-effective way. Timely professional advice would more than pay for itself, both in reduced claims for the insurers and by creating demand for a product that provided peace of mind in periods of extreme stress.

Consequently, a whole range of professional services sprang into existence to support insurers with managing cyber losses. Dedicated crisis responders offered bespoke services to manage the resolution and recovery process, from the minute a problem was detected to making the final claim. Before the rise of ransomware, the foremost concern (especially of US companies) was to insure against the problems arising from data privacy breaches. Therefore, insurers put privacy lawyers into the driving seat of crisis response. In case any mistakes were made, it was best to protect all communications between clients and their advisors from outside scrutiny. Client–attorney privilege served that purpose.[8]

In turn the crisis response firms created an intricate network of supply relationships to respond to the whole spectrum of cyber claims. They retained crack IT teams that identified the cause and extent of malware problems, ejected intruders and stopped leakages of data or money. If necessary, legal experts ensured that breach victims satisfied all regulatory requirements and fulfilled their duty of care. In other cases, advice was brought in to settle copyright infringements or compensate customers for harm caused by faulty software or inadequate services. Clients that faced extortion attempts were given assistance by professional ransom negotiators. Their tried-and-tested hostage recovery protocols – carefully honed by resolving hundreds of kidnap and hijacking cases – became an important touchstone for resolving cyberextortion.[9] Finally, most firms recovered much faster if their in-house IT team was boosted by recovery experts, who were used to the challenges of rebuilding systems and could recommend appropriate security enhancements to guard against future attacks.

Companies were thereby relieved of the burden of having to curate an emergency response under time and financial pressure. The convenience of having a single helpline number became a major selling point for cyberinsurance.[10] Meanwhile, the claims adjusters kept a beady eye on the evolving cyber incident resolution ecosystem. Every insurer wanted to hire or retain the best-value incident responders. Many firms competed to find the most cost-efficient solutions to the multi-dimensional challenges of recovering from a wide range of crises: minimising the sum of business interruption costs, recovery and rebuild expenses, fines, compensation payments, as well as strengthening the client's IT systems against future incidents. Each responder in turn evaluated their suppliers, retaining and rewarding the best performers and sacking those that let them down. Firms bringing in successful innovations grew, while others either adapted or failed.

It is important to note that the standards for cyber-crisis response evolved well before ransomware became a serious threat. The protocol for dealing with cyber losses focused on three main cost factors: regulatory fines, business interruption and system recovery. Cyberextortion was extremely rare and when it happened, criminals' demands were either low from the offset, or they could be bartered down by professional ransom negotiators. When CryptoLocker and its imitators burst on to the scene from 2013 onwards, the established protocol benefited the criminals in three ways.

First, crisis responders tended to advise companies to resolve minor security breaches privately, and ransomware was no exception. It quickly transpired that the police and intelligence services could not offer practical help with reversing sophisticated asymmetric encryption. In fact, involving the cops was likely to make the problem worse. If called in to investigate a crime scene, law enforcement would seize infected computers to carry out a full forensic investigation. IT staff were left to twiddle their thumbs rather than restoring their systems. Meanwhile, ambulance-chaser law firms would do their best to put a class action lawsuit together. It was much better to say nothing or as little as possible. This attitude created a veil of secrecy around data breaches, which provided an ideal opportunity for ransomware actors to develop their product under the radar of the law and the media. By the time policymakers fully recognised the threat of ransomware at the end of the decade, it was already endemic.

Second, crisis responders were laser-focused on minimising business interruption. Each day spent offline or operating in pen-and-paper mode contributed significantly to total recovery costs. When a company was hit by ransomware, doing a deal with extortionists was almost always preferable to recovering (slowly) from backups. The quicker the payment, the faster the repairs could begin. Early ransomware campaigns priced decryption keys at a few hundred dollars, so the decision to pay made perfect business sense for each individual victim. Yet a far-sighted spokesperson for the Lake City Police Department in Florida lamented the city council's decision to pay a ransom to 'save time and money' and end the city's paralysis. 'Our insurance company made [the decision] for us ... At the end of the day, it really boils down to a business decision on the insurance side of things: them looking at how much is it going to cost to fix it ourselves and how much is it going to cost to pay the ransom.'[11] Anyone looking at the bigger picture knew that normalising and speeding up payments would make ransomware more profitable and attract more crooks to create or join ransomware-as-a-service gangs.

Third, ransomware gangs benefited from the experienced IT professionals drafted in by crisis responders to ensure that corporate clients didn't mess up what was often a complex, multi-step decryption procedure. For the criminals it was easier to address the occasional problems faced by highly skilled recovery experts than to coach quaking novices through the entire process. In fact, one ransomware gang – SamSam – was so pleased with the services provided by a legal IT company called Proven Data Recovery that they specifically recommended that their victims work with them.[12] The less time the gangs spent helping their victims with the recovery, the more time they had to infect more computers.

Few people stopped to ask whether it was in the public interest to outsource ransomware recovery to private companies focused on their clients' immediate problems rather than the social consequences. Doing so inevitably set a vicious cycle in motion. At first, only a tiny minority of (generally large) companies had cyberinsurance, and very few cyber responders existed. When ransomware-as-a-service produced a sudden and unprecedented surge in attacks, most of the victims were not insured. Seeing the enormity of the task ahead, many of them concluded that they needed professional support too. However, the established responders were expensive and quickly reached capacity. There were simply not enough outstanding IT security specialists on the job market for the existing firms to expand and keep delivering the top-notch product that insurers had come to expect. Rather than diluting their carefully curated brands, established responders started to turn down additional work.

The underlying features of the existing resolution protocol could be copied by others though: keep shtum, pay fast, help clients with the decryption. It did not take long before new private resolution services sprang up at every price point. Few businesses haemorrhaging money took a long-term view or asked searching questions about the rescuers' means and methods. Most victims wanted decryption keys as fast as possible, so they could recover before their customers, staff and suppliers became fully aware of the breach. The most profitable way of delivering this was for responders to develop surprisingly cosy relationships with ransomware gangs.

If an uninsured victim looked for 'ransomware removal' help online and entered their attacker's brand name, the sponsored links were mostly what came to be known as ransomware payment mills. These typically offered 'guaranteed decryption without having to pay the hacker' – though at a multiple of the gangs' asking price of a few hundred dollars.[13] Such offers looked like an ethical way out of a tight spot. Yet, having obtained the details from the victims' lockscreens, the operators of payment mills went straight to the ransomware gangs' TOR portals and bought a decryption key for their anxiously waiting clients. It was easy money – and if the clients needed help with implementing the decryption keys, some of the mills offered that too.

Since underworld business runs just the same as any other, the intermediaries began to negotiate better terms with the gangs. After all, they were bringing in business from victims opposed to paying ransoms and saving the criminals time and effort. Soon, the mill operators were offered 'discount' codes that not only improved their profit margins (the savings were rarely passed through to the customers) but also gave them access to private chat lines in case of queries. It was a win-win situation, with higher profits and time savings for both payment mills and gangs. Predictably, this fuelled fresh waves of attacks, drew further rounds of victims into the net, and produced more business for the mills.

Even though many victims hushed up ransomware incidents, law enforcement became aware of the increased frequency of attacks. Some citizens called the police or intelligence services as a matter of course after being victimised. But a growing number of victims called them because no functioning decryption keys had materialised after paying the ransom. Not all denizens of the underworld were sophisticated coders or capable of running the kind of tight ship that asymmetric encryption requires to match public and private keys.

What was the police going to do about that? They were caught between a rock and a hard place. On the one hand, paying ransoms encourages extortive crime. If nobody paid ransoms that would be the end of ransomware – so the top-line official advice was not to pay ransoms. On the other hand, asymmetric encryption as practised by the top ransomware gangs was almost unbreakable and the authorities realised that paying the (still low) ransoms was a pragmatic way to get out of a pickle that might otherwise turn into a disaster. Indeed, it was a situation in which government agencies and police forces around the world had found themselves too.

One outcome was a curious situation in which US police forces and former FBI staff endorsed a company that routinely channelled ransoms to criminals.[14] MonsterCloud promoted its business by resolving ransomware attacks in paralysed police stations in the US. Its slick website was full of video testimonials from officers with a carefully crafted storyline and a fairytale quality. The protagonists universally start off in a state of despair. A burly Texan sheriff recalled his horror from deep beneath the shelter of his white hat: 'It shut everything down, it crippled us is basically what you could say. It just crippled us.'[15] The weight of the officers' responsibility was immense. 'We could not access anything. Even our backup system was destroyed in the process … That put the health and safety of the public in danger.'[16] It wasn't just the computers in the police stations that were affected; communications with patrol cars were disrupted and arrests could not be processed. 'All of our incident reports, all of our jail files, everything that we use day to day in this department to take care of the citizens of Lauderdale County was now in jeopardy.'[17] The failure felt personal, as the Chief of Police at Trumann, Arkansas, remembered: 'There is a data breach and to know that I am the one that's in the seat and it's my responsibility to safeguard that, it's an incredibly disgusting feeling.'[18]

When the chiefs turned to their IT departments for solutions, they found their staff equally perplexed and helpless. The camera cuts to the system administrators admitting their defeat. 'This was a very advanced attack, and I realised very quickly I could not resolve it on my own.'[19] Tough guys felt overwhelmed: 'Your heart drops into the pit of your stomach. I mean you are pretty much hijacked. It cripples your agency.'[20] Feelings of guilt, shame and fear intermingled: this was an IT manager's worst nightmare. Proud and self-reliant men freely express anxiety and panic: 'So now we were freaking out ... We are not sure what we could do.'[21]

Giving in to extortion was anathema to law enforcement, but time was of the essence. Calling their colleagues around the country, a certain company was recommended: 'MonsterCloud can do this. Here is the number, contact them now.'[22] Once the stressed-out police departments signed on with MonsterCloud, decryption keys materialised near instantaneously and they were coached through every aspect of the recovery. 'MonsterCloud started telling me everything we needed to do. And it was amazing because he already knew what to do, he already had a plan of action ... Man, these people really know what they are doing ...'[23] Other IT managers were content to let the cybersecurity experts log in remotely and just stood by, watching in amazement as one server after another came back online and their corrupted files were restored. 'To be able to be that skilled in every area of a recovery from a cyberattack, I have never seen anything like it. It's like a huge corporation – almost like the Department of Defense to have that expertise.'[24] One grown man expressed an almost childlike sense of wonder and relief: 'The only question I had for the representative from

MonsterCloud was simply what colour capes do you wear? Because every superhero I have ever known had a cape and I guess they all walk around their office with capes on. Because to us, MonsterCloud is a bunch of superheroes.'[25]

The MonsterCloud website proudly proclaimed that they were 'The #1 Ransomware Removal Experts In The World. Trusted by Federal & Municipal Agencies All Over The World'.[26] To prove it, the company's landing page showed a video featuring John Pistole, a former deputy director of the FBI, looking any dithering potential customer straight in the eye and saying to the camera, 'MonsterCloud will help you ...'[27] But where did MonsterCloud get the decryption keys? It seemed that either it did not matter, or the officers really believed in superheroes. MonsterCloud offered a free service to the police. Accordingly, not a dime of US taxpayers' money went to the criminals. All MonsterCloud wanted was a glowing testimonial for their website to entice other companies to pay for their services.

These website testimonials foreground the magic and relief of the recovery process while glossing over its technical details. MonsterCloud's CEO Zohar Pinhasi was evasive when asked detailed questions about their recovery methods. He was only prepared to tell journalists that the company's approach 'varies from case to case' and 'it's a trade secret'.[28] His business was to sell peace of mind to victims who knew not to ask awkward questions: 'We work in the shadows ... How we do it, it's our problem. You will get your data back. Sit back, relax, and enjoy the ride.'[29]

When your organisation faces financial or reputational ruin, it's hard to turn away from this promise. For companies and individuals willing to pay ransoms, it was clear that the 'FBI frowns on it officially – and winks at it in practice'.[30]

For those who did not want to engage with criminals, police endorsements suggested that data recovery companies offered an effective and ethical solution to ransomware attacks. Paying a multiple of the ransom bought a service that obscured whether ransoms were being paid ... but surely nobody could complain if someone employed the patriotic superheroes who had brought US law enforcement back online, could they?

Meanwhile, with extortionists large and small boasting in underground forums about the Bitcoin flooding into their crypto wallets, it was only a matter of time before other hostile actors started to get interested in ransomware.

9

Ransomwar:
Automatic, Rapid, Indiscriminate, Reckless

Usually, the term 'organised crime' suggests shady characters concealed behind dark sunglasses, clandestine meetings in smoky, ill-lit back rooms, a pervading atmosphere of danger, immorality and secrecy. Not so in North Korea, where crime is organised by the state. As early as 1995, the late leader Kim Jong-Il had predicted that 'In the 21st century, war will be [waged as] information warfare.'[1] Accordingly, the government set out to build up its own elite cyber-military units. This required a massive effort in a country with only the most rudimentary digital infrastructure. The recruitment drive started in primary schools, looking for kids who stood out for their mathematical abilities. A life of privilege was promised to those who proved themselves competent and loyal to the regime. Parents had little option but to give up their small children to be educated at physically and academically demanding state-run boarding schools. There the young contenders spent their lonely childhoods studying how to code. For years they mostly did so using pen and paper, only occasionally testing their mettle on a real computer owned by their school (on days when there was electricity).[2] At age seventeen, all students entered a tough competition for a place at Military College or the University

Kim Jong-Il and advisers in a press photo released in January 2008

of Automation for further training. From there, the most gifted students were hand-picked for deployment in China.

The computers in China had internet access, giving the isolated North Koreans their first glimpse of a different world. The recruits had been trained to view the West with suspicion and hostility and were assigned to various jobs: cyber-espionage, disrupting enemy nations or earning funds for the regime through fraud, theft, money laundering and extortion. Everyone works hard in the knowledge that only the most successful and trustworthy cyber-operatives will be allowed to return to Pyongyang. The majority serve out their days in China as mere IT foot soldiers. A chosen few, however, are recognised as their country's cyber-elite and handsomely rewarded. The prize for decades of hard work and dedication is the best life North Korea can offer: modern apartments, pleasant offices and a high social status. The agents' families are granted permission to move to the capital, and everyone has enough to eat.[3] When cyber-officers are posted abroad, they not only earn a handsome diplomatic stipend but can engage in side hustles such as smuggling drugs, gold, ivory or counterfeit currency.[4] The hope of achieving this golden goal sustains the entire recruitment scheme.

The infamous WannaCry ransomware attack of 2017 was masterminded by one of these North Korean cyber-units, known internationally as the Lazarus Group. Working tirelessly in the dank basement of geopolitics, the Lazarus operatives had already committed countless wire frauds and drained the bank accounts and ATMs of their country's enemies around the world. Stealing money was their bread-and-butter business. Yet, at any moment they could be redirected by the government to focus their attention on a different project.[5] For example, in 2014 they had attacked the SONY corporation to prevent the release of a film that the North Korean government considered harmful to its international image. *The Interview* was a comedy about two bumbling journalists accidentally assassinating Kim Jong-Un, the leader of North Korea. Its plotline had caused a serious sense of humour failure in Pyongyang's corridors of power and the Dear Leader had considered it 'the most blatant act of terrorism and war'. When the US government declined to ban *The Interview* as North Korea had requested, it fell to the Lazarus Group to carry out their government's threat of 'merciless countermeasures'. These included wiping out the corporations' computers, leaking candid and highly embarrassing email exchanges and releasing several SONY films online for free download. It did not take long for SONY to cave: the producers edited the film to be more friendly to North Korea and its wide release in cinemas was scrapped.[6]

In 2016, the Lazarus Group pulled off an audacious online bank heist, draining $81 million from the Bangladeshi National Bank's reserves held at the Federal Reserve in New York. Even though they had intended to swipe the whole billion-dollar booty, their final tally still easily put them in the top ten bank heists in world history.[7] Was this cybercrime, modern slavery or an act of patriotism? The Lazarus team only did the Dear Leader's bidding and relied entirely on him to reward their efforts.[8]

In May 2017, the group was ready to press the button on a completely new venture: using ransomware at a scale that dwarfed all previous efforts. Ironically, the Lazarus Group were greatly aided in this endeavour by the US National Security Agency (NSA). American government agents had meticulously analysed the Microsoft operating code and spotted a weakness that allowed those who knew about it to enter any computer system in the world that ran the hugely popular software. Instead of telling Microsoft about this flaw, the NSA kept the information in their top-secret arsenal of espionage tools under the codename EternalBlue.[9]

This is exactly where a member of the ominously named hacking group the Shadow Brokers found and stole it five years later. Cue frenetic activity: the NSA informed Microsoft of the problem and advised them to fix it pronto – as well as closely monitoring the Deep Web for this explosive information to leak. Although displeased by the belated revelation, Microsoft reacted immediately to amend the code for all its current operating systems, sending an urgent message to all customers in March 2017 that running the update was of critical importance. By the time the NSA saw criminal groups chatting about the endless possibilities of EternalBlue in April 2017, Microsoft had also provided a software update to patch the problem in older programs that were no longer formally supported by the corporation. Once again, everyone was told to immediately update their computers and the agents and programmers stood down with a huge sigh of relief. Disaster averted.

Except, of course, many people had better things to do than update their computers. Aren't updates just a conspiracy by manufacturers to encourage customers to replace completely satisfactory computers by progressively slowing them down? In Pyongyang at least, the Lazarus malware coders thought it was still worth having a go fully two months after the first Microsoft updates had been released. Rather than using the traditional phishing approach to insert the ransomware into target computers one by one, they exploited the EternalBlue vulnerability by means of a 'cryptoworm'.* Once inside a computer, the worm – which would become globally known as WannaCry – encrypted the hard drive and posted a ransom note, but it also scanned the infected computer's portal to the internet to test whether any connected computers were also prone to the EternalBlue flaw. If so, the WannaCry worm would crawl across and install itself on these computers too – and so on, and on, and on.

As it turned out, the hackers had bet correctly and millions

---

* Releasing computer worms is reckless. The first of its kind – the Morris Worm of 1988 – accidentally brought the early internet to a halt as it spread uncontrollably from MIT's computer lab to Berkeley, Harvard, Princeton, Stanford and NASA. Although young Robert Morris was just a prankster and there was nothing obnoxious in the program, it slowed the affected computers to a crawl. The only way to stop its spread was to switch off all computers until an antidote became available. Yet disconnecting from the internet meant that Morris's abjectly apologetic email containing instructions on how to fix the problem also became stuck in the system.

of computers around the world had not fixed the EternalBlue bug. The WannaCry worm was designed to root them out all out. The first infection occurred on the morning of 12 May 2017 in Asia. Within a few hours, the worm had speed-crawled to tens of thousands of computers in a hundred countries.[10] As usual, organisations operating well behind the technology frontier were hit hardest. In the UK, WannaCry is remembered for paralysing the National Health Service, with hospitals and doctors' surgeries in more than a third of health trusts in the country forced to turn away patients, reroute ambulances and cancel operations.[11] In Spain, the malware compromised the telephone operator Telefonica, a power company and a gas provider. In Germany, train travellers faced chaos and confusion as the hub controlling arrivals and departures boards across the nation was taken offline. Companies and individuals throughout Russia and India, as well as students at Chinese universities, came to bitterly regret their reliance on outdated and pirated software that had not benefited from Microsoft's recent updates.[12] Commerce, education and public services all over the world were suddenly at the mercy of a previously unknown ransomware gang.

According to the deep red @WanaDecryptor lockscreen with the cheery heading 'Ooops, your files have been encrypted!', victims were given three days to cough up a standard ransom of US $300 in Bitcoin, with the price doubling thereafter.[13] However, Kim Jong-Un's cyber-soldiers were ransomware rookies and hadn't fully thought through the business end of their attack. They had neglected to automate the storage and delivery of decryption keys. They were quickly overwhelmed by an avalanche of decryption requests. It was hard for victims to take the moral high ground when the remedy was priced at $300. Lazarus did not have the capacity to deal with dozens, then hundreds, then thousands and tens of thousands of individual requests to unlock files. In every language. All at once. Even worse, sloppy coding made it extremely difficult to link victims who had paid the ransom to the correct decryption key. It did not take long for IT security and intelligence services to realise that although desperate people all over the world were stuffing money into the attackers' Bitcoin wallet, hardly any data was decrypted. The automatic holding message from @WanaDecryptor did not inspire confidence either: 'You did not pay or we did not confirmed [sic] your payment. Pay now if you didn't pay and check back after two hours. Best time to check is 9.00–11.00 GMT on Monday to Friday. OK.'[14] Soon, word went out that victims should press pause on paying ransoms until further information arrived.

Meanwhile, white-hat hacker forums were abuzz with commentary, information and speculation. Marcus Hutchins, a twenty-two-year-old British computer security expert, was among those who witnessed the horrifyingly fast spread of WannaCry infections in real time. He was hooked.

Marcus had grown up in the rural west of England, a potentially tough environment for youngsters of colour. He was obsessed by technology and computers and had had a lonely childhood, struggling to fit in with his football-playing classmates.[15] His parents eventually became resigned to their inquisitive six-year-old repeatedly dismantling and reassembling the family Dell computer and running weird and wonderful programs on it. Predictably, Marcus was light years ahead of his IT teachers. Bored to tears as they explained basic word processing skills to his peers, he quickly found his way on to the internet and into the world of online games – as well as learning to cover his tracks and evade the school's attempts to monitor his activities.

When Marcus turned thirteen his parents relented and

bought him the parts he needed to build his own computer. Soon, locked away in his bedroom, the young teen found people who seemed like true soulmates: hackers. He found teachers he could learn from, a community that shared his obsession, insider jokes and – perhaps most importantly – respect. At age fourteen Marcus posted his first 'cool idea' to his favourite hacker forum: a password stealer. He later said it never even occurred to him that others might use it for nefarious purposes.[16] Yet soon he was working on the criminal fringe himself. At fifteen, Marcus remotely hijacked some 8,000 computers that he rented out to other hackers. He also offered to host webpages for phishing and a platform for trading fraudulent software, but he quickly grew bored with attending to the whims of his 'whiny customers'.[17] He shifted into developing malware code to order, earning a few hundred dollars here and there: a fortune for a small-town boy. At sixteen, he found his first serious customer, a person he only ever knew as Vinnie. Vinnie knew about all about shady online markets. If Marcus could solve a few programming challenges for him, Vinnie would give him a 50 per cent profit share. Vinnie was kind and really listened to his teenage friend's grumblings. He even wanted to send him a birthday present. Young Marcus did not think twice about giving Vinnie his real-world contact details. Imagine the lonely boy grinning as he unpacked his seventeenth birthday gift box: a luxury collection of ecstasy, weed and shrooms.

Although Vinnie continued to pay Marcus thousands of dollars in Bitcoin for his freelance programming projects, he also started to blackmail him into coding ever more sophisticated malware for use in online bank fraud. Personally, Marcus had always drawn the line at theft, but with Vinnie threatening to alert the police if he failed to deliver the goods, he felt that he had no choice. He spent a stressed-out year coding a banking Trojan, which was marketed by Vinnie under the boastful name Kronos (after the mythological giant who fathered Zeus).[18] The software required constant updating and 24/7 troubleshooting – something a solitary coder who was also trying to finish college could only accomplish by self-medicating with amphetamines.[19] In 2015, at the age of twenty-one, Marcus was exhausted, sick and heartily fed up with the cybercriminal underworld. He went cold turkey and ended his business relationship with Vinnie.

When he recovered, Marcus resurfaced as a blogger. His incisive writing under the pen name MalwareTech soon attracted a mixed audience of criminal and white-hat hackers. Unaware of his background, a leading IT security company was so impressed by his analyses and coding samples that they offered him a highly paid job. Marcus was amazed that legitimate employment would pay a much larger and more regular income than Vinnie's handouts, and jumped at the chance of becoming a bona fide IT security expert. Working remotely – still from his childhood bedroom – he specialised in reverse-engineering malware code, mapping infections and tracing the command infrastructure that directed networks of hijacked computers.

Marcus was on a well-earned holiday when the first alerts about WannaCry came through, but he could not resist taking a look. He immediately got drawn into the drama and decided to focus on mapping the spread of the superworm.[20] When Marcus ran the code in an isolated environment, he noticed an oddity. There was a line in the code requesting that each infected computer contact a particular website. Marcus surmised that this was the malware's command centre, but on investigating further he found that the website had not yet been registered. So, for the price of $10.68, Marcus bought and registered the

WE KNOW YOU CAN PAY A MILLION

Marcus Hutchins: a hero with a dark past

domain name himself. At once, his new website received information about every new WannaCry infection in the world in real time. It was a triumph for the young man and his company.

Three and a half hours later his colleagues pinged him excitedly. The very minute that Marcus had registered his website, WannaCry seemed to have stopped encrypting files. Had Marcus accidentally stumbled on and triggered the 'kill switch' for WannaCry? More hectic programming and experimenting confirmed their hunch: if the WannaCry program successfully contacted Marcus's website it stopped running immediately and did not proceed to the encryption stage. When it sank in that Marcus had saved the world, he could not contain his jubilation. After a while though, jumping up and down in his bedroom began to pall, so he wandered into the kitchen, where he found his mother busy fixing supper. With classic British diffidence, Marcus calmly volunteered that he had stopped the world's most virulent cyberattack in its tracks. His mother had been out for the day and knew nothing about WannaCry's global trail of destruction or the drama in the NHS. She barely lifted her eyes from the chopping board: 'Well done, sweetheart.'[21]

It took another week for the WannaCry threat to pass fully. Although the WannaCry worm was neutered, it was still on the loose. Malicious hackers around the world kept attacking the website that Marcus had registered. If the servers hosting it were to be overloaded or somebody succeeded in taking it down, WannaCry would no longer receive the message to abort in newly infected computers and it would regain its destructive capacity. It took the combined power of the British National Cyber Security Centre and Amazon to provide the server capacity needed to repel the spate of attempts to take global commerce and public services to the brink again. Even when everything was shored up, Marcus was still so wired that his employers had to bribe him to go to bed – with a $1,000 bonus for every hour he slept.[22]

Waking from his sponsored sleep, our accidental hero was keen to celebrate properly. No better place to party than DEF CON – the famous annual hacker convention at Las Vegas. Here, the West Country boy would mingle with 30,000 industry insiders, who could truly appreciate his marvellous feat.[23]

It would be one hell of a party and Marcus its undisputed star. Marcus rented a luxury villa off the Strip so that he and his friends could dip in and out of the convention for quick doses of hero worship and plentiful free drinks. None of them paid any attention to the SUV permanently parked outside their villa.

Graciously, the three burly plain-clothes agents only struck at the very end of Marcus' week-long binge. The FBI had issued an arrest warrant for Marcus Hutchins, the author of the Kronos banking Trojan and other malware. When the officers clapped the cuffs on him 5,000 miles from home, Marcus only had one chance to summon help – but who would understand his complicated situation? He decided to call his boss before he was taken to a shared jail cell, where he spent the night shackled to a chair. Marcus's peers in IT security were confused. Had there been a mix-up? Had the FBI arrested an innocent guy? Or had Marcus coded WannaCry himself to take credit for flicking the kill switch? Nobody knew anything about Marcus's past, but he was likeable and it was clear that spending more time in a US jail wouldn't be good for him. His colleagues, fans and friends decided to put up bail. They also collected funds to house and feed him for nearly two years as his case slowly made its way through the court system. After a brief struggle, Marcus chose to plead guilty to his youthful sins and throw himself on the mercy of the judge.[24] With a five-year maximum sentence on the table, it was a big gamble. Fortunately, the judge decreed that the way Marcus had turned his life around, along with his subsequent work as a white-hat hacker, had compensated for his former crimes. His defeat of WannaCry bought him his freedom and passage home to his family in 2019.[25]

WannaCry probably fell far short of the expectations of the Dear Leader and the dreams of the Lazarus Group. Victims stopped paying ransoms after finding out about the coding errors, so total takings were estimated at a paltry $80,000.[26] Yet, in its brief life, WannaCry had caused an estimated $4 billion of damage by irretrievably trashing 230,000 computers and bringing the businesses relying on them to a standstill. This confirmed that ransomware could be used as a powerful weapon of war. It was surely only a matter of time before another nation followed suit. One might therefore hope that companies would have taken WannaCry as an urgent warning to patch their software. Yet many firms still failed to install the freely available updates on all their machines – meaning that EternalBlue remained an exploitable weakness.

It should not have been a surprise to anyone that Ukraine became ground zero for the next ransomwar campaign. The country had long been Russia's preferred target for hostile cyber-actions, and especially so since its invasion of Crimea in 2014.[27] A ransomware strain called Petya had briefly made waves in spring 2016 for its novel, super-fast encryption process. However, the extortion scheme ended after a month when code and instructions on how to decrypt Petya appeared on a public messaging board. For reasons best known to themselves, the author posted under a pseudonym (leo-stone), making one wonder what skeletons in their cupboard made them reluctant to take credit for their public service.[28] Petya's successor, the infamous NotPetya, came with two 'improvements'. The coders made the encryption fiendishly complex and enhanced the spreading power of the malware. When the first computer in an organisation was infected, NotPetya used an old hacker trick to retrieve all the passwords stored in its memory. The stolen passwords were then tried on every other machine in the network so that the virus could jump to any that were accessible with the pilfered credentials. In addition, the code scanned all connected computers, checking whether the EternalBlue problem had been patched.[29] If a single unpatched computer was found in the same or an adjacent network the infection spread further, and the program cycle repeated, using stored passwords to jump to patched machines and EternalBlue to unpatched ones.[30]

The hackers then infiltrated M.E.Doc, a provider of software programs used by thousands of Ukrainian companies to file their tax returns.[31] Due to volatile inflation, tax rules changed frequently and M.E.Doc constantly adjusted their algorithms to reflect the latest changes. The easiest way for firms to avoid trouble over taxes was to choose the auto-update function. When the NotPetya coders sent their malware disguised as a legitimate software update on 27 June 2017, most customers installed it immediately and unquestioningly. The worm started to speed-crawl at once and within a few hours of NotPetya's launch, the entire commercial sector of Ukraine was paralysed. But this was not a precisely targeted attack against a specific enemy: major international companies with business interests in Ukraine had also subscribed to M.E.Doc software. Perhaps NotPetya's Western victims – such as the shipping company Maersk, the freight company FedEx, the pharmaceutical giant Merck, the construction company Saint-Gobain and the food company Mondelez – were seen as fair game on account of their trade with Ukraine. But was this true for their suppliers and customers too? NotPetya did not spare Russian companies either. The oil giant Rosneft, a bank, and a mining and manufacturing conglomerate caught the bug too and passed it on further. The number one rule for cybervandals to give Russian interests a wide berth had been broken. As with WannaCry, it seemed as if NotPetya's coders had not fully thought through their scheme.

Those who watched NotPetya rip through their enterprises were taken aback by the speed at which the catastrophe unfolded. An employee at Maersk's head office in Copenhagen recalled the surreal experience of watching his open-plan office going offline in a matter of seconds: 'I saw a wave of screens turning black. Black, black, black.'[32] Within seven minutes, 55,000 Maersk devices were locked. Every computer in the company that was not shut down at the time of the attack was disabled. After rebooting, the computers showed a lockscreen with a $300 ransom demand. The paralysis not only afflicted 49,000 laptops but also the most basic applications such as the system operating the gates used by thousands of trucks bringing goods to the ninety Maersk freight terminals around the world. Maersk's global shipping operations came to a sudden halt.[33] Other companies that were lucky enough to receive advance warning switched their systems off voluntarily.

Once again, everyone anxiously awaited developments as the computer security world kicked into hyperdrive. Amit Serper, a cybersecurity researcher from Boston, heard about NotPetya on the radio on the way to visit his parents. Windows malware was not really Amit's speciality, but on arrival his father looked up from the TV and asked him what he thought about this latest cyber-atrocity. Amit was so charmed by his dad's unusual curiosity about a computing matter that he asked a colleague to send him a copy of the source code. As his friends were already waiting for him in a bar, Amit quickly decided that he could do nothing about the devilishly complex encryption.[34] He decided to focus on whether he could limit the malware's spread instead. One of the program's first actions was to search for a marker showing a previous infection with NotPetya. There is no benefit to repeatedly encrypting computers, so NotPetya put a file in the computer's directory at the end of each successful attack. This served as a sign to leave the computer alone thereafter. Keen to join his mates, Amit signed off with the suggestion that computer users who were not yet infected should also put a copy of this file into their file directories. It turned out to be a 100 per cent effective vaccine – and by all accounts Amit had a very good night out.[35]

For those for whom the vaccine came too late, there was no remedy. The encryption code was nonsensical and hence irreversible (which Amit had guessed might be the case). Nobody – not even the attackers – could recover data or unlock the affected computers. Those who paid the $300 ransom never heard back. It could have been another case of shoddy coding, but many surmised that NotPetya was not ransomware gone haywire but a cyberweapon designed to sabotage and destroy.[36] Any payments from desperate victims were just the icing on the cake for whoever was responsible for NotPetya. Although it ran for only a few hours, NotPetya became the most damaging cyberattack the world had ever seen, with the White House estimating total global damages at billions of dollars.[37]

The events of 2017 led to major soul searching in the West. So far, governments had been content to consider ransomware a private-sector problem. Clearly, this stance was no longer tenable and some stark conclusions were drawn. Western economies had to become more resilient against ransomware. Cybersecurity protocols failed far too often, and ransom payments had become so normalised that malware coders could make money even if they had no decryption keys to sell. Somebody had to take charge and change public attitudes to cybercrime. Next, the rising costs of resolving ransomware incidents (and politically motivated malware masquerading as ransomware) threatened to exceed the private sector's capacity to absorb them. Businesses and insurers would have to renegotiate with governments how future catastrophic losses would be shared. Worst of all, even Western governments' own cybersecurity capabilities looked inadequate. Much as we enjoy heroic rescue stories featuring people like 'leo-stone', Amit and Marcus, policymakers could ill afford to put national security in the hands of private software and cybersecurity companies and a ragtag collection of hackers of ambiguous backgrounds and unknown allegiances. Would the authorities step up to the challenge at last – or continue to bury their heads in the sand?

10

No More Ransoms?:
A Fractious Alliance Against Ransomware

The ransomwar campaigns of 2017 brought public and political attention to a problem that IT security companies had been quietly struggling with for some years. WannaCry and NotPetya had surprised insiders with their speed and recklessness, but incident responders were only too used to destructive malware posing as ransomware. Recovery experts routinely checked whether an encryption was reversible and what backups were available, searched hacker forums for free decryption information, and explored whether the attackers had a reputation for delivering functioning keys before pressing the pay button. However, victims who lacked in-depth IT knowledge were rarely so circumspect, nor did they have the skills to implement the cryptic multi-step recovery instructions the white hats posted for each other. For a typical computer user, the directions published by the likes of leo-stone under 'hack-petya mission accomplished!!!' were useless, even if they knew where to find them.[1]

Meanwhile, the business grapevine began to buzz that some ransomware gangs were escalating their ransom demands to thousands and tens of thousands of dollars. Even relatively small firms started stockpiling the highly volatile Bitcoin in preparation for cyberattacks.[2] Service providers sprang up offering to source large amounts of cryptocurrency at short notice. This meant there was little downside for ransomware gangs to raising prices. The days of the $300 ransom were numbered: ransom inflation was the next disaster waiting to happen. Unless the gangs started to meet meaningful resistance to rising ransom demands, prices would continue to go up – and there was no obvious upper limit. Stopping money being thrown at extortionists required a sea change in attitudes and public services to provide realistic alternatives.

The unstable dynamics of ransomware – with both numbers of attacks and prices in upward spirals – and the large-scale losses from WannaCry and NotPetya brought a powerful new lobby on to the political scene: insurers. While demand for the insurance-cum-recovery product benefited from increased awareness of cyber-risks in the corporate world, it was also clear that rampant ransomware would destroy the business model. Insurance relies on spreading risk. However, if current trends continued, all cyberinsurance clients were going to be breached sooner or later and another ransomwar campaign could potentially wipe out major insurers' capital reserves in one fell swoop. Insurers therefore lobbied their governments to engage in large-scale counter-ransomware efforts and share in the financial burden of state-sponsored attacks. Conversely, governments expected insurers – who had in any case cornered the market in top security and recovery specialists – to take the lead in dealing with a problem that was at least partially of their own making. After all, law enforcement had insisted from the start that paying ransoms should only be considered a last resort. That advice had rarely made financial sense to insurers and had therefore largely been ignored. In these circumstances, building trust and hashing out what equitable burden-sharing might look like was extremely difficult.

NO MORE RANSOMS?

There was one area on which everyone agreed though: far too many victims (falsely) jumped to the conclusion that cooperating with an attacker was the only way forward.[3] In the early days of ransomware, many cybercriminals made money with malware that either could not be decrypted, that only pretended to have encrypted files, or used superficial encryption protocols that could be reversed by security technicians.[4] Some gangs had more sophisticated code, but a single master key could be used to unlock all victims. Once this was released to the first victim, it could be shared. Even when asymmetric encryption was used, law enforcement sometimes seized servers used by criminals and recovered decryption keys or source code. White-hat hackers then analysed the gangs' source code with the aim of reverse-engineering the encryption programs.[5] This process could take days or weeks without guarantee of success, but as soon as some cyber-Samaritan had produced a decryption tool for a specific ransomware strain, subsequent victims could use it. In short: (some) free recovery options existed, but far too few (and especially uninsured) victims knew about them.

A consortium of international law enforcement, insurers and major IT security companies had therefore already joined forces to found the No More Ransom initiative in July 2016. They launched a website, which is still operational today, providing detailed help and advice with the objective of radically reducing the pay-off to ransomware for criminals.[6] Victims who find themselves locked out of their computers can upload two small encrypted files or the text of their lockscreen, or type in any email, website or Bitcoin address from the ransom note.[7] From this the system recognises what type of ransomware was used – or whether it is malware masquerading as ransomware and no effective remedy exists. If a free decryption tool is available, victims are given detailed instructions on how to restore their systems.[8]

However, the 2017 malware events showed the ways in which the No More Ransom initiative was flawed. First, too many victims still jumped to the conclusion that they had to pay. Second, even if every victim refused to pay for poorly designed, faulty, outdated or shoddily administered ransomware, that still left sophisticated gangs using asymmetric encryption in the game. Cybercriminals never ceased innovating. Although the No More Ransom project declared that 'the battle is over' for dozens of ransomware strains, everyday people were struck by malware that could not be decrypted without paying the extortionists.[9]

Turning the tide on ransomware therefore required a complete change in business practices: that is, ensuring that potential victims became less vulnerable to attacks and more able to rebuild their systems without their attackers' help. Many victims were already reluctant to pay the criminals but thought there was an easy alternative: employing a ransomware removal firm promising 'data recovery without paying the hacker'.[10] However, these incident responders (with their sponsored links and glowing testimonials) had always been cagey about their methods. For anyone working in cryptography, the very idea that anyone (never mind unsophisticated provincial IT businesses) could effortlessly reverse the advanced asymmetric encryption used by major ransomware brands was preposterous. Perturbed by the opaque claims of this business model, two Californian computer security specialists, Bill Siegel and Alex Holdman, who were looking to set up their own crisis response firm, decided to see if they could catch these apparent IT superheroes red-handed.

Bill and Alex rounded up a few trusted associates to run a

little experiment. The group contacted several data recovery specialists posing as desperate victims of ransomware attacks who did not want to pay their extortionists. To create a cover story, Fabian Wosar – a well-known malware analyst – created a few batches of sample files encrypted with a top-notch ransomware strain.[11] These were accompanied by fake screenshots of ransom demands showing a fictitious ransomware gang's contact details, which were actually being monitored by Alex and Bill's group. Each enquiry used a unique victim ID number so they could identify the recovery companies even if they communicated from anonymous accounts. Sure enough, it did not take long for various 'superheroes' to get in touch with the made-up ransomware gang, offering to pay their ransom. Having ascertained that a deal was on the table, the so-called decryption experts swiftly returned to their potential customers. They were most eager to help – at a price that was a multiple of the fake gang's original demand. Funnily enough, no mention was made of paying a ransom. Fabian Wosar recalled: 'They all claimed to be able to decrypt ransomware families that definitely weren't decryptable and didn't mention that they paid the ransom ... Quite the contrary actually. They all seemed very proud not to pay ransomers.'[12]

Alex and Bill's initiative exposed these data recovery firms as 'usurious and predatory'.[13] Their firm, Coveware, was one of the first to test the market with an ethical alternative: transparent data recovery. They tell their customers honestly if paying the ransom is necessary to decrypt their files, and then give them a choice of recovery paths. If customers decide that they need the extortionists' help but are reluctant to deal with them directly, Coveware facilitates the ransom payments – passing on any discounts the ransomware gangs offer to repeat customers.[14] Rather than sweeping the problem under the carpet, the firm gathers precise information about each attack and cooperates closely with law enforcement. Since 2018, Coveware has published their data and analyses on current ransomware trends, as do a range of other IT security specialists. Although the number of attacks, top ransomware brands and average ransoms paid reported by different firms diverged (depending on what was happening in their customer base), one thing was clear: the No More Ransom initiative was at best an aspirational slogan. Ransomware gangs could still extort at will.

A consensus therefore emerged among all parties that better cyber-hygiene and more effective back-up routines needed to be widely adopted. Unfortunately, there was no agreement on who should take the lead on making this happen. Governments were reluctant to legislate in a domain where they readily admitted that their own expertise trailed far behind that of the private sector. Fiscal purse strings had been tight at least since the 2008 financial crisis and market-oriented salaries for IT experts seemed unaffordable in public service. Moreover, the creaking public infrastructure would need serious investment if it was to comply with regulations that meaningfully improved on the status quo. Couldn't the private sector move on ahead under its own steam? IT security companies found that most of their customers were reluctant to change. Upfront investment and higher running costs were immediately obvious, whereas the benefits were debatable and long-term. Even when software providers offered a choice of secure settings that could be implemented with one mouse click, organisations generally resisted putting up additional barriers that might reduce productivity or alienate customers.

Politicians and IT experts therefore hoped that insurers would lead the charge for raising standards – if only to reduce their own losses. Indeed, many insurers offered better terms for customers that upgraded their security, but doing so was only financially worthwhile for a few technology-forward firms. Otherwise, the old stand-off between buyers and sellers of insurance continued. Firms did not want to be forced into specific safety protocols and were prepared to shop around for policies with lax conditions. As underwriters around the world fought tooth and claw for market share in the growing cyberinsurance market, most avoided tightening their security requirements. Why couldn't governments just legislate and set benchmarks that would stop competition driving underwriting standards inexorably towards the bottom? As the ball kept being passed back and forth between the various interest groups, security improvements remained incremental. Usually, the best (or only) opportunity for meaningful progress came just after a business had been victimised. However, this organic process was not going to turn the tables on ransomware gangs; breaking and entering remained laughably easy and if a gang kept delivering the goods, they would keep getting paid.

With efforts to reduce victims' reliance on buying decryption keys mired in controversy or difficulty, thoughts turned to raising the risk of getting involved in the production or spreading of ransomware. Law enforcement had several potential tools at their disposal to deter cybercriminals, such as arrest warrants, asset freezes, travel sanctions, infiltration and takedown of gangs' servers and websites and release of decryptors.[15] But monitoring and identifying the culprits, tracking their movements into areas where capture was possible, extraditing and trying them or taking direct actions against their virtual infrastructure required massive financial and personnel resources. The people with the greatest skills and insights into ransomware were working in the private sector. Some were raring to inflict damage on their adversaries, but they had to be very careful not to make themselves liable for damages should their vigilante actions end up harming the gangs' victims. Although law enforcement was recruiting staff with advanced IT skills, ransomware was not yet near the top of their list of concerns. When the US government established its Cybersecurity and Infrastructure Security Agency (CISA) in 2018, it was given a broad brief to deal with the whole range of foreign cyberthreats to the United States. Predictably, politicians made election security its top priority.[16] The first CISA Insights paper on ransomware in 2019 was a mere one-pager recommending some basic security precautions and urging victims to seek experienced help and advice – including a link for contacting CISA, the FBI or the Secret Service.[17] It would take significant time to build up the personnel, tools and protocols that would persuade the commercial sector that the state could offer meaningful help in the event of an attack – or indeed deter cybercriminals and their states from using ransomware to make money or wreak havoc.

With minimal state involvement in managing cyber-risks either by legislation or through law enforcement, there was just one more option for governments to support the private sector in dealing with the rising tide of ransomware and ransomwar: formal backstop insurance to cover extreme losses.[18] There was every reason to expect that the threat actors responsible for WannaCry and NotPetya would re-emerge with better-functioning ransomware strains. Yet insurers and governments were at loggerheads over who should bear the cost of ransomwar. It was expected that future cyberwar losses could be comparable to those of global terrorism, where governments had stepped in to prop up private insurance markets.[19] A necessary condition for triggering state support would be a clear-cut definition of what constituted a cyberwar. Without this, firms and insurers had only a vague assurance that ad hoc assistance might be made available in the right circumstances. NotPetya was an important test case: Russian state involvement seemed very likely, losses were huge, and its main victims were insured multinationals. For example, the food and beverage company Mondelez totalled their NotPetya losses at $188 million.[20] The shipping company Maersk's estimated losses were even higher: somewhere between $250 million and $350 million.[21] At the top end of the scale was the drug producer Merck with a whopping loss of $1.4 billion.[22]

Cyberinsurers had wisely prepared themselves for this kind of calamity by limiting the amount each customer could claim for an individual attack. So, their clients opted to claim on their 'all risk' property insurance instead. If the firms' brokers had done a good job, property policies included cover for loss of or damage to computer equipment – and any costs arising from the disruption of business as a result.[23] Property insurers were aghast when they suddenly found themselves on the hook for huge cyber-exposures. The only way of wriggling out of these unexpected financial commitments was to invoke the famous 'war clause'. The circumstances in the case – the deliberate release of the malware into Ukraine, multiple clues pointing to Russian authorship of the malware, and the common knowledge that Russia-linked hackers had already been implicated in a string of previous cyberattacks against Ukraine – lent themselves to the assertion that NotPetya constituted a 'hostile or warlike action in time of peace', as the standard policy wordings put it.[24] However, no insurer had ever tried to invoke a war clause for a state-sponsored cyberattack. If NotPetya was acknowledged as an act of war, it would mean that compensation (if any) had to come from the firms' governments. But cash-strapped politicians were resolved against using taxpayers' money to bail out well-resourced insurance companies on this occasion – and understandably unwilling to assume responsibility for incalculable future ransomwar losses. If insurers failed to step up, the courts would have to decide whether to make them pay.

All was up in the air when, in the summer of 2018, the Zurich Insurance Group denied a $100 million claim from Mondelez[25] and a group of American insurers jointly denied a $700 million claim from the pharma giant Merck.[26] Short of the Russian government formally taking credit for the NotPetya attack – which nobody expected them to do – a court case to prove a hostile action by the Russian government beyond reasonable doubt could take for ever. In 2018, the courts could only go by hearsay evidence and a few smoking guns. It took until October 2020 for the US Department of Justice to gather sufficient evidence to indict four Russian intelligence officers for suspected involvement in the 2017 NotPetya attack.[27] However, it is a completely different matter to move from a criminal charge to a criminal conviction – especially when the suspects cannot be arrested, extradited and tried. The question of 'was NotPetya an act of cyberwar?' simply could not be settled within a practical time frame.

Merck and Mondelez therefore pursued a different tack when they sued their insurers for breach of contract.[28] They asked a more basic question: what is war? Just because some events trigger inconveniently large claims, that does not automatically make them acts of war. The claimants argued that unless and until insurers defined what constitutes an act of war in their contracts, they should not be allowed to trigger a war exclusion. So, what is 'war'? Ask any elite military officer and they will wax lyrical and quote at length from the works of the Prussian general and military theorist Carl von Clausewitz. A mercifully short summary of the general's definition of war – published in 1832 – might be: in war opposing sides use violence causing extensive disruption as a means to an end, guided by a political objective.[29] 'Cyberwar' does not neatly fit into these criteria. NotPetya was not violent, the intention of the disruption was opaque (given its indiscriminate nature and spillover into Russia) and, since the alleged aggressor denied all responsibility, it had no obvious political goal.[30]

But why should von Clausewitz's definition of war – based on conventional warfare – still reign supreme nearly 200 years after it was first published? There was an excellent reason for this, according to the leading insurance law professors in the United States.[31] War clauses in commercial insurance were first used at Lloyd's of London in the late eighteenth and nineteenth centuries in marine insurance. Once the wordings had been proven to work well, they had become standardised and came to be applied across other insurance divisions. They were copied unrevised into subsequent contracts down the centuries. Both Merck and Mondelez therefore argued that, given the ancient pedigree of the policy wordings, the war clause in their policies should be understood in its historical sense: violent conflict between states using military forces.[32] Moreover, war clauses were never understood as a get-off-scot-free option for insurers in case circumstances became unexpectedly prickly. They were intended to clarify what is or is not insured under an insurance policy. In normal insurance practice, either a war is formally declared before or very soon after the event (which triggers the war clause), or insurers have a protocol to decide and publish whether a geographic area is deemed a 'war risk'. In the latter case, either an additional war premium is charged, or clients choose to avoid the danger area. Everyone knows the risks and prices before they make their decisions. A good example is the many ships that took long detours in the Indian Ocean or even around the Cape of Good Hope to avoid traversing the area declared as a war risk by Lloyd's of London in response to Somali piracy.

In short, if insurers want to exclude 'cyberwar' or 'warlike cyber-hostilities in times of peace' from their cover, they can – but before the contract is signed. Unfortunately, insurers had forgotten to do so (or had chosen not to rock the boat) on their 'all risk' commercial property policies. It was too late to do so after the NotPetya losses had occurred. Legal opinions, briefing notes and scholarly arguments went back and forth, racking up bills that looked like they might eventually rival the claims at stake. After years of wrangling the insurers therefore decided to settle the Mondelez and Merck disputes behind closed doors in November 2022 and January 2024 respectively.

As a result, more than seven years after the catastrophic NotPetya attack, insurers still did not know how to write cyber-war clauses for their policies that would stand up in court. Without a formal definition of what qualifies as a cyberwar, it is not worth tackling the question of how large-scale future losses might be apportioned between the private and the public sector. On the one hand, kicking the can down the road saved the bureaucratic effort required to create a government safety net. Politicians knew how much work was required from propping up the insurance market in the aftermath of the terror attacks on commercial centres of the 1990s and especially 9/11. One might also congratulate governments for not rushing in to commit scarce public resources to dealing with a problem that – at least on the surface – looked like it could still be resolved by private insurance.

However, in the meantime, underwriters had quietly reduced their cyber-exposure. Even major insurers had reached the limit of their willingness and capacity to absorb the losses of a geopolitical problem that politicians were reluctant to discuss in parliamentary debates or committees. Property insurers solved their problem by excluding cyber-risk from their policies altogether. Cyberinsurers further limited the maximum amount each insured could claim per attack and per year. So, just as ever more companies realised that they desperately needed comprehensive cyberinsurance, it ceased to be available and the prices for limited cover were high and rising. This left private companies to manage the rising cyber-risks on their own or with very partial insurance. Unfortunately, ransomware gangs had more tricks up their sleeves to make life even more difficult.

11

Big Game Hunting: Second- and Third-Generation Ransomware

Losses from ransomware attacks accelerated sharply in early 2018. Digging into victim reports and complaints data, FBI analysts observed a decline in indiscriminate (spray-and-pray) campaigns, but an increase in 'big game hunting': the deliberate targeting of large firms, the healthcare sector, transportation and state and local government.[1] For many of these organisations, data decryption was worth a lot of money. Gangs like Dharma, Phobos and SamSam had therefore steadily raised the price of their decryptors. But whereas five- and six-figure ransoms still represented excellent value for major businesses, smaller enterprises often chose different recovery options when faced with excessive non-negotiable demands. Business-minded ransomware coders therefore decided to dispense with their one-size-fits-all fee structure. Rather than fully automating their platforms from the moment of breach to the delivery of the decryption key, they added a function that allowed the affiliates to check out who had taken their bait before encrypting their systems and setting their ransom demand.

Ryuk – first observed in August 2018 – was the trailblazer for what would become known as second-generation ransomware. They encouraged their affiliates do a little research on the victims' ability to pay. It was not difficult to Google a company and get a good idea of their size and revenues.[2] Ryuk primarily targeted small to medium-sized businesses that could probably afford a six- or even a seven-figure ransom but did not have terribly complicated computer networks that would be a nightmare to decrypt afterwards. The Ryuk gang were not sophisticated in their attacks and mostly used phishing emails, credentials bought on darknet marketplaces, and known software vulnerabilities to gain entry.[3] Once inside one computer terminal within an organisation, the malware program would terminate local antivirus operations and seek to infect as many computers in the network as possible. The program then deleted any backups it could find. Ryuk's code also had the capabilities of a banking Trojan, so the criminals could view the data held on the network (though in 2018 they did not routinely do so). When they pressed the button to encrypt their victims' files, they set a ransom demand they deemed on the painful side of affordable. They reckoned that even if some victims refused to pay, the occasional large gains would more than compensate for any lost business.

Ryuk's second-generation ransomware business model created several new challenges for its victims. The cybercriminals took a rough-and-ready approach to estimating affordable ransom amounts – and in many cases they were wildly optimistic. Many firms simply could not raise the money demanded by the extortionists. Moreover, the criminals' ability to sniff around in the victims' systems created massive data privacy issues. To top it all, Ryuk's decryption program was sloppily coded and unless great care was taken to follow a process only vaguely outlined by the criminals, a victim could easily end up with a wiped hard drive despite having dug deep into their pockets for the ransom. Cybersecurity firms offering data recovery services and privacy lawyers were soon overwhelmed with requests for help. This provided a prime opportunity for the ransomware ecosystem to expand.[4]

Victimised firms needed help in three broad areas: digital forensics, deciding whether to ransom and setting a price, and data recovery. First, the digital forensics teams identified the threat actor, assessed the scope of the damage and investigated how the criminals gained access and what exactly they had done in the computer or network. Ransomware gangs' ransom demands were still a fraction of the whopping penalties a firm might face for breaching data privacy regulation.[5] US regulators had sweeping powers to levy punitive fines on firms with a cavalier attitude to safeguarding personal information and cracked down hard on firms that tried to cover up data leaks. It was therefore crucial to find out whether an outsider had looked at any of the data held by the firm – and if so, who was affected and what safeguards had to be put in place. Forensic experts also gave the victim (and their insurers) information on how to secure the network in the future, made sure that the malware was not still lurking in the network and checked that the criminals had not left themselves a back door open for the next raid.

Second, professional crisis responders could not afford to waste their clients' ransom money. Based on the scope of the damage, the availability of backups and the sophistication of the attack, responsible incident responders advised the victims whether and how to engage with the extortionists. Seeing the same ransomware strains repeatedly, they knew which gangs permanently destroyed data or struggled to provide functioning decryption keys. The most sophisticated data recovery experts closely studied the malware code for tiny flaws that allowed them to reverse-engineer the encryption programs and create their own decryption keys.⁶ These were then posted on the No More Ransom website, depriving ransomware gangs of future revenue streams from that strain of malware. Systematic data collection, sharing of decryption tools and naming and shaming gangs that failed to deliver on their promises meant that ransomware gangs had to innovate.⁷ Inept or lazy malware coders and administrators could no longer rely on the PR stigma associated with attacks to hide their disappointing performance. Realising that reputation and trust-building mattered, the top gangs soon offered a new service. They invited their victims to upload any two small files from their servers for free recovery – thereby proving their ability to reverse the damage ahead of payment.

When victims decided that they would pay, they did not necessarily want to pay the asking price. Yet nobody really knew what sort of price reductions might be available and how long a victimised company would have to wait to strike an acceptable bargain. Research into ransomware negotiations was urgently needed. Hostage crisis responders working for kidnap and ransom insurers had developed sophisticated models of bargaining that kept hostages safe and ransoms low and stable.⁸ Some hoped that the surprising order and predictability that characterises the trade in human hostages could also be replicated in ransomware. Innovative responders, including Bill Siegel and Alex Holdman's firm Coveware (which we met in the last chapter), therefore added ransom negotiations to their list of services. The alarming proliferation of Ryuk ransomware from the late summer of 2018 gave the Coveware team the opportunity to build a ransom payments database and populate it much more quickly than they had expected.⁹

Ryuk victims were driven to seek professional advice in droves: the affiliates had either not graduated from business school or had weak language skills. Their ideas of the kind of ransom a firm could afford were often vastly inflated. Coveware found that if their clients were able to operate in pen-and-paper mode for a while, ransomware affiliates grew impatient or nervous about losing the deal altogether and would offer them a 'discount'. But what was the best way to close a deal? The newly minted ransomware negotiators had the opportunity to experiment with different approaches: starting low or near the victim's limit, raising their offers fast or slowly, being friendly, businesslike, ingratiating or confrontational. The Ryuk operators were people of few words. The ransom note did not pop up with a flourish but was left as the only readable file on the network drive. When small companies opened RyukReadMe.html they only saw an email address, the brand name Ryuk and the enigmatic tag line 'balance of the shadow universe'.[10] Victims with more complicated networks were treated to a slightly more detailed ransom note to warn them against actions that might scupper their eventual recovery. Here the tagline read 'no system is safe'. When the victims contacted their extortionists, the reply was simply the number of Bitcoin demanded and the address of the wallet to send them to.

Even victims that had prepared for a ransomware attack with a hoard of Bitcoin were caught off guard by Ryuk's opening gambits. Small companies were touched for six-figure ransoms while for larger companies demands were in the $1 million to $5 million range. The highest demand in the Coveware dataset was close to $24 million. Some of these demands were completely unaffordable, and even if they were affordable (for example, if there was insurance) victims at least wanted to know if they could potentially reduce the price. Ransomware crisis responders soon spotted some patterns. Lizzie Cookson, one of Coveware's recovery experts, developed four essential insights from repeatedly negotiating with the Ryuk gang.[11] First, you could not outwit the extortionists, you could only outwait them. As in real-life hostage crises, patience is key to driving a bargain. Second, it was best to stay calm and businesslike. The criminals were in it for the money, but they did not respond well to insults and appeared largely immune to sob stories. Third, extortionists generally responded to demonstrable facts and patiently repeated communication about why a victim was not able to meet their demands. Fourth, discounts could be considerable – but they had to be weighed against the cost of running the enterprise on pen and paper for the duration of the negotiation. These insights became the foundation of Coveware's ransomware negotiation strategy.

There were also some features particular to Ryuk negotiations. There was no point in trying to tempt these extortionists with a counter-offer at the start. All the negotiator would get back was a 'no' – and they would keep getting a 'no' whenever they raised the offer. Ryuk affiliates would just sit and wait for the victim to bid the price up all by themselves. To get the hoped-for discount, the victim had to explain why the demand was not affordable without making a counter-offer. A brief 'OK' from the affiliate would signal the start of a proper bartering process. From this point on, large discounts were possible: Ryuk was not in the business of flogging dead horses. If they had made a genuine mistake in their assessment, they would re-evaluate and take what they could. Spotting these patterns in negotiations was extremely valuable. Coveware could advise their cash-strapped clients not to jump in too early with a counter-offer but to establish their credibility with the extortionists first.

The third area where victims needed help was in rebuilding their systems. Even if a victim's data was recoverable and the price affordable, it did not mean that the journey would be smooth. Many IT experts were underwhelmed by Ryuk's sloppy coding and unhelpful instructions. Although Ryuk offered a free test to prove that the encryption was reversible with two small files, decrypting large files on a complex network was an entirely different matter. Victims would often end up in an endless loop or with a mixture of decrypted and permanently lost files. Moreover, some of the criminals' instructions looked alarmingly like a ruse to gain even better access to their networks. Victims needed reassurance before switching off their security systems and reconnecting all computers that were taken offline to protect them at the attack stage. It took Coveware's recovery specialists considerable effort to develop a workable protocol that avoided the many potentially fatal pitfalls. Even so, it was always worth making a complete copy of all the encrypted files before attempting to run the decryptor. When the decryption hit a hitch and the program accidentally deleted their files, the recovery attempt could be restarted ... again ... and again ... and over again.

Despite this painful trial-and-error process, data recovery firms agreed that the Ryuk gang broadly kept their promise: the decryption program did indeed remove the malware. Eventually, Coveware published a free step-by-step DIY recovery guide on their website to help victims make an informed choice about whether they were brave enough to attempt a decryption themselves or whether it was wiser to invest in professional help.[12] If the victims had cyberinsurance, their insurer would make that decision for them. The answer was always a resounding yes: the overall cost of ransomware resolution was greatly reduced by bringing experienced recovery specialists on board.

In this way, second-generation ransomware accelerated the trend towards the professionalisation of ransomware incident response. However, this process unfolded in an ad hoc, unregulated and uncoordinated way. At the top end of the market, crisis responders developed best practice protocols for their brand-new business area. This often included suggesting some resistance against outsize ransom demands in a bid to slow down the threat. Yet good practice was not applied uniformly for three reasons. First, demand for data recovery services outstripped the capacity of ethical responders. Ransomware victims that were turned away by reputable companies often clicked nervously on a random sponsored link online and ended up on the payment mill route. Second, many firms pragmatically chose to pay the asking price at once to reduce their downtime and shorten the recovery period – taking such shortcuts was tempting if ransoms remained a relatively minor part of overall resolution cost. Third, when affiliates started to meet resistance to their demands, many decided to have a quick sniff around hijacked systems for financial data before launching the encryption stage. It was difficult to plead for clemency with extortionists who were au fait with the company's turnover and profit, and especially those who could forward a pilfered insurance certificate to the negotiator. As a rule, it did not take long to extract big payments from insured victims, leading some commentators to advocate banning ransomware insurance altogether.[13]

Ryuk proved extremely lucrative for its coders and affiliates, topping the 2018 charts at the FBI Internet Crime Complaint Centre.[14] With a reported US $60 million rolling into the Ryuk coffers between February 2018 and October 2019 (and multiples of that in unreported payments), more criminals applied to join Ryuk's affiliate ranks. For crooks with basic foreign language and business skills, 'second-generation' ransomware offered a much higher return than the 'first-generation' fixed-price model. As the Ryuk franchise grew, other ransomware gangs took note. The resulting wave of second-generation ransomware inflated firms' expected cost of recovery through higher ransoms, time delays if they had to negotiate, and the burden of investigating and mitigating data privacy breaches.

Many firms found that this was no longer an insurable problem. The cost of cyberinsurance was not only rising fast, but the claim limits on affordable policies were often well below expected losses. Although insurance was still worth having – if only to get quick access to a reliable and comprehensive recovery service – chief financial officers knew that a successful ransomware attack would cost them dearly. This created a long-overdue correction in terms of prevention and resilience. Chief information officers were promoted to seats on executive boards, which transformed company culture regarding IT security. Organisations rolled out multi-factor authentication requiring one-time codes sent through trusted devices or biometric identification in addition to passwords to prevent entry and impede criminals' lateral movement through company networks. Backups were made more regularly and systematically, and due attention was paid to ensuring that the information was not only held securely but was readily accessible in the aftermath of attacks. Having made significant investments in their systems and processes, many firms felt confident that they could bounce back from attacks without the extortionists' help in the future.

But the criminals were not sitting idly by when promising prey slipped through their nets with a smug 'thanks but no thanks' to the offer of a decryption key. They started to combine ransomware with an entirely different business model: data exfiltration extortion. In the 'double extortion' business model, the criminals identified data that the victims would most like to keep private and downloaded the most 'interesting' files to their own servers before encrypting their systems. This gave them two ways to put pressure on their victims: first to purchase a decryption key and – if this failed – to purchase a promise to delete the exfiltrated data. In 2019, an enterprising gang called DoppelPaymer did an experiment on their victims alternating between two versions of their lockscreens: one had a text threatening a data release, the other made no mention of the stolen data.[15] It soon became obvious that victims were very sensitive to the enhanced threat and soon the data release version became standard. But one question remained: how would the gangs name and shame their victims in practice? Responsible journalists and editors did not lightly publish tip-offs coming from criminals.

A group called Maze found an elegant solution: a public online shaming board. The header of Maze's darknet 'leak site' explained in broken English: 'Represented here companies dont wish to wish to cooperate with us, and trying to hide our successful attack on their resources. Wait for their databases and private papers here. Follow the news!'[16] Checking a leak site for the latest victims of cybercrime provided an easy scoop for opportunistic bloggers and freelance journalists on slow news days. Ransomware gangs easily found willing volunteers to make their successful attacks public knowledge. 'Third-generation' ransomware was born.

With the threat of naming and shaming, the hope of sweeping a data breach under the rug dwindled. If a company's name was leaked by the extortionists, the regulators would not only investigate the victims' failure to prevent the breach and evaluate their efforts to safeguard personal data but would also punish them for being tardy in owning up. The criminals were keenly aware of how much power the regulators had to impose punitive fines; they now weaponised this threat. Even large ransom demands could be made to look like a low-cost alternative to being fined. As a REvil ransomware operative explained during a ransom chat: 'In case of refusal of payment – the data will either be sold to competitors or laid out in open sources. GDPR. Do not want to pay us – pay x10 times more to the government. No problems.'[17]

Maze's innovation of the leak site provided an easy-to-use infrastructure for causing maximal embarrassment to companies – and stress and anxiety to anyone whose personal data was suddenly up for grabs in the economic underworld. Maze's 'wall of shame' intimidation tactic was soon copied by other gangs. Usually, a countdown timer on a leak site shows the victims how little time is left to raise and pay the ransom – presumably with journalists keenly watching the clock for their next scoop. When the time is up, the criminals either release the data for free download, or – having made the victim's name public – auction them off on the darknet to the highest bidders, whether financial fraudsters, identity thieves or good old-fashioned blackmailers.

However, paying a ransom does not solve a data leak problem. Unlike a real-life hostage situation where the captive eventually walks free, there is no 'clean finish' to a ransomware incident. Exfiltrated data can be copied and stored multiple times. A 'proof of deletion' screenshot sent by a ransomware gang is meaningless. A company's name not appearing on a leak site or being shown without leaked files for public download is somewhat valuable but no guarantee that the data has in fact been kept safe. The criminals may have sold a copy of the data even before they engaged in the negotiation and there is nothing the victim can do to prevent them from doing so afterwards. All a victim can cling to is a vague hope that the gang's leadership cares sufficiently about their malware's reputation to keep their promises. In addition, the crooks require the discipline to avoid mistakes and the ability to contain opportunism among their loosely connected affiliates – indefinitely into the future. With a particularly juicy dataset there is every temptation to touch the individuals concerned directly, in addition to extorting the company. Some gangs were not willing or able to maintain such discipline, engaging in re-extortion or leaking data belonging to companies that had paid, while at least one is known to have faked a 'proof of deletion'.[18]

Law enforcement and ethical crisis responders therefore repeatedly warned victims that a breach is a breach is a breach. Any company that lost control of personal data had to go through the entire process of regulatory oversight and engage in appropriate damage limitation, regardless of whether they had paid the extortionists a ransom.[19] Firms that had implemented reasonable precautions and informed and protected those whose data was compromised had little to fear from information commissioners.[20] No state wants to give the impression of systematically victimising the victims of crime.

Despite all these cautions, third-generation ransomware worked well. The tweak in the business model gave cyber-extortion new legs despite massive improvements in firms' cybersecurity stance.[21] For a CEO making a hard choice between a slow rebuild and a faster recovery with a decryption key, preventing public exposure might just tip the scale – whether to avoid embarrassment or reputational damage, to preserve people's safety or safeguard commercial secrets. Paying a ransom at least prevents an immediate release – even if future leaks are beyond one's control. By mid-2021, most ransomware gangs were using the double extortion tactic, with around 50 per cent of victims opting to pay in the hope of suppressing or delaying data leaks.[22]

Double extortion is especially effective if the damage is not only financial, but the organisation also holds sensitive personal data.

In early October 2021, the Los Angeles branch of Planned Parenthood, a charitable organisation that offers a range of reproductive and sexual health services including abortions, fell victim to hackers. The hackers spent over a week inside their network before the suspicious activity was detected and the system shut down, by which point the criminals had already managed to steal the names, addresses, insurance numbers and health records of over 400,000 patients.[23] The organisation became aware of the full extent of this disastrous privacy breach on 4 November. Yet it was only on 30 November that Planned Parenthood mailed out a letter to affected patients admitting that their diagnosis, treatment and health insurance details could no longer be considered confidential. Planned Parenthood did not admit to paying a ransom but stated that no data had been leaked to the public. They explained that they were only mailing out the notification letters 'out of an abundance of caution', encouraging patients to 'review statements from their healthcare providers or health insurers and contact them immediately if they see charges for services they did not receive.'[24]

In the context of the ferocious political divide over abortion rights and reproductive health in the US, the organisation's focus on unexpected medical bills was beside the point. Exposure had the potential to tear families apart, disrupt marriages, lead to job loss or leave patients open to blackmail and harassment or, far worse, life-threatening violence.[25] The affected patients had been badly failed in respect of their privacy and the organisation was slow to explain what it would do to help or compensate them – or indeed how it would prevent future breaches, given that this was already the third data breach at Planned Parenthood since 2015. However, Planned Parenthood is a not-for-profit organisation, hardly flush with cash, which presented the claimants with an ethical dilemma: any compensation would come directly out of Planned Parenthood's healthcare or education budgets, diminishing the care available to other patients in need.

In December 2021, patient K.O. (clinging desperately to the tattered remains of their anonymity) filed a complaint against Planned Parenthood at the Superior Court of the State of California in Los Angeles: personally, and on behalf of the other 409,758 patients whose records had been exfiltrated. The class action claimed that patients suffered imminent threat of harm, given Planned Parenthood's position as a 'lightning rod in the public debate on abortion restrictions'.[26] The claimant also alleged that the organisation had been negligent in storing their highly private data and had unreasonably delayed notifying patients of the problem. K.O. sought compensation for the stress and anxiety they and other patients had suffered because of the breach, reimbursement for the time and cost of monitoring and securing their accounts, and insurance protection for medical identity theft and extortion well into the future.

The proposal put forward by K.O.'s lawyers of $4,000 in damages plus costs seemed on the low end of what was reasonable, considering the uncertainty and worry caused by the breach. Yet with more than 400,000 patients affected by the breach the LA Planned Parenthood group couldn't feasibly fund anything close to this figure. On the other hand, fighting the case would further impair the reputation of an organisation that – despite all of its problems – provided healthcare that was deeply valued by many. A legal settlement was laboriously hashed out behind the scenes over the next two years. In January 2024, Planned Parenthood made a final offer of $6 million to settle the case without admission of wrongdoing

– which worked out to a disappointing average of less than $15 per affected individual.[27] However, even this paltry amount would not be paid automatically: patients had to submit documents proving financial losses, time spent and out-of-pocket expenses incurred as a direct result of the breach.[28] The small and very late payments are barely a sticking plaster for the anxiety and worry that patients like K.O. had suffered when threatened with the potential disclosure of a most private secret. The only clear winners were the lawyers who started, negotiated and eventually settled the lawsuit.

Unfortunately, Planned Parenthood was just one of many healthcare providers compromised by third-generation ransomware gangs. The highly sensitive nature of the personal information held by healthcare providers, as well as the desperate need to guarantee patient safety and keep downtimes to a minimum, makes hospitals, medical centres, emergency services, health insurers, clinical software providers, vaccine manufacturers and pathology laboratories particularly attractive targets. Over time, ransomware gangs met increasing resistance to double extortion in the commercial sector. Best practice protocols increasingly focused on containing the damage from data leaks rather than on wishful thinking regarding the trustworthiness of criminal gangs' promises to handle personal data responsibly. Healthcare providers by contrast were generally putty in the hands of the gangs, some of which specialised in compromising and threatening to expose healthcare records.[29] If an organisation refused to pay – like Synnovis, the pathology services provider to the UK NHS, in summer 2024 – it was only a matter of time before sensitive patient records were leaked online.[30]

Even during the Covid-19 pandemic, cybercriminals decided to exploit the humanitarian crisis for their personal gain. A new suite of protocols enabling remote and hybrid consultations created new and badly understood IT vulnerabilities. Phishing emails promising important Covid-19-related information, benefits or lifesaving equipment preyed on the fears of a nervous public and harried health workers. The success rate of attackers rose. More than 1,500 successful healthcare-related breaches were reported to the US Department of Health and Human Services between April 2020 and June 2022 alone, with more than 100 million personal health information records compromised.[31] In a global survey of healthcare providers in 2021, over a third of respondents reported at least one ransomware attack in the previous year – and of those a third reported paying a ransom. In late 2024, ransomware was flagged as a critical risk to the world's healthcare infrastructure by the World Health Organization at the United Nations Security Council.[32]

Gallingly, the healthcare sector had already been sounding the alarm loudly and clearly since at least 2020. In May of that year, the American Hospital Association's (AHA) cybersecurity advisors warned that ransomware was no longer a mere economic crime but had crossed the line to a threat-to-life crime. Critical infrastructure was at risk and ransomware was a direct threat to public health and safety. They were frustrated that this crisis was not 'aggressively pursued and prosecuted' by governments.[33] The AHA cybersecurity experts urged the government to help them in tackling what was ultimately a geopolitical problem. They drew a parallel to 9/11 and the subsequent all-of-government approach against terrorism – including those outside the US and beyond the reach of the FBI. Yet, it was abundantly clear that the US administration did not want to get involved in a major geopolitical offensive. It would take a catastrophic attack for the US government to find the political will to grasp the nettle of ransomware.

12

A Matter of National Security: Proactive Counter-ransomware Policy

Opportunities for cybercrime expanded exponentially during the Covid-19 lockdowns.[1] By late 2020, many citizens were genuinely concerned about ransomware that compromised hospital care and pushed firms over the brink at a time of global crisis. Politicians knew they could no longer ignore the issue, but most felt lost among the conflicting policy advice they received. Although experts broadly concurred on what best practice in IT security and ransomware recovery would look like, they disagreed on whether governments should encourage or force the adoption of improved cybersecurity standards. Ransomware policy hawks advocated for a complete ban on paying ransoms to cut off the gangs' profits, but industry leaders warned that doing so would massively escalate economic damages. It was also unclear if a ban would be enforced if lives or public services were at stake. If not, there was a real danger that a ransom ban would divert the crime towards those least able to bear its costs. The geopolitical dimension of ransomware caused further headaches. Cybercriminals would only be deterred from deploying ransomware if bad things started to happen to them. Yet, many cybercriminals seemed to be privateers operating with the implicit or explicit backing of their governments.

Targeting such gangs might break international law and generate unpredictable diplomatic consequences. White-hat hackers were keen to join the fray and take direct action against ransomware gangs, but unleashing them came with incalculable risks. Various law enforcement agencies clamoured for additional resources, but it was unclear how money should be allocated between different branches of government and what initiatives should be prioritised. Lacking easy answers, the first Trump administration (2017–2021) had been at best half-hearted in tackling cybercrime, leaving the Western alliance without effective leadership.[2]

Megan Stifel at the Global Cyber Alliance and Phil Reiner at the Institute for Security and Technology (IST) saw the change in the US administration as a prime opportunity to orchestrate a fightback. They both understood the workings of the US government inside out and knew that the incoming Biden–Harris administration would greatly benefit from a 'cheat sheet' of widely supported counter-ransomware policy proposals.[3] They therefore decided to bring together a broad coalition of stakeholders to develop a consensus on what should be done. The political calendar gave Megan and Phil just four months to complete the project in time for spring 2021. But rather than quickly rounding up the 'usual suspects' in the various branches of government, they envisaged their Ransomware Task Force as a 'big tent'.[4] Megan and Phil particularly wanted to hear from people who worked on ransomware every day: providers of threat intelligence, software engineers, blockchain experts, insurers, negotiators, privacy lawyers and academic researchers. It was well known that the different groups had diverging viewpoints, objectives and priorities – and did not necessarily like or trust each other. However, the IST's promise was that all stakeholder opinions would be heard properly and that any policy recommendations would reflect the industry's consensus.[5]

The Task Force was structured around four themes: Preparation, Response, Disruption and Deterrence. The four working groups were led by eight co-chairs from private or public sector backgrounds with decades of legal, policymaking, technical and commercial experience between them. In asking Microsoft's counter-ransomware lead Kemba Walden to head one of the groups, the IST immediately signalled that this would not be yet another consultation exercise with 'just four white guys running the discussion'. Pairing the very correct retired Major General John Davis with the irreverent computer security specialist Jen Ellis as co-chairs was equally inspired. Appointing a young insurance specialist – Michael Philips – as a penholder brought the response and underwriting community on board. The diverse leadership recruited more than sixty volunteers from their networks, willing to spend many unpaid hours in online meetings to discuss various policy proposals – including any 'wild ideas' that surfaced during the debates.[6] With the chairs (and academic observers like me) in listening mode, the group members quickly gelled. Day by day a more detailed picture of the ransomware ecosystem emerged – as did the mutual trust and respect required for effective collaboration.

The members of the Deterrence group puzzled out ways of changing the risk–reward profile of ransomware. The various gangs lured potential recruits with the promise of easy money and in countries with few well-paid job opportunities, such offers were difficult to resist – unless there was a credible threat of punishment. Yet, many crooks knew that their governments either tacitly encouraged them or lacked the resources to pursue them. How could this perception of easy, riskless profits be changed? Somehow, ransomware needed to be linked in criminals' minds with having their identity exposed, their assets raided and their foreign holidays ending in arrest, extradition and long prison sentences. The Deterrence group identified who was already active in the counter-ransomware space. They found plenty of experts and resources, but they were thinly spread across countries, where they were further divided among various government departments and private companies. If this knowledge and power could be pooled, however, law enforcement would become hugely more effective. Doing so required a profound culture change as well as completely new networks, information-sharing hubs and coordination mechanisms. This transformation could only be achieved with decisive and sustained political leadership – and realistically, the campaign would have to be headed by the White House.

The Disruption working group explored completely novel ideas for breaking the ransomware gangs' business model. The dry final presentation of the group's recommendations barely conceals the fun the participants had in discussing their desire for a gloves-off fight. Private sector specialists offered law enforcement a whole catalogue of suggestions and practical help in hacking back. If governments want to unleash a whirlwind, they just need to set different rules of engagement for private companies (and live with the consequences). White-hat hackers were raring to identify, infiltrate and inflict massive damage on the gangs and their service providers. All the private security companies asked for was not to be held liable for collateral damage. Blockchain experts had the technology to freeze or retrieve ransoms – if they were correctly flagged. Cryptocurrency dealers, exchanges and brokers could become subject to the same regulations as other financial service providers regarding money laundering. If victims were routinely required to report ransom payments, such regulations could be checked and enforced. Another suggestion was for governments to provide incentives for whistle-blowers to let investigators into the communication channels or IT networks of the gangs. Lastly, if governments expected big companies to pull together against ransomware, they would have to give them safe spaces to collaborate. If governments remained laser-focused on preventing collusion, powerful firms could not pool information or work together – even for the common good.

The experts in the Prepare working group knew how to improve computer safety. The group took no time at all to agree on around five to seven security measures that would create an immediate step-change in cybersecurity and reduce successful ransomware attacks. However, they also knew from working with their clients that many organisations chose to underestimate risks, prioritised ease of communication over safety, or relied heavily on insurance for peace of mind. The group's objective was therefore to explore measures that would encourage public and private sector organisations to upgrade their security stance. Having shared their experience of the common roadblocks to the adoption of better cyber-hygiene, the group recommended that governments should become more proactive in promoting higher security standards. Governments could help improve awareness, make information and training resources available, communicate expectations regarding organisations' cyber-hygiene clearly, and enforce standards appropriate to a firm's size and sector where necessary. The group also recommended that organisations that conformed to their industry standards should not be penalised for having been breached by malicious actors. Such clarity would reduce the fear of double victimisation that hampered cooperation and information flow between victims and law enforcement.

Finally, the Response group discussed how to reduce ransom

payments. On balance, participants felt that small companies mostly needed encouragement and hands-on support to refuse payment. If they were offered clear advice, practical help and financial assistance, many more victims would refuse to engage with the extortionists. Setting up a functioning victim support network required serious investment though. Small businesses needed immediate assistance to empower them to stand up to the extortionists. Large organisations with complex networks and the sketchy end of the crisis response sector probably needed a strong steer to drive them away from paying the criminals. They could, for example, be obliged to report incidents and formally explore alternatives to paying ransoms. Payments might only be authorised after a detailed cost–benefit analysis and if all crypto wallet addresses were revealed to law enforcement.

The panel co-chairs led, recorded and summarised the lively and often robust group discussions and framed them as a set of policy recommendations. These were brought back to the participants for further discussion and endorsement. Some proposals received broad support at the outset while others needed to be refined to gain traction. The complete ban on paying ransoms favoured by many in the policy community was the most controversial proposal of all. Although the underlying reasoning of cutting off the gangs' profits was sound, the devil was in its practical application. Should a ransom ban apply if lives were at risk? What level of economic pain was tolerable to uphold the principle of non-payment – at the individual, firm or state level? Should there be compensation for those whose well-being was sacrificed for the greater good? Would a ban divert attacks to the most vulnerable? Time was running out and opinions remained divided. With the deadline approaching fast, the Task Force leaders decided to put only

Launching the Ransomware Task Force
recommendations into a locked-down world

recommendations with broad stakeholder support forward. The prohibition of ransom payments was placed in a separate section, summarising the experts' reservations and setting out how a ban might eventually be phased in.[7] When they finally pressed the send button the panel chairs were hugely proud and utterly exhausted. They 'had sprinted a marathon'.[8]

The Ransomware Task Force report was launched into a locked-down world preoccupied with the Covid-19 pandemic on 29 April 2021 via a video conference. However enthusiastic the Task Force members were about what they had achieved, it was clear to them that their 'cheat sheet' would be a hard sell. With forty-eight recommendations in total, policymakers could see at once that there were no quick wins or easy fixes to the ransomware problem. Moreover, the authors of the report insisted that this was not a list to pick and choose from. The measures would be most effective if implemented together – ideally internationally. Only the White House could pull this off. Unless the US president named ransomware as a national security threat, beefed up the US cybersecurity budget, banged heads together where necessary and brought diplomatic pressure to bear on cybercriminals' safe havens, counter-ransomware efforts merely rearranged the deck chairs on the *Titanic*. This call to arms seemed like a long shot in a political world preoccupied with overstretched healthcare, increasingly unpopular lockdowns and ailing economies. Yet, it turned out that the IST's report was launched at the perfect moment. Just over a week later, on 7 May 2021, the Task Force was entirely vindicated in its doom and gloom predictions. A ransomware gang called DarkSide had infiltrated the network of Colonial Pipeline, a 5,500-mile energy artery carrying natural gas, diesel and gasoline from Texas to New Jersey.

Colonial's attackers had found their way into the network through a former employee's account using a compromised password. To cope with the Covid-19 lockdowns, Colonial had massively invested in their IT infrastructure to enable their employees to work from home. They knew the dangers of doing so. Crooks could find billions of leaked passwords on darknet sites.[9] When required to dream up ever more complex concoctions of words and numbers, many people reuse passwords across accounts and over time. Thus, an old password from someone's social media account may also be their current one for their employer's network. Colonial had added further layers of identification (such as one-time codes sent by smartphone or generated by a digital security key) to bolster security. However, IT had neglected to upgrade (or terminate) accounts that were no longer in use. Patiently trying out pre-loved passwords sourced from the darknet was a simple way for low-tech affiliates to gain access to company networks. One DarkSide affiliate had struck oil at Colonial in exactly this way.[10]

When the first Colonial employees saw the ransom notes popping up on their screens, they raised the alarm at once. NotPetya and WannaCry had taught companies to shut down their networks at the first sign of a ransomware attack and ask questions later. For Joe Blount – Colonial's CEO – this was a tough call. He had decades of experience in running products through pipelines. He was painfully aware that pipelines not only lacked convenient off switches, they also don't have an on switch to bring them swiftly back into operation once a danger has passed. A pipeline can only fully resume duties after every segment has been inspected for potential damage and hundreds of skilled staff have safely brought each section back into operation. Thousands of companies and millions of individuals along the Eastern Seaboard depended on Colonial to transport 2.5 million barrels per day of gasoline, diesel and jet fuel from the oil refineries of Texas. Yet, there was no point in hoping against hope that somehow the ransomware would not affect the pipeline itself. Reluctantly, the decision was taken to halt operations.

As soon as rumours of an 'incident' at Colonial spread, lines of cars began to build up at gas stations. Newsflashes and social media showed images of drivers pouring petrol or diesel into whatever empty vessels were to hand, which triggered a wave of panic-buying.[11] Fuel shortages became acute in seventeen states. As backup stores dwindled, airlines scrambled to get enough jet fuel. Prices spiked, adding to the woes of poor households already reeling from the economic impact of the Covid-19 pandemic. Suddenly ransomware was a kitchen-table issue. US citizens were outraged. Profit-motivated hackers had done what no foreign military or intelligence agency had so far dared to do: cripple US critical infrastructure.

Colonial's management entered recovery mode at once. They would do whatever it took to get products pumping through the pipeline as soon as possible – including paying the ransom demanded by DarkSide.[12] For the US government, the immediate priority was to deal with the energy supply crisis. On 9 May, President Joe Biden declared a state of emergency for the affected states.[13] Two days later, the US government launched a comprehensive federal response to get sufficient fuel to their increasingly restive people. But the White House – at last – was also ready to tackle the underlying problem. A presidential executive order on cybersecurity was issued, promising forthcoming 'bold changes and significant investments in order to defend the vital institutions that underpin the American way of life'.[14] The FBI became 'laser-focused' on the ransomware threat and the gangs targeting US national infrastructure.[15] Although he refrained from directly blaming the Kremlin for the attack, President Biden was very clear that Russia had 'some responsibility' in dealing with ransomware attacks that emanated from their territory, and he would personally raise the issue with President Putin in their next bilateral talks.[16]

The crooks at DarkSide watched with concern as the US government behemoth stirred itself into action. They put out a communique on their website that they were 'apolitical' and in no way linked to a nation state: 'Our goal is to make money and not creating problems for society'.[17] They promised moderation and social responsibility going forward – including closer oversight before their affiliates pressed the button to encrypt a company's servers. The target audience for this message was unlikely to be the American public: the prospect of Russian security forces calling round must have been infinitely more terrifying. Indeed, it did not take long for bad things to happen to DarkSide. On 13 May, DarkSide made an announcement to affiliates that the company hosting its webservers had taken them down 'at the request of law enforcement authorities'.[18] The group thereby lost control of their own critical infrastructure: namely their payment website, their 'name-and-shame' blog and the leak sites for victim data. Even worse, the cryptocurrency stash on their payments server had also disappeared. DarkSide folded at once. The group administrators handed out any remaining decryption keys to affiliates, gave everyone forty-eight hours to finish their outstanding business in whichever way they chose and then signed off: 'The affiliate programme is closed. Stay safe and good luck.'[19]

A takedown without anybody taking credit was very unusual. Western security agencies had typically gone out of their way to broadcast their successes to criminal and domestic audiences. A discreet request from an unnamed agency shook up the ransomware scene: it looked like the Russian government had become involved. Several Russian-language cybercrime forums reacted by banning ransomware gangs from posting recruitment ads on their sites, to avoid getting drawn into the fray. Ransomware-as-a-service gangs overhauled their operating procedures and introduced new restrictions on their affiliates. The notoriously aggressive REvil group formally banned their affiliates from targeting anyone in the health or education sectors or government agencies. Afraid to lose the informal support of the Russian authorities, the REvil management also ordered their partners to run every target past them before launching the encryption program – backed by the threat of releasing free decryption keys to unauthorised victims.[20] When the Irish Health Service was paralysed in May 2021 by a ransomware attack carried out by affiliates of the

Russian-based Conti ransomware group, the hackers quickly offered a free decryption tool.[21]

Western cybersecurity experts were under no illusion that the ransomware threat had receded, however. Only a few weeks after the Colonial attack – at the end of May – American citizens already faced the next major disruption. The world's largest meat supplier – the Brazilian multinational JBS S.A. – had to temporarily close its production facilities in North America to limit the spread of a ransomware attack on its computer network. Supply shortages of beef burgers and steaks may not seem like a huge civic issue. However, with better-off consumers substituting chicken for their favourite meats poorer Americans were quickly priced out of making nutritious dinners for their families. Although JBS had managed to safeguard their backups and could have recovered (slowly) on their own, the political sensitivity of the shortages left them beholden to the extortionists. The management therefore decided to pay an $11 million ransom.[22] This compounded citizens' outrage: the US was exposed to catastrophic risks and – so far – politicians had done precious little to address the underlying threat.

Much finger-pointing ensued. Computer security experts blamed poor cyber-hygiene at JBS. As with Colonial, password leaks were at the root of the incident, and the attackers had spent more than two months roaming around JBS's global network without triggering an alert.[23] The company in turn directed the blame at REvil and Russia's cybercrime industry. A White House spokesperson concurred, pointing out that ultimate responsibility lay with the Kremlin, arguing that 'responsible states do not harbour ransomware criminals'.[24] But this time there was no sign of the Russian government even gently pulling on the leash. A representative of REvil explained in a Dark Web forum that their gang had not broken the new rules of engagement to avoid US critical infrastructure. REvil had tried their best to avoid being put 'on the agenda with Putin [...] The parent company is located in Brazil, where the attack was directed. Why the US intervened is not clear ... In connection with the recent events with fuel, the United States [is] in every possible way avoided ... Brazil was attacked, and the United States was outraged. We do not want to play politics.'[25] It seemed that the Russian authorities agreed that this was a criminal case that did not require state interference. They evidently defined 'critical infrastructure' quite narrowly, giving tacit (or explicit) consent to Russian cybercriminals to disrupt Western commercial enterprises.

With a sense of crisis brewing among a previously apathetic public, American politicians had to get a grip; 2021 was on track to become a record-breaking year for cybercrime. Ransomware had come out of the shadows and was now visibly ruining and endangering citizens' lives.[26] Senior politicians therefore decided to personally learn the lessons from the Colonial Pipeline attack. A month after the attack – on 8 June – the company's CEO Joe Blount was summoned to appear in front of a senate committee to tell his (somewhat inglorious) side of the Colonial ransomware attack.[27]

Mr Blount was visibly uncomfortable. It did not matter that he was a victim of crime. US officials were clearly far from happy with him and his company.[28] Mr Blount would be grilled on his company's cyber-hygiene and the 'process' his company adopted in dealing with the crisis – when in fact he and his people had made a series of snap decisions as the catastrophe unfolded. Colonial's management had worried about containing the damage and solving the energy crisis rather than following best practice protocols for ransomware incidents – to the extent that they were even aware of them.

Perhaps the sorest point was that Mr Blount had personally authorised a $4.4 million ransom against explicit FBI advice. His advisors and responders had not seriously tried to barter with the extortionists and Colonial had paid the criminals the day after the attack occurred. Unfortunately, the decryption key had turned out to be a disappointment. A full month after the attack, the company was still in the process of decrypting files and bringing important software back into play. The crisis might have been handled better – and the buck stopped with Joe Blount.[29] There was just one piece of good news in this grave and often tense meeting. The day before the committee convened, the US Department of Justice had recovered 63.7 Bitcoin (at this time worth $2.3 million) of the 75 Bitcoin ransom paid to DarkSide.[30] Detectives had closely charted the criminals' money-laundering operation on the Bitcoin ledger. At one point, whoever had control of the ransom had made a mistake and transferred a sizeable amount of the tainted cryptocurrency to an address that the US authorities had a spare key for, and the Special Prosecutor had swooped immediately.

The senators interrogating Mr Blount had a threefold agenda. First, they wanted to send a message to US citizens and organisations about improving their cyber-hygiene and resilience. Politicians wanted to drive home that paying ransoms perpetuates ransomware, that it was illegal to pay certain threat actors, and that decryption keys were often unhelpful. Second, they wanted to develop a better understanding of how US companies dealt with cyberattacks. They needed to know which resources were valued and trusted by the private sector and which were seen as a distraction in moments of crisis. Third, politicians wanted to explore what business leaders expected of their government. Blount sat ramrod straight as he faced the senators' tough questions. He remained vague on what kind of cyber-crisis response plan the company had rehearsed before the breach, leaving his audience with the impression that the recovery operation could indeed have run more smoothly. Yet, he also made clear that some of the rules and regulations for reporting cyber-incidents were unhelpful. There were far too many government departments that had to be alerted in the right order at the appropriate time. At a time of crisis, a CEO does not have the bandwidth for separate conversations with seventeen state governors as well as the White House, the FBI and the CISA. Blount stood by his decision to ignore the FBI's advice on ransoms and buy a decryption key. Although the decryption key wasn't 'perfect', it was still much better than rebuilding from scratch. He was certain that a ban on ransom payments would have compromised the US energy infrastructure for considerably longer. When asked for his own impressions on the public–private partnership in tackling ransomware, Blount focused on several issues where the private sector needed better support. It was true that Colonial had failed to secure its system, but perfect security was impossible. Government should define 'good enough' cybersecurity standards – and fully support the victims of crime if sensible precautions did not stop a determined, sophisticated and innovative attacker. Companies needed a single point of contact into government networks. Too many reporting requirements, pointless box-ticking exercises and limited practical support put many companies off sharing their problems with the authorities altogether. Finally, Blount had a stark warning: the people who knew how to operate a pipeline manually were retiring. Soon his company would no longer have the know-how to run even the most critical sections of pipeline in the old-fashioned way. With every passing month, the nation was becoming more reliant on its IT systems. The private sector could no longer deal with this escalating threat on its own: government had to step in or prepare US citizens for the next rounds of catastrophic ransomware attacks.

It was clear that nothing short of a complete overhaul of US cybersecurity policy, regulation and the ransomware response infrastructure was needed. The Colonial Pipeline attack became a major turning point in engaging governments in the fight against ransomware – with the US taking the lead. The White House delivered a range of policy initiatives under the leadership of the formidable Anne Neuberger, President Biden's Deputy Assistant and Deputy National Security Advisor for Cyber and Emerging Technology. Her team decided to implement many of the IST's Ransomware Task Force report recommendations. A new inter-agency body – the Joint Ransomware Task Force (JRTF) – was founded to coordinate counter-ransomware efforts across different levels and parts of the US government and cooperate with international partners as appropriate.[31] The US Department of Justice elevated the priority given to investigating cyberattacks to the same level as terrorism.[32] To enhance the private sector's cybersecurity, previously voluntary guidelines became mandatory for companies and sectors that delivered services of critical national importance – including water, transport, energy, communications and healthcare.[33] Experts on international law carefully studied what else the US could legally do to disrupt criminal threat actors operating from foreign soil.[34]

President Biden made ransomware a major topic in his only face-to-face meeting with President Putin in Geneva in June of that year. He emphasised that certain sectors were off limits to Russian cybercriminals and that the US held the Russian government responsible for enforcing international norms in this respect. Although President Putin did not make any promises,

A MATTER OF NATIONAL SECURITY

US law enforcement was invited to share information about any cybercriminals they had identified as active in Russia. Understandably, the US police and military did not rely on Russia to call off their privateers and instead beefed up their own cyber capabilities. Law enforcement received millions in funding to hire additional staff, enhance preparedness and help ransomware victims. If ransomware groups crippled Western critical infrastructure again, the US would be able to retaliate.[35] To what extent these policies and threats would deter profit-motivated cybercrime, however, remained to be seen.

13

In One Fell Swoop:
The Supply Chain Attack on Kaseya

'I was staring into the abyss ... Suffocating, drowning – or both at the same time – is what it felt like in those moments.'[1] As a Managed Service Provider (MSP), Robert Cioffi's job was to keep his customers safe from cybercrime: to take on the daily worry of updating and patching their software, monitoring their systems for intrusions and ensuring that they had robust back-up processes. His company – Progressive Computing – sold peace of mind to small and medium-sized businesses. His staff were always on call to solve their clients' IT problems, ideally before they impacted on their day-to-day business activity. Yet here he was, frozen with shock and fear, as he realised that a ransomware gang had got past him and his trusted crew and had taken the systems of every single one of their eighty customers hostage. As the attack unfolded, he sat watching, breathless and crumpled, as one icon after another on his own computer turned white.

The Kaseya ransomware attack on 2 July 2021 was a world away from the Colonial and JBS hacks only a few weeks earlier, which were made possible by using leaked passwords bought on the darknet. Nor was it a clever but uncontrollable worm like WannaCry or NotPetya. Instead, a sophisticated hacker had probed and eventually pierced the soft underbelly of an IT security ecosystem, in which companies that could not afford high-quality in-house 24/7 computer support had subcontracted their ever-increasing IT problems to specialist companies. Underlying these outsourcing relationships is a software that facilitates the remote management of clients' IT systems, allowing unseen IT professionals to monitor client servers, implement software updates, and run those magical individual user support sessions where expert hands undo careless damage, find missing files and solve mind-boggling problems in a trice.

It was exactly this off-site monitoring and management function that the Russian cybercrime gang REvil targeted. One of their team established a tiny foothold in the IT system of Kaseya – a software company that provided tools for tens of thousands of MSPs. Each MSP in turn served dozens or even hundreds of small or medium-sized companies. Such supply chains are – of necessity – built on complete trust. Kaseya pushed updates to the MSPs who bought their software, and the end users in turn were directly connected to their MSP's servers. Any code, remote management session or download that bore the electronic signature of Kaseya bypassed all the usual security barriers in this supply chain.[2]

To successfully contaminate this system with malware, the attackers had to spend significant time inside Kaseya's network. The first step was to bypass the authentication procedure used by registered Kaseya employees to log into the company's servers. A tiny flaw in the login protocol's code meant that if a registered Kaseya agent did not put anything into the password box, the system would still treat them as a registered user. Anyone who knew a valid Kaseya username could therefore enter the system at any time of their choosing.[3] Somehow, a REvil hacker had found this open door, obtained administrator privileges and established an undetected link between Kaseya's

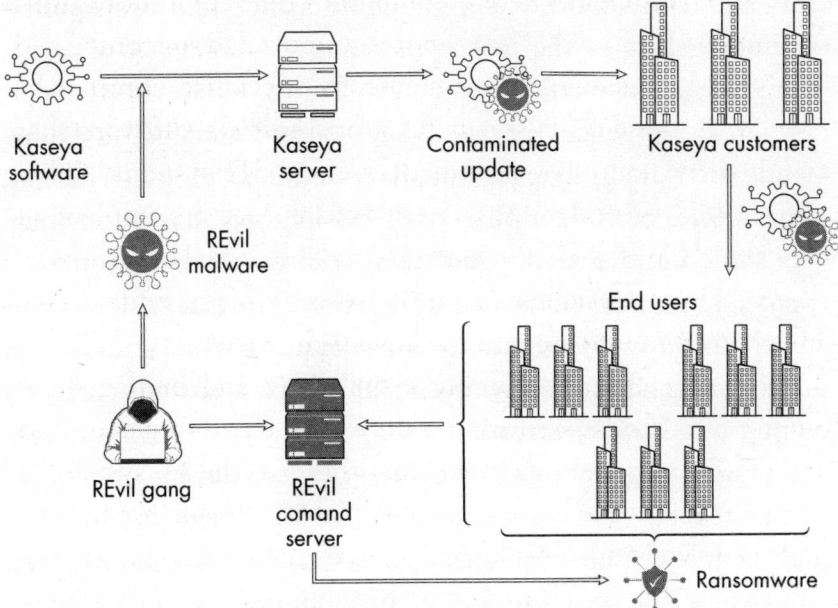

How the Kaseya attack unfolded

system and their own server. They then secretly downloaded their digital toolkits to study the Kaseya software in meticulous detail – as well as when and how the company sent its software updates. Once they were ready, they pushed a software update to all customers connected to the compromised Kaseya server. The update included a malicious function allowing REvil operatives to directly open remote management sessions – just as if they were authorised Kaseya agents. Once inside the end users' systems, they downloaded a ransomware program that had been made to look like it came from Kaseya too.[4] Any client that installed and deployed the initial tainted update and remained connected to the internet while the REvil affiliates completed their unauthorised remote access session could thus be hacked and extorted.

This audacious kind of supply chain attack had been pulled off once before in the infamous SolarWinds breach of 2020. A highly sophisticated adversary – most likely the Russian Foreign Intelligence Service (SVR)[5] – had switched a Solar-Winds software update for one that contained a few additional, elegant lines of code milliseconds before the software package was signed and sealed – and then sent on to the company's clients. The SolarWinds attack, however, was designed to open a back door for spying, not for immediate financial gain. It was hugely successful. By striking SolarWinds, a trusted software company whose electronic factory seal was unquestioningly accepted, around a hundred companies and dozens of government agencies were compromised. The firms were hand-picked high-tech and high-profile companies, such as Microsoft, Intel and Cisco. The breached government agencies included the US Treasury, the US Departments of Justice and Energy, the Pentagon and even the Cybersecurity and Infrastructure Security Agency (CISA) – the very group tasked with monitoring cyberthreats against the US. As the intruders were extremely patient and careful to keep a low profile, it took nine months before the full extent of the breach was uncovered and the spies were finally evicted.[6]

By contrast, the motive in the Kaseya attack was purely financial. The attack had been intended to unleash a tsunami of devastation, but it had also been carefully calibrated not to touch any US critical infrastructure that might provoke a political backlash.[7] REvil had read the new political rulebook and was ready to play the game just as profitably as before. Once the Kaseya mothership was breached, the faulty software would cascade down to every (small and politically insignificant) customer of every MSP that used Kaseya software – unless the problem was spotted and stopped in its tracks. To reduce the chances of the victims being on high alert, the REvil gang sent out the contaminated software update on 2 July 2021, just as businesses across the United States headed off for an extended holiday weekend. The criminals' calculation was that only a skeleton IT crew would be on call during this major public holiday, and at least some of the experts would be a few beers down and feeling slightly worse for wear by the time they stumbled into the briefing room.[8] If REvil had counted on Kaseya's customers being too busy firing up their barbecues to notice the intrusion, they were disappointed, however.[9] The alarm was raised almost at once and the problem was swiftly traced back to its root. Kaseya identified and immediately shut down all potentially problematic servers, and alerted their customers by email, telephone and online notices to take their own systems offline pending further investigation.[10]

With many US clients shuttered for the holiday weekend, it was difficult to estimate the scale of the problem in the first instance. The final tally only came in when the Kaseya software was patched, all servers were up and running again, when clients coming back from a break had successfully logged in, and their systems had been investigated for intruders and properly swept clean. Thanks to the vigilance of those who raised the alarm and shut down the compromised servers, the problem was relatively contained: only 50 of over 35,000 MSPs that were direct Kaseya customers were compromised – and in turn only 800–1,500 of up to a million potential final users were shut down.[11] However, this was little consolation to MSP owners like Robert Cioffi, who were sitting disconsolately in the smouldering ruins of their businesses wondering how on earth they would recover.

Of course, the very point of outsourcing IT to an MSP was that the providers' security experts would be prepared for the eventuality of a breach and have a remediation strategy in place. The unforeseen circumstance here was that some MSPs were hit extremely hard: Robert Cioffi simply did not have the staff to run the forensics, manage the incident response and rebuild the IT systems of eighty customers at once. Yet, for companies like the Swedish supermarket chain Coop, whose cash registers were paralysed by the attack, time was of the essence.[12] With checkout screens locked in most of the Coop's 800 stores, disappointed customers were unable to pay for their weekend groceries. Online orders were jammed, too. The company's only possible response was to close most of their shops until expert help arrived to clean and restart their systems and recover and reload their data.[13] Not ideal when the milk is turning sour and the bread is going stale. Perhaps the moment had come to ignore the FBI advice on refusing ransoms once more and make a deal with the extortionists. REvil had a reputation for fiendish encryption as well as delivering workable decryption keys, so the expectation was that enterprises that paid up could be rescued. Accordingly, REvil had put out a full menu of ransom demands: $44,999 to unlock a single enterprise desperate to quickly resume their operations, a few million dollars for hard-hit MSPs who needed help with decrypting all their customers' files, or a 'bargain price' of $70 million for a universal decryption key that would see everybody right.[14]

One surprising and heartening observation in the Kaseya attack was the change in victims' responses to ransomware incidents. When Robert Cioffi had recovered sufficiently from the initial shock to gather his staff in the conference room, he knew that only exceptional dedication and team spirit would see them through the demanding, sleep-deprived weeks ahead as they tackled the task of cleaning and restoring their clients' networks.[15] What Cioffi did not know as he tried to motivate his dispirited little band was that reinforcements were already on the way. Rather than turning their backs on their afflicted colleagues with a sigh of relief that they had escaped this attack, other MSPs rallied round. A friend immediately put six of his own staff on planes bound for New York to help as volunteers at Progressive Computing. In the end, twenty-seven companies in Cioffi's MSP peer group (that is to say, his competitors) provided a total of fifty volunteer helpers. They helped to restore 250 servers and were able to recover 95 per cent of the 2,500 computers entrusted to Progressive Computing's care. After just seventeen days the company's customers were back online. Robert Cioffi's business was saved.[16]

The other sea change was the trust that the affected companies placed in law enforcement, particularly the FBI. The Kaseya breach was too spectacular and far-reaching to be swept under the carpet. However, there was still a choice about how closely to involve the authorities in the various levels and stages of the recovery process. In the past, crisis responders had often advised minimising engagement with law enforcement. If the business priority was to manage reputation, keep the incident quiet and get back online as fast as possible, the last thing a company wanted was crime scene tape festooned across the front door and police officers seizing computer equipment for forensic analysis. However, the Colonial Pipeline incident had changed that attitude. The FBI was now fully engaged with identifying and disrupting ransomware gangs. Giving ransomware a similar priority to fighting terrorism encouraged greater cooperation and information sharing, including reporting when ransom payments had been made. Establishing which servers and cryptocurrency accounts were used by REvil provided valuable information for future law enforcement actions. Victims that volunteered relevant information were consequently not penalised for having been breached or for engaging with the extortionists.

The acute phase of the Kaseya crisis was largely resolved within three weeks. By the end of week one, the software bug at Kaseya was fixed and their servers were secured. Most of the affected companies had either rebuilt or ransomed their systems on an individual basis. Kaseya had taken the moral high ground and made it clear that they would not cooperate with REvil. However, it was known that the extortionists had tried to tempt them by lowering their initial demand from $70 million to $50 million.[17] On 13 July 2021, all negotiations ended. REvil's negotiation portal, helpdesk, public website and payment infrastructure vanished. Nobody took credit for this outage. Was it a technical blip, an exit scam of the REvil management, the work of the Kremlin or a covert Western law enforcement operation?[18] Further unexpected news came on 22 July: Kaseya announced that they had obtained an effective universal decryptor. Individual keys were offered to all Kaseya clients still in need of them and Kaseya staff offered hands-on help with the decryption process. The company's tight-lipped explanation was that the universal key had come from 'a third party'.[19] Rumours started to swirl: had Kaseya folded and paid the criminals after all? The company was at pains to stress that 'in no uncertain terms ... Kaseya did not pay a ransom ...'.[20] Nonetheless – somehow – they had got a universal key. It was all rather mysterious.

Several weeks later, the *Washington Post* surprised its readers by revealing the source of the universal key: the FBI. Even more intriguingly, the FBI had apparently held back the decryptor for several weeks – allegedly to avoid jeopardising a planned law enforcement campaign.[21] This is a classic problem in intelligence operations: at what point do you show your hand? Using information (especially from undercover sources) to help victims or prevent an individual incident can potentially endanger the success of a future decisive strike against organised crime. Identifying and going after a gang's (hidden) leaders rather than the replaceable crew toiling at the coalface takes time. If the leaders get wind of an operation too early, they tend to regroup after a tactical withdrawal. In this case, the authorities had evidently concluded that letting the Kaseya attack run on for another week was not that damaging. The affected companies were small and already well on the way to recovery. The FBI therefore only released the key after the mysterious shutdown of REvil's online infrastructure, when it was clear that REvil's notorious leader Unknown (aka UNKN) was no longer active.

The unexplained appearance of a free decryptor had interesting repercussions in the ransomware underworld. In September 2021, when REvil was ready to make a comeback, awkward questions were asked in underground chat forums. Had the old REvil leadership scammed their staff out of their hard-earned ransoms? REvil's new public representative O_neday argued fiercely on the illicit Russian-language forum Exploit that it had been a classic case of human error: a cock-up, not a conspiracy. The coders had to create a recovery key for each encrypted machine. Depending on the size of a network, up to several hundred keys were required to unlock individual computers. One employee had slipped up: 'One of our coders misclicked and generated a universal key, and issued the universal decryptor key along with a bunch of keys for one machine. That's how we sh*t ourselves.'[22]

The urgent tone of the conversations illustrates the problem of maintaining mutual trust in cybercrime firms. The Kaseya attack should have been spectacularly lucrative, even though it was stopped far too quickly for the criminals' liking. The $70 million ransom demand was unprecedented, and 1,500 firm-level decryptors at $45,000 each should have netted $67.5 million. But somehow it looked like the hype and effort had not generated much profit. REvil employees and affiliates were disappointed and suspicious. Some of them asked the administrators of darknet forums to investigate the shenanigans of the REvil leadership. Allegations of fraud and scams were taken seriously by forum administrators to maintain trust in their own platforms: anyone unable to clear their names risked being banned from future participation. The REvil leaders were therefore at pains to reassure fellow crooks that everything was above board. 'The payments totaled over 10kk [sic] and everyone knows about them ... No one was scammed. We are in contact with our affiliates, we aren't hiding anything.'[23] (10kk is underworld shorthand for 10 million. A respectable if not astonishing haul for such a sophisticated attack. In fact, it was short of the $11 million a much less sophisticated REvil affiliate had extracted from the Brazilian meatpacker JBS in June of that year.[24])

As REvil was observed working through its reputation management exercise, international law enforcement agencies were preparing their own surprises for the crooks. The US military was finally ready to implement its 'defend forward' doctrine, including the option to 'disrupt or halt malicious cyber activity at its source', which had been formally on the books since 2018.[25] International law certainly prohibited Western agents from hunting down Russian cybercriminals in Russia's territory. However, legal scholars argued that limited and proportionate actions in cyberspace that did not use 'force' fell into a conveniently grey area of international law and were not explicitly forbidden (even if the targeted infrastructure was located on Russian territory).[26] In October 2021, an international law enforcement consortium took the REvil servers down, with the intention of putting the group out of business. This time the agencies involved not only took full credit for the disruption but put other gangs on notice that REvil was just number one of a long list of ransomware groups that should expect retribution.[27]

The new offensive doctrine led to the precipitate departure of O_neday, the operative who had led REvil's short-lived resurrection: 'The server was compromised and they were looking for me ... Good luck everyone, I'm off.'[28] The REvil boss had correctly seen the writing on the wall. In early November, the FBI announced multiple successes. They had arrested and charged Yaroslav Vasinskyi, a Ukrainian REvil affiliate directly involved in the Kaseya attack. He was extradited from Poland to the US and eventually pleaded guilty, accepting a hefty prison sentence of thirteen years and seven months and a fine of over $16 million.[29] The FBI also named and indicted Yevgeniy Polyanin, a Russian national, for multiple counts of extortion and deploying REvil malware. Western law enforcement agencies managed to seize $6.1 million of his cryptoassets that could be traced back to various REvil ransom payments.[30] The Romanian authorities arrested two more suspected REvil affiliates, who were deemed responsible for 5,000 infections and had pocketed half a million euros in ransom money.[31] It looked like the only safe place for REvil gang members to hide was in Russia. But even that faith was about to be shattered.

In mid-January 2022, Russian security services surprised the world with the news that they had 'neutralised' the REvil group and their IT infrastructure at the request of the US authorities.[32] Russian TV channels showed dramatic footage of raids on flats, of people being pinned to the floor and arrested.[33] The man considered responsible for the attacks on both Colonial and JBS was said to be among fourteen suspects remanded in custody.³⁴ Charging and sentencing the REvil operatives was a lengthy process, but two and a half years later several former REvil operatives were indeed convicted of illegal use of payment cards and malware distribution.³⁵ Clearly it was possible for Russian privateers to cross a line with the authorities and be punished for it. The optimists who breathed a sigh of relief at this unexpected sign of Russian cooperation with the FBI had their hopes for further arrests dashed, however.³⁶ On 24 February 2022, just a few weeks after the raid on the infamous REvil gang, Russian tanks started to roll towards Kyiv. The Russian bear was on the prowl and all bets were off regarding President Putin's commitment to rein in cybercriminal activity directed against Ukraine's Western allies.

Indeed, REvil attempted a comeback in April 2022. However, its web presence was a ropey pastiche of its former glory. Its infrastructure looked like it had been inexpertly restored from old backups.³⁷ With a breach website that failed to lay claim to important past successes and an unstable leak website, those trying to hire new affiliates were scraping the bottom of the barrel. REvil never regained its reputation and faded into relative obscurity far behind its former competitors Conti and Hive and newcomers that included LockBit, BlackBasta, KaraKurt and ALPHV.³⁸

The decline and fall of REvil demonstrated that Western law enforcement, having finally woken up to the scale of the challenge, would not rest until criminals and enterprises that posed a threat to national security were hunted down. The cybercriminals' narrative of impunity had been fundamentally challenged by Russia's unexpected cooperation with the US authorities. Moreover, the war in Ukraine did not bring a return to normal privateering business. Instead, it shook up the cybercriminal underground.

14

Conti 'at War' with Costa Rica: The Implosion of a Multinational Criminal Enterprise

Corruption scandals, high and rising poverty, inequality and unemployment, and a tourism industry battered by the Covid-19 pandemic: Costa Rica was not in a happy place in early 2022. Many Costa Ricans were disillusioned with politics and some even with democracy. In the run-off for the presidential election on 3 April, a disgruntled electorate voted out the scandal-ridden centrist Carlos Alvarado Quesada in favour of a right-wing anti-establishment maverick: Rodrigo Chaves.[1] The nation collectively held its breath, waiting to see if and how the populists would deliver on their fulsome election promises. In the various ministries experienced bureaucrats reluctantly cleared their desks, making space for whoever the appointees of the new administration would be. If someone wanted to wreak havoc in Costa Rica, this period of political transition was an ideal time.

Indeed, nobody noticed when the Conti malware group found their first foothold and began crawling around the servers of the Ministry of Finance – known as the Ministerio de Hacienda – sometime in the week of 10 April 2022. The victims only realised the intrusion in the early hours of 18 April, by which time the gang had already exfiltrated huge amounts of sensitive data and proceeded to encrypt the ministry's key IT systems: digital tax administration and customs and excise. This immediately created massive disruptions for the commercial sector as well as fiscal disorder. Import and export duties make an important contribution to the Costa Rican budget, and customs ensured that goods could not enter or leave ports without proof of payment. Cue for complete paralysis in the country's international trade as these permits could no longer be issued. Moreover, without access to the Ministry of Finance computer system, the government didn't know who had paid their taxes and what was being spent. Small businesses that relied on the Ministry of Finance's system to invoice goods and services had no alternative way of getting paid. It took more than a week to switch to workarounds using emails and clumsy paper alternatives. In the meantime, perishable goods spoilt on the docks and Costa Rican families went hungry. When the port gates opened again, some people and businesses could no longer afford imports as the shipping companies had raised prices to cover the additional costs.[2]

The direct financial impact of just the first forty-eight hours following the attack was estimated to be in the region of $125 million – with every further day costing the government around $30 million.[3] The human cost was of course incalculable: in stress, worry and meals and purchases foregone in households at and below the poverty line. Yet the outgoing government refused to pay the $10 million ransom demanded by the criminals. In response, Conti escalated the problem by encrypting computers at local authorities and municipalities, state-run utilities and further ministries.[4] In total, twenty-seven institutions were compromised, with nine of them severely affected. Conti had achieved this wide coverage by sending hundreds of plausible and unique phishing emails – in perfect Spanish – to government agencies several weeks prior. When officials double-clicked on infected links, their computers connected to the Conti command-and-control servers. In addition to downloading their malware into the breached systems, the attackers looked for connections to other state organisations running on unpatched legacy software. Wherever they went, the Conti crew left their encryption malware lying dormant until they were ready to raise the stakes.

As the criminals successively crippled more of the country's institutional infrastructure, the asking price for the decryption key – and an end to the attack – rose to $20 million. Wasn't this still a small price to pay to unlock an entire country? To apply further pressure, the gang also leaked 670 gigabytes of stolen data on its 'name-and-shame' blog and threatened to reveal even more. Yet, Costa Rica was still in a state of political limbo: there was no one at the end of the line ready to take responsibility for resolving the crisis. Seemingly exasperated with the lack of a response, the criminals used their leak site to appeal directly to the Costa Rican people: 'Just pay before it's too late ... we are determined to overthrow the government by means of a cyber attack ... we have defeated you! I appeal to every resident of Costa Rica, go to your government and organize rallies so that they would pay us as soon as possible if your current government cannot stabilize the situation? Maybe it's worth changing it?'[5]

When President Chaves was finally sworn in on 18 May 2022, he immediately – if belatedly – declared a state of national emergency over the ransomware crisis. He indicated that his government would resolve the attack without negotiating with the 'cyber-terrorists'.[6] In response, the attackers pulled out another trump card. On 31 May, printers at the Costa Rican Social Security Fund started to spew out unintelligible messages. It appeared that the Hive ransomware gang had joined in the Conti attack, and they demanded $5 million in Bitcoin for their own decryptor. This time, the country was on high alert. The fund's 1,500 servers were switched off immediately to limit further spread of the malware. The shutdown came at a massive political and personal cost. As the Social Security Fund is responsible for running the country's public health service, officials also made the decision to take the computer systems of 1,200 hospitals, clinics and GP practices offline.[7] Medical care was deeply disrupted: stressed doctors had to work from mould-spotted medical files retrieved hurriedly from hospital basements, pharmacies were unable to dispense medications, Covid-19 test results were delayed, and some rural clinics were entirely cut off from communication. In addition, salaries and pensions due at the end of the month could not be paid. Public servants who had already struggled to survive on meagre and irregularly paid salaries fell into in dire hardship, waiting anxiously for the authorities to respond to pay claims submitted on paper forms. Desperate teachers, who were expected to purchase additional teaching materials for their students out of their own pocket, formed an 'Alliance for Immediate Payment', threatening demonstrations in front of the presidential office unless they were paid in full.[8] The final cost of the attack was estimated in the region of half a billion dollars – a huge sum in a nation of just over 5 million people.[9] What was the point of creating this scale of trauma and disruption in a small and far from wealthy Central American country?

Conti was an infamous and highly profitable ransomware brand. Its founders had specialised in hacking healthcare and education facilities – including a callous plan to simultaneously disrupt hundreds of US hospitals they had previously infected with malware in October 2020.[10] The Conti staff behind that attack had no moral qualms whatsoever. 'Fuck the clinics in the USA this week ... There will be panic. 428 hospitals ...' one of the managers wrote to the group.[11] By holding vulnerable institutions to ransom, Conti became the top-earning ransomware group in 2021, raking in more than $180 million in revenue. Its nearest 'competitor' in this underworld league table – DarkSide, the group infamous for the Colonial Pipeline breach – trailed in a distant second place with earnings of less than $80 million.[12] Alongside its in-house hacking team, Conti also bought from initial access brokers – hackers who specialise in getting a foothold in valuable companies and selling the access credentials to the highest bidder. One of Conti's frontmen was known under the alias Reshaev. A direct translation is 'problem solver', but the nickname also references 1990s Russian gang culture in which *reshaly* were underworld authority figures who settled conflicts, enforced decisions and dealt with corrupt authority figures. Reshaev was a talented and experienced coder who had previously been involved in the Ryuk group that had revolutionised ransomware in 2018 by dispensing with flat fees and tailoring ransoms to their victims' ability and willingness to pay. He was renowned among business insiders as an outstanding organiser. 'It was Reshaev who set the foundation for Conti's dominance in the cybercrime business by creating an organizational system based on skill, teamwork, clear business processes, hierarchy, and clear foresight.'[13]

Conti had between sixty and a hundred salaried employees, organised in six distinct groups each with its own budget and leadership.[14] There were coders to write or improve malware programs and a group of testers to assess the malware's efficacy against security and detection tools. With antivirus software updating every few hours, the ceaseless cycle of coding and testing could be a repetitive and boring task. However, as Conti had to stay one step ahead of the defenders, they needed their staff to be on hand and keen as mustard 24/7 – with the testers and coders constantly handing back and forth newly identified problems and proposed solutions. Meanwhile, the reverse-engineering group searched for vulnerabilities in the hardware, software and cloud services used by potential victims. A whole department of hackers was dedicated to big game hunting. This was where high-profile attacks on corporate victims and concerted campaigns against multiple agencies or facilities (such as the one on Costa Rica) were prepared. The fifth group were the administrators of Conti's attack infrastructure: the Trickbot malware, its botnets and the servers that Conti relied on for spreading its ransomware around the globe.[15]

The sixth group was Conti's very busy human resources department. New talent had to be recruited for every major campaign. Conti employed headhunters and paid employer subscriptions on various internet job-hunting websites, as well as scouring the CVs posted there for untapped IT talent. Coders and penetration testers don't necessarily need to find out exactly how their employer turns their work into profits and salaries.[16] Where the criminal nature of the job could not be disguised, the group recruited on Russian-speaking darknet cybercrime forums.[17] Conti did not routinely lease malware to affiliates but employed its own social engineering specialists. A common ruse was to craft phishing emails that directed potential victims to phone a call center for help with a fictitious problem, whereupon the Conti operators talked their unsuspecting prey into downloading malware. Paying Russian call center wages was cheaper than the cuts expected by affiliates. However, recruits had to be screened for their computer and social skills, work ethic and for being dependably criminal. Checking out underworld applicants is a demanding job in an organisation facing the threat of infiltration and lackadaisical or disgruntled employees harming the brand. Whenever security was compromised staff were purged in large numbers and the hiring process was ramped up again. Criminal HR is a fast-moving, high-stakes job.

With the start of the Russian invasion of Ukraine, Conti's HR headaches suddenly intensified. A notice went up on the Conti News site, pledging its 'full support' to the government of Vladimir Putin.[18] Furthermore, the group threatened to target the Kremlin's enemies: 'As a response to Western warmongering and American threats to use cyber warfare against the citizens of Russian Federation, the Conti Team is officially announcing that we will use our full capacity to deliver retaliatory measures in case the Western warmongers attempt to target critical infrastructure in Russia or any Russian-speaking region of the world …'[19] Although the message did not stay up for long, it created a deep rift in what had once been a pan-Central European crime group. Conti's Ukrainian members, Ukraine supporters and those holding anti-war views found themselves questioning their allegiance to an organisation that had publicly pledged its support for the Russian invasion.

This tension led (at least) one Ukrainian patriot to take direct action. To the delight of Western security researchers, bloggers and journalists, a Twitter account with the name 'ContiLeaks' appeared in late February 2022 with the byline 'fuck ru gov'. Its anonymous author described themselves as a 'boring security researcher' whose heart was 'breaking over my dear Ukraine and my people'. They said they were not a Conti member. Yet, somehow, they had gained access to thousands of internal documents, cryptocurrency account numbers and conversations between Conti employees and their bosses spanning several months in 2020 and 2021. So, over the course of

March 2022, they detonated one bombshell after another with the gleeful message: 'Glory to Ukraine!'[20]

The conversations revealed that over the months covered by the leaked chats Conti did not run a tight ship and morale was often low. Staff numbers fluctuated wildly. Many employees groused that Conti didn't offer them a good or fair deal. Coders were offered a basic salary of $2,000 a month for a job that required them to be available for shift duties 24/7, and their bosses could be grumpy about staff taking leave or changing their hours. Team leaders also counselled their members against taking foreign holidays. 'It's up to you, of course, but I wouldn't fly abroad' was the sage advice of Mango (a mid-level Conti manager) to an employee called Skippy who did not like the idea that they would 'sit in Russia' for the rest of their life. To counter the impression that coders were mere 'galley slaves' Conti held out the promise of incentive payments. Mango tried to lure someone in by assuring them that those who 'bring results can earn more ... there are examples of coders who work normally and earn $5–$10k salary.'[21] Even though this is a respectable salary in Eastern Europe, we are not talking about yachts and supercars here. Skippy once happily bragged that they had spent their earnings on a 27-inch iMac ... apparently something they had 'wanted all [their] life'.[22] It does not exactly sound like the high-roller experience.

Some Conti staff left to work for other cybercrime groups, while others simply burnt out under the pressure of the gruelling shift work. Of those that stayed, many vented or grumbled while others wilfully neglected their day-to-day business. Mango was often frustrated: '... we constantly have one or the other: Either we write nonsense in chats, or we don't answer patients [victims] for half a day. Naturally, our affiliates are nervous after that.'[23] Having spent (too) many hours studying the ContiLeaks cache, the security researcher Brian Krebs concluded: 'Conti is a highly effective – if also remarkably inefficient – cybercriminal organization.'[24] It was a sentiment that was shared by the Conti bosses themselves: 'We have all the opportunities and conditions, we just need to be more professional …'[25] Indeed, a large amount of management time was spent checking up on employees. Reshaev's anonymous hirelings developed valuable code that competitors and security researchers would pay good money for. They handled hugely sensitive data that could be copied and sold on underground forums and implemented large Bitcoin transfers. Their terminals were therefore bugged, insulated with strong firewalls and regularly monitored. 'You check on me all the time, don't you trust me?' asked one upset employee of their overseer when they realised how closely they were being watched. Their boss was unapologetic: 'When that kind of money and people from the street come in who have never seen that kind of money, how can you trust them 1,000%?'[26] It takes a crook to know one.

The backlash to their pro-Russian stance probably did not hit Conti entirely unexpectedly. However, with many of their workforce already hovering somewhere between uncommitted and disgruntled, the group was not resilient to a fault line of this magnitude. The Conti management could not readily fix ContiLeaks: the secret source kept posting taunting messages for an entire month. It looked like they were still in the system, observing bosses as they tried to work out what was going on.[27] Conti's staff and affiliates must have felt extremely insecure. Thanks to the details that had been divulged, Western law enforcement now had a wealth of information connecting their nicknames to specific attacks. Had they left any trace connecting their real names with their online aliases somewhere? Also, what was the point in trying to extort ransoms, if the police might pounce on their cryptocurrency accounts whenever they made the slightest mistake? Perhaps it was time to disappear ...

Indeed, this is what Western commentators eventually concluded about the unusually political attack on Costa Rica. Alongside several other Caribbean and Latin American countries, Costa Rica had been an early and vocal supporter of Ukraine. It is likely that this put them into the cybercriminals' firing line. When Conti launched its high-profile attack, its payments infrastructure was already in disarray. With the Russian government subject to strict economic and financial sanctions, many US and European companies decided they could not risk paying ransoms to an underworld organisation that had made its pro-Kremlin stance on the war in Ukraine so abundantly clear. Although the leaked chats do not provide direct evidence of links to the Russian state, the 'patriotism' of Conti's leadership and their awareness of how cybercrime serves Russia's interests was obvious.[28] Paying ransoms to Conti was no longer simply a question of disregarding a widely flaunted FBI recommendation but potentially a criminal offence. Conti ransomware had become a toxic brand.

Yet, the Conti group still had many assets that could be used profitably elsewhere: powerful malware and small groups of managers and computer wizards who trusted each other and knew how to make crime pay. So, it was a question of retiring the Conti brand while quietly salvaging and reorganising the assets of the parent company. The management decided against switching off their servers and popping up again a few weeks later under a new name. It would be impossible to obscure the Conti DNA in the malware, and law enforcement would soon turn against any large and hierarchical successor enterprise – with all the information from ContiLeaks to help them along, Conti II would be extremely vulnerable to proactive law enforcement. The group leaders therefore decided to restructure as a network of independent cells – like many terrorist and separatist organisations before them.[29] Not wishing to be closely observed in the process of disbanding and reforming, they came up with a devilishly ingenious idea. They would keep everyone talking about the Conti brand when it was already an empty shell with a spectacular attack on Costa Rica – as well as continuing to post victim data from their pipeline. They reckoned that the more spectacular the smoke signals they sent from their deserted camp, the more law enforcement would focus on what was left of Conti rather than watching its leaders form new enterprises or join or take over existing ransomware groups. As for the second- and third-order effects of paralysing a middle-income nation's government, economy and social institutions for weeks and months on end, the criminals were too self-absorbed and cynical to care.

In the end, the plan only worked partially. As Conti's messaging became more erratic and deviated ever further from the established norms in ransomware, security researchers became suspicious. The US-based cybersecurity firm AdvIntel noticed in mid-May that Conti's infrastructure was defunct.[30] When forensic computing experts started to look more closely, they saw several groups whose technology looked suspiciously like that of Conti. Black Basta came from nowhere in early 2022 and soon became one of the most active ransomware groups in the world.[31] Blackbyte specialised in big game hunting. It became the subject of an FBI advisory in early 2022 but expanded its operations regardless.[32] KaraKurt (which means black widow spider) experimented with a new (fourth-generation) ransomware model focused on pure data exfiltration. The extortionists found that they could successfully harass their victims into paying to avoid sensitive data being leaked, and therefore decided to ditch the technical hassle associated with encryption and decryption.[33] Other former Conti infiltration specialists apparently moved to groups like BlackCat, AvosLocker, HelloKitty and Hive – a potential explanation for Hive's sudden participation in the Conti attack on Costa Rica. And throughout this complex rebranding exercise the Conti leadership's crypto wallets kept receiving payments from attacks launched nominally under other names.[34]

Behind the scenes, however, the police were slowly putting the information from ContiLeaks to good use. In September 2023, the United States indicted nine Russian individuals involved in Conti and the Trickbot malware campaigns.[35] Arrests, extraditions and convictions may eventually follow. We know from ContiLeaks that the arrest and trial of the Trickbot coder Alla (Klimova) Witte, who had made the mistake of travelling abroad in 2021, had caused great concern in the Conti group.[36] Several chats feature Mango discussing arranging legal representation for the well-liked Alla, the best tactics to minimise her punishment and how to transfer the necessary funds to the US.[37] 'The number of core individuals involved in ransomware is incredibly small versus perception, maybe a couple hundred ...' reckons Bill Siegel of Coveware, based on the incident response sector's experience of repeatedly interacting with the same people and recycled code. 'It's the same criminals, they're just repainting their getaway cars ...'[38]

Judging from the REvil and Conti group members' behaviour after the groups' implosions, incapacitating a few key players probably has some deterrent effect, but it is limited. The real game changer would be to meddle with gangs' ability to attract new followers after a catastrophic leak or law enforcement campaign.

15

The Lockbit Takedown: Undermining Trust in the Ransomware Business

Cooperation between international police forces on counter-ransomware projects became increasingly routine after 2021. Police efforts were also discreetly boosted by private sector volunteers and received tip-offs from anonymous whistle-blowers. As a result, law enforcement became ever more successful in disrupting gangs' attack infrastructure. Software engineers secretly helped hundreds of victims recover without payment by finding flaws in gangs' malware code or using decryption keys recovered from infiltrated websites.[1] Blockchain analysts tracked down and helped the police snatch ransoms from criminals' crypto accounts, reducing the gains from extortion even further. Hurting gangs in their wallets or tearing down their virtual architecture reduced their effectiveness, but most rebuilt or rebranded eventually.[2] In a hectic world where attention spans barely outlast the camera flashes in the briefing room, naming and shaming foreign criminals felt almost pointless. Arrests and convictions remained exceptions to the rule.

The Operation Cronos team – led by the UK's National Crime Agency (NCA) – therefore pursued a different approach. The break-up of Conti had raised the spectre of 'Frankenware' – an endless cycle of takedowns and resurrections of ever more (if ever smaller) adversaries.³ However, a new opportunity for rattling the ransomware scene presented itself when law enforcement managed to infiltrate the inner workings of LockBit, the gang that had taken down the Royal Mail in January 2023. Law enforcement officers spent time hanging out undetected in the wires (like the phreaks and hackers of the olden days), closely studying the day-to-day operations of the world's current top ransomware group. As the silent observers collected ever juicier titbits, the leaders of Operation Cronos realised that they could fundamentally change both criminals' and victims' perceptions of the ransomware business.

The LockBit code had first reared its ugly head in September 2019 as a proof-of-concept operation run by an innovative and skilful hacker who encrypted their victims' files with the unimaginative extension .abcd. Once they had optimised and demonstrated the speed, potency and convenience of their malware they rebranded it under the name LockBit. The leader – who took the nickname LockBitSupp – started to recruit affiliates in underground forums in January 2020. Their attack team members weren't necessarily computing wizards: all an affiliate had to do was establish an initial access point into a company's network – by whatever pedestrian or high-tech means available to them. Once a patient zero was infected, the LockBit program automatically took care of the rest. The malware propagated itself through the victim's system and encrypted it at great speed as soon as the affiliate sent the command. Each affiliate could organise their workflow from attack through negotiation and payment from a nifty management platform, which also pinged them every time there was a new development. Not only was the ransomware package so user-friendly that a child could have been taught to run it, but LockBit had also remedied one of ransomware's fundamental trust problems.⁴ Turning the payments model back to front, affiliates received the ransom in full and paid a 20 per cent share to LockBit afterwards. This eliminated a common (and well-founded) fear among affiliates that the gangs' leaders would breach their contract if an underling struck gold.

As double extortion took off, LockBit created StealBit: a program that automatically collected certain file types from breached networks and stored the exfiltrated data on servers controlled by LockBitSupp. Affiliates therefore didn't need to worry about the risk of moving or storing large amounts of data on the darknet themselves. For further peace of mind, LockBitSupp claimed that they carried the most sensitive data on a memory stick on a chain around their neck – i.e. well away from file servers that could be seized or instructed to terminate criminals' access and leave them exposed or empty-handed. Finally, LockBitSupp made a point of being accessible and approachable. They could generally be relied upon to be online for troubleshooting, advice and sexist banter. They were clearly workaholic(s), in love with their job and perhaps more motivated by fame than money.

To create a buzz around their brand name, LockBitSupp ran several contests and challenges in darknet forums. They started with a strangely highbrow essay contest in the summer of 2020, offering five prizes worth a total of $15,000 for essays on all subjects related to cryptolockers and networks – and even more if LockBitSupp had a particular favourite among the entries.[5] In June 2022, LockBit announced a bug bounty program: any hacker – ethical or otherwise – who could demonstrate a flaw in their malware would receive a renumeration of between $1,000 and $1 million for bringing it to LockBitSupp's attention. This offer mimicked and compared favourably to prizes offered by major legitimate software developers. In September of the same year, LockBit offered $1,000 to anyone who had the LockBit logo tattooed on their bodies, and at least twenty (mostly Russian) individuals came forward to claim their prize.[6] However, the top prize was reserved for revealing information about the real-world identity of LockBitSupp – to them rather than the police: 'We pay exactly one million dollars, no more and no less, for doxing [disclosing the identity of] the affiliate program boss. Whether you're an FBI agent or a very clever hacker who knows how to find anyone, you can write us ... and get $1 million in Bitcoin or monero for it.'[7] In January 2024, LockBitSupp raised the price on their name to $10 million.[8]

LockBitSupp was a frequent commentator on cybercrime forums, occasionally gave interviews to journalists and readily chatted with cybersecurity experts. Those who regularly engaged with the LockBitSupp account realised that there was more than one person behind the nickname. The correspondent who appeared to be at the helm of the enterprise came across as abrasive and narrow-minded. Their language and cultural references indicated that they were beyond the first flush of youth and liked portraying themselves as a supervillain. Although they were mostly grumpy and aloof when interacting with strangers, their messages to favoured correspondents were often playfully peppered with cat stickers and memes. The kitties became their rather incongruous underworld trademark. At other times LockBitSupp seemed much younger and kept their interactions professionally friendly and cat-free.[9] Not everyone in the underworld enjoyed the older LockBitSupp's apparent addiction to controversy and publicity. Their irritable nature, arrogant and racist comments, opportunism and smear campaigns against rival gangs made them some bitter enemies – and even saw them banned from a darknet forum. Armchair psychologists were tempted to diagnose a narcissistic personality disorder.[10] Security at LockBit suffered on several occasions when disgruntled staff members left and took valuable code or data with them to start their own spin-off operations.[11] Even so, new affiliates continue to flock into the LockBit affiliate programme. After the Conti group broke up in 2022, LockBit became the most prolific strain of ransomware. LockBitSupp was crystal clear about the reason for their success: 'This secret is very simple, an impeccable reputation. We are the only ones who have never scammed anyone or changed our brand. People trust us.'[12]

Operation Cronos therefore aimed at destroying that trust, a central ingredient of the business model. In ransomware-as-a-service, affiliates rely on gang leaders to keep their identity, crypto wallets and details of their crimes confidential. They are permanently on the lookout for scams and betrayals. Victims only pay to keep their data confidential if exfiltrated files are deleted after payment, rather than sold or kept for a later extortion attempt. Unless law enforcement believes a gang's promise that they have robust procedures in place to avoid targeting critical infrastructure, they keep them on their list of priority targets – exacerbating the concern of affiliates that they will eventually be rumbled.

Superficially, LockBit seemed like a large, well-oiled crime machine. There were nearly 200 affiliates in the programme. However, only a third of them were prolific offenders. Others seemed to do little or no business with the LockBit malware. Between them the affiliates were responsible for over 2,500 successful attacks. These had netted them around $500 million in ransom payments.[13] The money side of the business was clean: LockBitSupp had taken no more than their agreed share of $100 million and had ploughed a lot of that back into the business. As one online acquaintance of LockBitSupp said, 'The person that I know, while he certainly is motivated by money, he is not a flashy person, he's not the type of person I would expect to be obsessed with material items ...'[14]

On the other hand, LockBitSupp clearly took a cavalier attitude to security. For example, Jon DiMaggio, an enterprising analyst at a threat intelligence company, had once mischievously applied for an affiliate position at LockBit. Although he did not get the job after an unsuccessful interview, his membership in LockBit's private communication channel was never revoked, even after he published a detailed report on the gang's operations.[15] Similarly, nobody spotted or interrupted law enforcement when they spent happy weeks mining the gang's virtual infrastructure, digging up gritty material to bring the LockBit engine to a sudden, painful and shuddering halt. The undercover team identified nearly three dozen servers used by LockBit, as well as 200 cryptocurrency accounts used for ransom payments. They also found a copy of LockBit's source code, so software engineers could create decryptors for all victims that had not (yet) paid the ransom.[16]

Intelligence officers also studied the affiliates' accounts and correspondence and carefully mapped their criminal records. Detectives chased up whether any of the nicknames could be traced to real-world identities. A handful of affiliates turned out to be within the reach of an allied police force and could be rounded up. Officials discovered that, contrary to their promises, LockBit still held copies of stolen data of victims that had paid ransoms.[17] Neither had LockBitSupp kicked affiliates off the programme who had violated the supposed code of conduct. For example, the prolific offender who had compromised the SickKids hospital in Toronto in 2022 was still working for LockBit in 2024.[18]

The Cronos leaders decided against firing off all this

damaging evidence in one impressive volley. They would use just enough force to stop LockBit's day-to-day operation and thereafter trickle in the rest of the information slowly to – hopefully – permanently damage the trust that lubricates the wider ransomware business. The first challenge was to get eleven law enforcement agencies on board with this unusual approach and agree a time frame for (in)action. This was easier said than done. Even within agencies there are usually divisions: while intelligence officers tend to prefer operations to run long to maximise the chances of delivering a lethal blow to an organisation's leadership, police officers tend to focus on stopping harm as soon as possible. Once a plan was agreed in principle, the Cronos collaborators had to sequence their actions, craft their communications and keep everything secret until its allotted reveal time.

As the various aspects of the plan came together, the UK's NCA got ready to have some fun with trolling their opposition. By carefully crafting and timing the release of damning information, the NCA aimed to maximise media interest, make a laughing stock of LockBitSupp and destroy their reputation – not just in the underworld but among their victims too. On 20 February 2024, the NCA posted a message on X: 'Official announcement in four hours #Cronos'.[19] Shining out from the sombre black background, an icon in the top left-hand corner showed eleven flags surrounding the logo of the infamous ransomware group LockBit. A timer counted down the minutes and sixteen police emblems graced the bottom line.

After sending this tantalising teaser the NCA automatically redirected everyone who wanted to reach LockBit's site to a different webpage which was marked 'seized'. Closely modelled on LockBit's own infamous leak website, the spoof site displayed timers promising various revelations about LockBit and its operatives. As each timer ran down to zero, the icon turned green, and visitors could click on the link for further information. One of the top-line icons taunted LockBitSupp directly: 'You have been banned from LockBit 3.0'.[20] Two icons offered free decryption and recovery tools to victims. There were links to press releases about Operation Cronos and a behind-the-scenes account of LockBit's business practices. Another link pointed to the US Department of Justice indictments of five LockBit affiliates, while further icons led to details on the arrest of three LockBit operatives in Ukraine and Poland. But some of the most intriguing icons showed countdown timers against red backgrounds, whetting appetites for further revelations. The main teaser was embargoed: 'Who is LockBitSupp? The 10 million dollar question …'[21]

Next, each time an affiliate logged into the LockBit control panel, the Cronos team sent a personalised 'welcome' message. Greeting them by their nickname, the police informed them that law enforcement not only knew the ins and outs of their (frozen!) cryptocurrency wallets but also every IP address they had ever used to log into the LockBit system. With the police having exfiltrated their negotiation chat logs too, there was no way any LockBit affiliates could protest their innocence if they were caught.[22] Cronos then signed off with a flourish: 'You can thank LockBitSupp and their flawed infrastructure for this situation … we may be in touch with you very soon.'[23] Was this enough to undermine the trust relationship on which the operation depended? LockBitSupp didn't seem to think so: 'I don't need to restore their trust, because there is no reason not to trust me – these people do not leave any personal information on my website. The generated nicknames are of no value to law enforcement agencies.'[24] However, the indictments and arrests revealed on the spoof website told a very different story. Clearly, not everyone had been 100 per cent successful in keeping their online and offline lives separate. And it looked like the LockBitSupp(s) themselves might be among the careless ones. An ominous countdown timer threatened to reveal their identity – or was the Cronos team bluffing?

When LockBitSupp tried to log into their servers, they too got an error message. All the information on their hard drive was gone. Everyone who was not laughing at their misfortune had good reason to be furious with them. However, if anything the humiliation made them more determined to stage a comeback: 'I will prove that not even the FBI can stop me ... the FBI just motivated me to work harder. They can't stop me ... Once I reach one million businesses on my blog, I will retire ...'[25] They claimed to journalists that they had found and fixed the security breach and business was continuing as usual: 'I have new attacks, more attacks, more updates.'[26] If the affiliates expected an apology, they may have been disappointed by LockBitSupp's nonchalance and braggadocio: 'I didn't pay much attention to it, because for five years of swimming in money I became very lazy, and continued to ride on a yacht with titsy girls ...'[27] LockBitSupp was far from cowed: they remained ambitious and optimistic for the future: 'I plan to continue working until my death. I don't have a goal for a year or for five years. My only goal in life is to attack one million companies around the world and go down in human history as the most destructive affiliate program.'[28]

Within a few days, LockBitSupp rigged up a new website to lure greedy risk-takers back into the programme. The site announced LockBit's latest attacks and announced forthcoming revelations from a recent breach in Fulton County in the US. Yet, insiders were quick to point out that the supposedly fresh attacks predated the LockBit takedown. Moreover, if the

National Crime Agency's claim was correct, LockBitSupp no longer had access to the Fulton data. Someone was bluffing – but who? Indeed, it did not look good when the Fulton data never materialised, but then Operation Cronos also went back on their word to reveal the identity of LockBitSupp. What had been touted as a big reveal turned into a disappointing anticlimax: no name – just more promises: 'We know who he is. We know where he lives. We know how much he is worth.'[29] The post was decorated with a cat sticker – clearly poking fun at LockBitSupp's fondness of felines. The final line of the post delivered an ominous threat in the direction of criminals tempted to join a resurrection of LockBit: 'LockBitSupp has engaged with law enforcement :)'[30] Commentators did not know what to make of the Cronos team's change of plan, but even so the holding message was first-class psychological warfare. The unexplained delay kept everyone guessing and speculating for longer. As the slow burn continued, attacks using LockBit malware persisted but at a much lower rate than before. Elite hackers had better options than joining the enterprise of a disgraced potential traitor, who couldn't even keep their own chat logs private.[31]

Those who understood LockBitSupp's huge ambition and ego still expected them to bounce back with a more convincing rebuild. So they weren't surprised when word went round in early May 2024 that the LockBit darknet site was back online. Those who rushed in to check it out, however, found a new leak website hosted by Operation Cronos. Apparently, the big identity reveal was back on, and the new timer was set for 7 May.[32] This time there was no messing around. At the appointed time, an eight-second video message appeared. 'LockBitSupp is ...' Then a heavily pixilated picture turned into two photographs of a smiling, muscular young man as his name appeared above: Dmitry Yuryevich Khoroshev.[33]

The NCA reveals the identity of LockBitSupp

On the same day, the US Department of Justice released an indictment for Khoroshev on twenty-six counts of extortion, wire fraud and conspiracy.[34] In addition, the US, the UK and Australia put Khoroshev on the list of sanctioned individuals, making it illegal for their citizens and companies to make payments to any (criminal or legal) enterprise associated with him. They also helpfully provided his street address in Voronezh – a provincial city in southwest Russia – and his tax ID, in case the

Russian authorities wanted to re-examine the income Dmitry had declared since 2019. Within hours of the release, more sleuths piled in with further details, including Khoroshev's phone number and birthday.[35] Others contributed credit card and bank account numbers and further underworld nicknames that Khoroshev had used in the past.[36] Dmitry was out of reach of Western security forces, but if one of his enemies wanted to call round to see him, they had all the information they needed. In a blog post security analyst Jon DiMaggio appealed with surprising gentleness and warmth to his vanquished adversary: '... sometimes you need to know when to walk away. It is that time, my old friend. Take your money and go enjoy your life before you end up in a situation where you can't ... It's time to move on.'[37] LockBitSupp, however, remained unintimidated. Writing from their old account, they claimed that the FBI had got it wrong, they didn't even know Dmitry. 'The FBI is bluffing, I'm not Dmitry, I feel sorry for the real Dmitry))) oh, and he'll get fucked for my sins))).'[38] They showed themselves so worried about the 'poor guy' that they offered yet another $1,000 reward for anyone who found out whether Dmitry was 'alive or not, healthy or not so healthy anymore.'[39]

Undeterred by only being able to name one of the people behind the LockBitSupp account, Operation Cronos kept up the pressure by naming, indicting, sanctioning and tracking down former LockBit staff. In July 2024, the US Department of Justice secured convictions against two LockBit affiliates, who pleaded guilty to all charges.[40] In August, one of LockBit's malware coders was arrested in Israel and extradited to the US.[41] When the US and UK sanctioned the members of the infamous Russian cybercrime firm Evil Corp in October (the successors of the Business Club that had run the GameOver Zeus campaigns) they linked a key member of its leadership team to specific LockBit attacks, further limiting the ability of LockBit victims to legally make ransom payments.[42] In December, the Russian authorities arrested Mikhail Matveev, one of the LockBit affiliates on the FBI's most wanted list.[43] LockBitSupp had let their staff down in the most fundamental way.

Unsurprisingly, LockBit went through a fallow period in 2024: attacks dwindled, and only relatively minor breaches were posted on their new leak site. As intended by Operation Cronos, many affiliates deserted the programme and perhaps some were lying low for a while. Even so, LockBit ransomware was still counted among the top threats of 2024. Some malware developers had built their own businesses with the leaked LockBit source code, and security companies were still logging these as LockBit attacks. Meanwhile, LockBitSupp remained determined to reverse their bad fortune. A call for new affiliates advertised an improved version of their code – LockBit 4.0 – and offered the same casual misogyny and easy riches as before: 'Want a Lamborghini, Ferrari and lots of titty girls? Sign up and start your pentester billionaire journey in 5 minutes with us.'[44] If the malware is sufficiently powerful, greedy chancers might just give even a disgraced hacker like LockBitSupp the benefit of the doubt once more.

As law enforcement focuses on disrupting and dismantling the biggest and most brazen gangs, it gets more dangerous for groups to raise their head above the parapet with spectacular or prolific attacks. In 2025, one group that formerly specialised in big game hunting – Hunters International – announced that it was looking to wind down its ransomware operations and rebrand and reorient towards data theft extortion, claiming that 'development in the ransomware direction had become unpromising, low-converting, and extremely risky.'[45] Gangs are worried about affiliates breaching the 'wrong' – i.e. politically sensitive – targets and being subject to sanctions that would wipe out their profits. Meanwhile affiliates are concerned that they can no longer rely on the gangs' managers to guarantee their operational security and anonymity.[46]

Yet, despite the effort and creativity that goes into every takedown, the threat of ransomware to firms and individuals is greater than ever. So far, the main upshot of arrests, disruptions and takedowns has been the proliferation and splintering of ransomware brands and cut-throat competition for competent affiliates. In 2024, IT security experts spotted seventy-five different ransomware strains, with an average of forty-five groups active each month.[47] When big gangs disband, new platforms and rival groups get a chance to recruit seasoned affiliates. Some developers bounce back as lone wolves. Among the top ten ransomware groups were two Conti successors and a group that had built a new affiliate programme from the old Hive source code. A further two slots were taken by groups that had also previously operated under a different name. Only one group in the top ten had operated for more than three years. The top slot, however, was taken by a brand-new group called RansomHub, founded in February 2024.[48] RansomHub's profit split reflects the rising risk of arrest and exit scams for affiliates. By offering affiliates a 90 per cent share of each ransom they were able to tempt former LockBit and scammed BlackCat/ALPHV hackers back into the game.[49] As LockBitSupp himself put it: 'This business works – and will always work ... [A] takedown isn't an indication of a systematic problem with ransomware. It won't have that kind of effect.'[50]

CONCLUSION

Big Money – Minimal Risk?: Dialling down the Ransomware Threat

Since its first hesitant appearance in 1989, ransomware has gone through many astonishing transformations. Until the rise of cryptocurrencies it remained a rare curiosity. Yet as soon as the criminals' payments problem was resolved, ransomware quickly advanced from a low-level nuisance to a problem touching all facets of society. Gangs continuously experimented to improve their 'product': enhancing their breach technology, making encryption more complex and discovering how to best exploit their victims' vulnerabilities. Entrepreneurial hackers copied successful business models while others joined flourishing enterprises as coders or affiliates. As rogue states used ransomware to make money, needle their opponents and circumvent international sanctions, it became an epidemic. Yet it was only in 2021 that ransomware was fully recognised as a serious threat to national security. Despite the concerted efforts of Western cybersecurity experts and international law enforcement consortia to tackle ransomware since then, the tide has not been stemmed. The director of the UK's National Crime Agency urgently warned lawmakers in 2023 that ransomware is 'the one serious organised crime that could bring the country to a standstill – and has not yet.'[1] Similarly, Anne

Neuberger, the US Deputy National Security Adviser for Cyber and Emerging Technology in the Biden–Harris administration, named cybercriminal gangs in the top three cyber challenges for the US, calling them 'the most disruptive set of adversaries today in cyberspace'.[2]

Yet, conveniently for the criminals, despite its ubiquity, ransomware has faded from public consciousness and the political agenda. Between 2021 and 2024, the US alone counted 4,900 reported attacks leading to at least US $3.1 billion in ransom payments.[3] In a relentless twenty-four-hour news cycle, people who are not directly affected by attacks barely have the bandwidth to register even major incidents. Unless the extortionists put children's lives at risk or compromise medical care for hundreds of thousands, create juicy data leaks, target popular brands or halt operations at major retailers, attacks are only fleetingly reported in the popular media. For people outside the technology, cybersecurity, insurance and law enforcement communities, ransomware is an occasional disruptor of healthcare, flights or deliveries, and a long-term excuse for providing substandard public services. Most citizens have become accustomed to the idea that their addresses and social security numbers are sloshing around the darknet alongside those of hundreds of millions of others. After the second or third data breach, a further violation of privacy no longer feels like the end of the world.

However, for anyone tracking the daily stream of global ransomware attacks, the extreme vulnerability of global and local supply chains, public services, transport and critical infrastructure is abundantly clear. Ports, trains and airports have already been subject to temporary shutdowns. Firms regularly lose access to their ordering, shipping and warehousing facilities. Every year, massive resources are spent rebuilding mission-critical services at major corporations and public utilities as fast as possible. Services for society's most vulnerable, local government and small and medium-sized businesses generally take much longer to recover. Although rich English-speaking nations remain the preferred targets for ransomware gangs, no internet-facing computers are immune from attacks. Ransomware developers have discovered rich pickings in emerging markets. They are ideal testing grounds for new campaigns, as many computers run pirated and unpatched software, and IT systems are often open and misconfigured. It is attractive to trial and refine malware in low-security environments where an intruder's presence remains unnoticed. Attacks in Africa and the Asia Pacific region have been rising rapidly, even though the true extent of the problem is masked by patchy reporting.[4] Gangs only progress to the extortion stage when they think it is worth their while, but the writing is on the wall for serious future disruptions. When Indonesia's national data centre was breached in 2024, government agencies were seriously disrupted and could not recover without a decryptor because only 2 per cent of the data in the affected servers had been backed up.[5] Further attacks were reported by Cameroon's energy provider Eneo, Telecom Namibia and the South African National Health Laboratory Services, which left the nation unable to process millions of blood tests for HIV/AIDS and mpox. As the ransomware strains involved could be the precursors of the kinds of threats that rich Western nations will face next, these problems concern us all.

It is also important to recognise that the damage and disruption we have seen so far was caused by uncoordinated and random attacks by disparate criminal groups. Annual losses of tens of billions of dollars (and rising) could be an acceptable cost of conducting global business via a free internet. So far global mass outages – like NotPetya and WannaCry – were caused by reckless experimentation and poorly coded malware rather than deliberate intent. However, one day our systems may face coordinated and targeted attacks, perhaps super-charged by AI. At that point, the goal of attackers may not be financial profit but causing shutdowns or spreading panic and misinformation. The leak of communications and contracts between the Russian technology firm NTC Vulkan and various Russian government agencies demonstrates the extent of the Kremlin's planning for a future cyberwar.[6] If a hostile nation successfully targets just one critical part of the transport, energy or communication infrastructure of a developed country, their interdependence will become evident extremely quickly. Immense physical damage could result from tampering with nuclear power stations, or the steering and control systems of ships or aircraft. We should also brace ourselves for mass data loss when attackers breach cloud servers.

We therefore live with a previously unimaginable level of catastrophic risk, to which many of us are blind or indifferent. In Western countries, politicians mostly focus on issues directly visible to voters, such as migration. As government bureaucracies have been instructed to do ever more with less money, public sector agencies remain saddled with legacy IT equipment. They also have very limited financial and human resources to respond to and recover from attacks. Other than in the US in the immediate aftermath of the Colonial Pipeline attack, tackling ransomware has not been the all-of-government political priority that the gravity of the situation would merit. Despite crime agencies demonstrating their ability to disrupt gangs such as LockBit, Conti and REvil, they have largely failed in their bids for adequate resources to deter foreign criminals from continuing in the ransomware business. Politicians and diplomats mostly tiptoe around the issue of states sheltering cybercriminals and encouraging cybercrime.[7]

Meanwhile individual computer users and organisations still take unnecessary risks in exchanging and storing data. When a breach occurs, between a quarter and a third of company directors still find themselves in the position where paying off the attackers is by far the best option.[8] A whole ecosystem of service providers stands ready to help them facilitate such transactions and in some cases the cost of doing so is covered by insurance. Despite the best efforts of law enforcement to disrupt ransomware gangs' operations, joining or creating a successful extortive malware brand remains extremely tempting for tech-savvy individuals who can rely on their governments to shield them from prosecution. The potentially large monetary rewards for relatively limited efforts with minimal risk of conviction and punishment compare favourably to the disappointing salaries for legitimate high-skilled jobs in countries that are isolated from the global economy by international sanctions. However, based on the knowledge of the criminals' modus operandi, these calculations can be changed. By making different choices, we can make ransomware more difficult to carry out and less profitable at every stage of the attack life cycle: the development of the malware and attack infrastructure, the recruitment of affiliates, accessing victims' networks, data exfiltration, encryption, extortion and ransom payment.

It is always tempting to think of policy levers to address national security threats. Setting a lever to zero ends a problem. Indeed, there are several policy options that could stop ransomware. The problem is that every one of them would either choke social and economic life to (near-) death or escalate geopolitical conflict. The most intuitive counter-ransomware policies – such as a ransom ban – come with severe side effects that are not in the interests of individuals, businesses or nations. A better image of the choices available is that of a control panel where judicious adjustments are made using dials rather than emergency circuit breaks. In adjusting a range of different controls, we can reduce the ransomware threat significantly – for ourselves and the communities we care about.

At the imaginary dashboard, choices are made at the personal, the enterprise or organisation and the state level. As individuals we have the power to make our online lives safer, even if we cannot avoid being caught up in attacks on businesses and public services that we use. In addition to enhancing our own security and resilience we can become more supportive of the security stance of the organisations we work for and interact with. We can also demand higher standards of cyber-hygiene from organisations we share data with, or withdraw from their platforms. Finally, we can vote for and lobby government to adjust the dials we cannot directly control towards a safer setting.

The counter-ransomware dashboard can be organised into four sections: penalties, openness, resilience and ransom payments.

The first section regulates the supply of ransomware by adjusting the probability of cybercriminals being held to account and the severity of punishment they face. Initially, cybercriminals' perception was one of almost complete impunity. However, this view has begun to shift. Western law enforcement agencies have landed major blows against ransomware gangs and their affiliates. It is now costly for criminal enterprises to come into the crosshairs of law enforcement. Even if malware developers have the skills and human resources to rebuild their virtual infrastructures and create alternative websites, re-establishing the trust of affiliates after a takedown is more complicated. By dialling up the threat of law enforcement and using takedowns to undermine trust relationships, ransomware gangs are encouraged to avoid drawing attention to themselves. Gangs that are prolific, excessively greedy, that fail to decrypt, leak data indiscriminately or disrupt critical infrastructure raise their probability of disruption.[9] With more investment in the staff and cyber capabilities of law enforcement, the parameters within which ransomware gangs operate could be restricted further.

Cybercriminals are only safe from prosecution in the jurisdiction of a handful of states that choose to protect them. Taking shelter comes with its own costs. Being made visible to the host government through a reward for information, indictment or an international arrest warrant can lead to unpleasantness, as the (admittedly rare) examples of Russia restricting gangs' activities on darknet forums, arrests and prison sentences demonstrate. At present, no government wants to escalate from ransomware to ransomwar.[10] A mixture of diplomatic pressure and political and economic sanctions has therefore succeeded in setting boundaries of (un)acceptable behaviour in the cybersphere. Over time, an international consensus may emerge – analogous to the 1949 Geneva Conventions – to set clear expectations and limits for the behaviour of conflict parties in cyberspace. So far there have been few positive incentives for nations to engage on this, but any improvements, especially in US–Russian relations, would mean that some dials could be turned towards more cooperative settings in the future. This might also affect the people behind the attacks, many of whom seem to be motivated by a mixture of thwarted dreams and state propaganda that designates anyone in the 'West' (or not using a Cyrillic keyboard) as fair game.

The second section of the dashboard controls the ease with which ransomware gangs enter their victims' IT systems. Here the trade-off is between openness and security. Cybercriminals took full advantage of technology that was originally developed by tech-obsessed explorers, idealists and anarchists for whom protection of private property and data privacy was at best an afterthought. Thousands of early computer users flocked to InterNet terminals for their promise of frictionless communication, ensuring that the most freewheeling and cooperative system won the 'protocol wars'. This could – theoretically – be rolled back. More secure systems are available. System access can be limited to a small number of trusted individuals and communications tightly monitored and controlled. We have a choice about whether mission-critical processes (for example, the operating system of nuclear power stations, pipelines or life support apparatus) are controlled by internet-facing computers. However, 'safe' arrangements are incompatible with global commerce and a whole swathe of online life depends on everyone freely accessing or sharing content. Security has real cost in terms of time, effort, money and foregone opportunities.

In practical terms, the many dials in this section regulate who can access a system, how many hoops they must jump to do so, and how far they can move before encountering the next verification challenge. Everyone makes decisions on their own cyber-hygiene: from the passwords they choose, to how often they update or recycle them, to whether they connect to 'free' and unsecured Wi-Fi in hotels and airports. Computer users choose what links to click, what files to open and what pop-up warnings to ignore. Organisations can opt into various multi-factor authentication systems and enforce frequent software updates. However, as hackers are constantly searching to find ways around the state-of-the-art defences, no technological innovation should be considered as a silver bullet. Enterprises also control what (automatic) safety checks incoming communication must pass and how free their staff are to access internet content on computers connected to their systems. Using legacy equipment online is a massive risk and this should be closely monitored if it is inevitable. Any organisation's overall safety stance is co-created with employees. Training and awareness campaigns help to reduce the risks that organisations must take to have an online presence.

Governments have been reluctant to regulate on minimum standards of cyber-hygiene. Where recommendations have been published, the roll-out has been patchy and half-hearted, especially in the public sector. Decades-long underinvestment means that raising security standards would require massive financial outlays. An up-to-date public digital infrastructure that can identify and neutralise incoming threats might seem unaffordable, but currently governments are at risk of repeating the mistake they made with Covid-19: the failure to prepare for a known risk with a high potential impact. Citizens and the media can hold elected leaders to account on how they treat cybersecurity in their budget allocations.

The third dimension of choice is between resilience and efficiency. Resilience to ransomware attacks refers to the capacity to recover from (partial) shutdowns, encryption and the data leak stage of an attack. Again, this comes at the cost of time, effort and financial resources. For individuals this may take the shape of printing a precious family photo album, keeping paper records of tax returns and storing their most important files on removable (and removed!) storage or in multiple cloud servers. Businesses become more resilient by closely monitoring suspicious activity in their IT systems and shutting them down to evict attackers before they can complete the data exfiltration or encryption stage of an attack. Organisations should also plan how they would operate in the event of an IT shutdown – well before it occurs in real life. Perhaps this requires switching to separate emergency equipment (which needs to be kept on standby) or operating in pen-and-paper mode. To build true resilience, each plan B should be practised so it can be implemented quickly and maintain critical business functions for however long is necessary. Making frequent and accessible backups, keeping them fully offline and regularly testing that they work reduces the reliance on the attackers' help with recovery.

Perfectly secure data storage would be infinitely expensive. As individuals we can reduce our exposure by only sharing information that we are happy about being revealed to families, friends, employers and on social media. The hacking and data leaks at Ashley Madison – an online dating agency for married people seeking affairs with partners of compatible kinks and preferences – and the subsequent waves of sextortion should give everyone pause for thought.[11] Similarly, organisations should question the value added by collecting data in the first place, store only what is absolutely necessary, and choose the appropriate level of storage security based on data sensitivity. There is plenty of scope for improving resilience in government bureaucracies where personal data is often held on highly insecure servers. In a world obsessed with making government services more efficient, obtaining additional resources for a more robust approach to security and resilience will be a big ask, but the case should nonetheless be made.

The final set of choices concerns the ease and confidence with which ransom payments are made. Here the main trade-off is between personal freedom and crime control. While most citizens would like their governments to do more to protect them, they also tend to dislike state surveillance, regulation and sanctions. A complete and strictly enforced ban on paying ransoms would negate all financial incentives to the attackers. Arguably it would end the scourge of ransomware, but governments have remained understandably reluctant to pull this lever. Unless security and resilience are fundamentally enhanced, the economic and social cost of such a ban would outweigh the benefit of maintaining some flexibility on payment. To the extent that ransomware gangs target their actions, partial bans could divert gangs' attention to (geographical or business) areas that are not covered by the restrictions. However, most ransomware affiliates still employ a broad spray-and-pray approach. If they breach a target that is formally unable to pay, they are likely to attempt the extortion anyway. If the cost of resistance is perceived as too high and payment is made, the ban's credibility will be compromised.

Yet even without an outright ban there are many options for dialling down ransom payments. The frequency of ransom payments will be reduced automatically with investment in security and resilience. In addition, governments can make corporate victims think harder about their recovery options by requiring that ransom payments are reported or even authorised. Individuals might be obliged to explore free recovery options such as the No More Ransom initiative before making a payment to unlock their home PCs. Governments could also offer greater financial and practical assistance to victims who choose to recover from backups. Smaller enterprises in particular are all too often left to their own devices at the crisis point. Unable to afford insurance or the services of crisis responders and lacking state support, the extortionist's offer of a quick recovery is a strong lure. Governments can also recalibrate the sanctions imposed on organisations that suffer data breaches, striking a careful balance between encouraging cautious handling of data and making the victims more vulnerable to extortion. If the data breach resolution protocol is shaped by avoiding lawsuits and fines, ransomware gangs exploit this to their own advantage.

The confidence of ransomware victims that gangs will keep their promises regarding decryption keys and the safety of exfiltrated data can also be further undermined. The 'trust paradox' – as Max Smeets calls it when victims turn to their abuser for help – is fundamental to the ransomware business model.[12] The supposedly deleted data found during the LockBit takedown and the Change Healthcare exit scam (where the malware coders kept a $22 million ransom to themselves and left their fuming affiliate to sell the personal data of 190 million customers on the darknet) speak volumes about the wishful thinking involved when victims pay ransoms to protect data privacy. If a victim nonetheless makes the decision to pay, there is still the question of how quickly and how much. When firms manage to keep their heads above water, most ransomware gangs are open to negotiating – and their 'discounts' can be substantial. Furthermore, although it is unlikely to cause a sea change in ransomware, cyberinsurers could be banned from reimbursing ransom payments while insuring all other costs arising from breaches. When company bosses fund ransoms from their own budgets, they may become less inclined to meet the terms of their extortionists.

Finally, cryptocurrencies are the lifeblood of the ransomware ecosystem. As governments around the world are racking up unsustainable debts, investors are increasingly attracted to assets whose supply is demonstrably outside the control of profligate politicians. Attempts to rein in cryptocurrencies can increase distrust of the state, and indeed laissez-faire political candidates have attracted big campaign donations in the US.[13] Criminals benefit from cryptocurrencies becoming more mainstream as their transactions are more difficult to track among a mass of legitimate sales. Even so, the very nature of the blockchain means that police can identify the proceeds of crime in crypto transactions, and they have a legal basis for seizing ill-gotten gains. Mandatory reporting of ransom payments would help to identify the cryptocurrency exchanges and accounts used by ransomware gangs. How much loot can be recovered depends on what resources governments dedicate to tracking the proceeds of crime and cracking down on providers serving the economic underworld.

In summary, there are many ways of causing friction in the mature and complex ransomware ecosystem. This will not only reduce the magnitude of the ransomware problem but will also increase economic and social resilience should ransomware technology be deployed in a future cyberwar campaign. However, it is impossible to throw grit into the well-oiled machine of ransomware without the risk of escalating geopolitical tensions, compromising other economic activities, redirecting spending away from current consumption and/or undermining freedom of choice.

The cost of stopping ransomware is prohibitive. In that way, ransomware is like Covid-19. It is not something that governments should seek to 'beat'. It is about agreeing on an acceptable level of risk and learning to live with the underlying threat. As with Covid-19, there are precautions we can take to avoid becoming a victim, measures that will help us cope and methods to prevent infection from spreading. People and organisations make choices appropriate to their circumstances. The most vulnerable reduce risky behaviour and invest heavily in prevention and remedies. The most resilient can enjoy their freedom but may be asked to modify their behaviour to shield the weak when necessary. Recovering from an infection is tough, as is being caught up in someone else's struggles. Governments provide a safety net for critical cases, monitor infection levels and decide when temporary emergency measures are needed. As populations learn to live with the hazard, treatments improve and eventually almost everyone who suffers an attack pulls through. Afterwards, most survivors are in a better position to defend themselves against whatever new mutation is already on the way. Improved (cyber-) hygiene and a more resilient infrastructure not only reduces the impact of the current threat but also defends against a wide range of future perils.

What is needed in the sphere of ransomware is a broad political debate about whether the current threat level is tolerable and, if not, what resources and policy tools will be devoted to reducing it. It would be very reassuring to know that a well-developed emergency plan exists for the potential of an economy-wide or regional 'standstill' predicted by cybersecurity experts. Nobody wants to see a repeat of the contradictory on-the-hoof policymaking of the first months of the Covid-19 pandemic when a catastrophic ransomware event occurs. Politicians must be pressed to formulate clear cybersecurity strategies and be held accountable for their implementation. But we don't have to wait for others to impose better choices on us. Everyone is free to make them now.

ACKNOWLEDGEMENTS

This book was inspired by the fascinating, dedicated and largely unsung heroines and heroes who spend their lives fighting cybercrime, containing its damage and aiding victims' recovery. Thank you for your work and for sharing your stories.

My peers at the Criminal Governance research group at Oxford, in the Mercatus Centre at George Mason University, the Insurance Law Centre, and the Society for Institutional and Organisational Economics laid the foundations for this book. I thank them all – and particularly Tom Baker, Peter Boettke, Paolo Campana, Jonathan Lusthaus, Mike Munger, Virgil Storr, Ed Stringham, Federico Varese and Daniel Woods. I tested my ideas and collected information in numerous seminars, workshops and conversations with colleagues at King's College, London, at Penn State, Duke, and Cambridge Universities, at the Royal United Services Institute, the National Crime Agency and in the Ransomware Task Force. I am especially grateful to Bill Siegel, Jen Ellis, Will Lyne, Michael Phillips, Chris Reiner, Megan Stifel, Michael Daniel, Elizabeth Cookson, Fabian Wosar, Jamie McColl, Eddy Willems, Ross Andersen, Roland Rosner and Robert Clark for their time, memories, and expertise. A big thank you to Elena Racheva, Zora Hauser, and Paul Sagar for their comments on the first draft of the manuscript and to Peter Frankopan, Paul

Greatbatch and Alice Sherwood for encouraging me to share the stories with a wider public.

I am grateful to my brilliant agent Catherine Clarke at Felicity Bryan, who has skilfully guided and shaped this book since its inception. I thank my editors Rowan Cope and Emily Taber for their thoughtful questions and comments and for mercilessly pruning superfluous material from the text – as will my readers. Thank you also to the teams at Profile Books and PublicAffairs – especially Leila Sackur, Emily Frisella, Clare Sayer and Susan Gollnick – for the efficient and friendly production process.

Everything I do and achieve is rooted in the loving support of my family and friends. Thank you for all the joy you bring into my life with music, clay, plants, garden visits, tea and cake, advice, spa-days, walks and bees. Thank you, Andrew, for encouraging, facilitating and tolerating my preoccupation with yet another parallel world. Henry, Ellie and Cristina: this book is dedicated to you.

IMAGE CREDITS

p. 5   Screenshot of Lockbit 3.0 Leak Site ransomware message. Royal Mail web post.

p. 17 'Blue box' developed by Steve Wozniak © Bonham's/Bournemouth News/Shutterstock

p. 28 Cropped version of *AIDS Information Introductory Diskette Version 2.0* photograph by Olle Gustavsson. Courtesy of Wikimedia Commons. Licensed under CC BY-SA 4.0. Available at: https://commons.wikimedia.org/w/index.php?curid=109486346

p. 39 Photograph of Kenneth Baker at the Rutherford Appleton Laboratory, 1981 © UKRI Science and Technology Facilities Council

p. 87 Screenshot of CryptoLocker malware screen display. Varonis blog post, https://www.varonis.com/blog/cryptolocker

p. 120 *Kim Jong-Il and advisers* © KCNA/Contributor/Getty

p. 128 Marcus Hutchins on the cover of *Wired*, June 2020. Ramona Rosales, *Wired* © Condé Nast

p. 173 Screenshot of ransomware task force Zoom meeting. Author's own.

p. 187 Kaseya attack diagram © Profile Books

p. 219 *LockBit Identity Reveal*, National Crime Agency

While every effort has been made to contact copyright-holders of the images reproduced in this book, the author and publisher would be grateful for information about any where they have been to trace them, and would be glad to make amendments to further editions.

NOTES

Introduction

1. Sophos, *The State of Ransomware 2024* (April 2024). Available at https://news.sophos.com/en-us/2024/04/30/the-state-of-ransomware-2024/
2. Chainalysis Team, '35% year-over-year decrease in ransomware payments' (22 February 2025). Available at www.chainalysis.com/blog/crypto-crime-ransomware-victim-extortion-2025/
3. 'Ransomware Damage To Cost The World $57B In 2025', Cybercrime Magazine (22 April 2025). Available at https://cybersecurityventures.com/ransomware-damage-to-cost-the-world-57b-in-2025
4. US Department of Health, *Lessons Learned from the HSE Cyber Attack* (3 February 2022). Available at www.hhs.gov/sites/default/files/lessons-learned-hse-attack.pdf
5. McGlave, C., Neprash, H. and Nikpay, S., 'Hacked to Pieces? The Effects of Ransomware Attacks on Hospitals and Patients', *SSRN* (4 October 2023). Available at http://dx.doi.org/10.2139/ssrn.4579292
6. Scroxton, A., 'Royal Mail spent £10m on cyber measures after LockBit attack', *Computer Weekly* (16 November 2023). Available at www.computerweekly.com/news/366559952/Royal-Mail-spent-10m-on-cyber-measures-after-LockBit-attack
7. Jolly, J., 'Royal Mail ransomware attackers threaten to publish stolen data', *Guardian* (12 January 2023). Available at www.theguardian.com/business/2023/jan/12/royal-mail-ransomware-attackers-threaten-to-publish-stolen-data
8. A cache of leaked ransomware chats is available at https://github.com/Casualtek/Ransomchats. The Royal Mail ransom chat can be

found at https://github.com/Casualtek/Ransomchats/blob/main/lockbit3.0/royalmailgroup_com.json

9. Espiner, T. and Tidy, J., 'Royal Mail hit by Russia-linked ransomware attack', BBC News (12 January 2023). Available at www.bbc.co.uk/news/business-64244121
10. See for example the ransomware chat between the Conti group and a medical provider at Github.com. https://github.com/Casualtek/Ransomchats/blob/main/Conti/20201109.json
11. Muncaster, P., 'Royal Mail to spend £10m on ransomware remediation', *Infosecurity Magazine* (17 November 2023). Available at www.infosecurity-magazine.com/news/royal-mail-spend-10m-ransomware/
12. Scroxton, A., 'Royal Mail stands firm as LockBit leaks data and renews ransom demand', ComputerWeekly.com (24 February 2023). Available at www.computerweekly.com/news/365531853/Royal-Mail-stands-firm-as-LockBit-leaks-data-and-renews-ransom-demand
13. Scroxton (16 November 2023).
14. Morgan, S., 'Global Ransomware Damage Costs Predicted To Exceed $265 Billion By 2031', Cybercrime Magazine (7 July 2023). Available at https://cybersecurityventures.com/global-ransomware-damage-costs-predicted-to-reach-250-billion-usd-by-2031/
15. Conversation between an anonymous victim and the ransomware gang Hive. Available at https://github.com/Casualtek/Ransomchats/blob/main/Hive/20211113.json
16. Conversation between an anonymous victim and the ransomware gang Akira. Available at https://github.com/Casualtek/Ransomchats/blob/main/Akira/20230815.json
17. Shortland, A., *Kidnap: Inside the Ransom Business* (Oxford University Press, Oxford, 2019).

1: Phreaks and Hackers

1. 'Telephone hackers active', *The Tech*, MIT (20 November 1963). Available at https://www.historyofinformation.com/detail.php?id=985
2. For more detailed information there is a good description on 'How

Telephone Phreaking Worked'. Available at https://www.youtube.com/watch?v=4tHyZdtXULw

3 Video: *World's Most Famous Hacker Kevin Mitnick & KnowBe4's Stu Sjouwerman Opening Keynote.* Available at www.youtube.com/watch?v=iFGve5MUUnE

4 *A Call from Joybubbles*, BBC Radio 4 (17 March 2018). Available at www.bbc.co.uk/programmes/bo8hlnjq

5 The Telephone Museum, 'Cap'n Crunch Bo'sun Whistle'. Available at https://telephone-museum.org/telephone-collections/capn-crunch-bosun-whistle/

6 Lapsley, P., *Exploding the Phone: The untold story of the teenagers and outlaws who hacked MA Bell* (Grove Press, New York, 2013).

7 Video: *Best of Kevin Mitnick: My Favourite Hack*, Cybercrime Magazine. Available at www.youtube.com/watch?v=Lat48rrtFto

8 Rosenbaum, R., 'Secrets of the Little Blue Box', *Esquire* (1 October 1971).

9 Lapsley, P., 'The Definitive Story of Steve Wozniak, Steve Jobs, and Phone Phreaking', *The Atlantic* (20 February 2013). Available at www.theatlantic.com/technology/archive/2013/02/the-definitive-story-of-steve-wozniak-steve-jobs-and-phone-phreaking/273331/

10 Ibid.

11 Video: *Steve Jobs Interview about the Blue Box Story*, Silicon Valley Historical Association (1997). Available at www.youtube.com/watch?v=HFURM8O-oYI

12 Video: *Hackers. The History Of Hacking – Phone Phreaking, Cap. Crunch, Wozniak, Mitnick, RCW39RJ.* Available at www.youtube.com/watch?v=FufYSx2_6Bg

13 United States Sentencing Commission, 'Offences against the person. Homicide' (2018). Available at www.ussc.gov/guidelines/2018-guidelines-manual/2018-chapter-2-c

14 Encyclopaedia Britannica, 'A packet of data', ARPANET (23 September 2023). Available at www.britannica.com/topic/ARPANET/A-packet-of-data

15 Computer History Museum, First Issue of Computer Club Newsletter. Available at https://www.computerhistory.org/revolution/personal-computers/17/312/1138

16 Computer History Museum, The Homebrew Computer Club. Available at www.computerhistory.org/revolution/personal-computers/17/312/2312
17 *Jobs, Interview about the Blue Box Story*
18 Babaria, K., 'The Demonizing of a Hacker', *Forbes* (19 April 1999). Available at www.forbes.com/forbes/1999/0419/6308050a.html
19 Burkeman, O., 'Why did I do it? For Fun!' *Guardian* (13 December 2002). Available at www.theguardian.com/technology/2002/dec/13/g2.usnews
20 Bondü R. and Esser G., 'Justice and rejection sensitivity in children and adolescents with ADHD symptoms', *European Child & Adolescent Psychiatry*, 24(2) (February 2015), pp. 185–98.

2: The World's First Ransomware Attempt

1 Popp, J. L., 'Ecological determinism in the life histories of baboons', *Primates*, 24 (1983), pp. 198–210. Available at https://doi.org/10.1007/BF02381082
2 Waddell, K., 'The Computer Virus that Haunted Early AIDS researchers', *The Atlantic* (10 May 2016). Available at www.theatlantic.com/technology/archive/2016/05/the-computer-virus-that-haunted-early-aids-researchers/481965/
3 McKinney, C. and Mulvin, D., 'Bugs: Rethinking the History of Computing', *Communication, Culture and Critique*, 12(4) (December 2019), pp. 476–98.
4 Ibid.
5 Fosket, J. R. and Fishman, J. 'Constructing the millennium bug: Trust, risk, and technological uncertainty', *CTheory* (1999). Retrieved from https://journals.uvic.ca/index.php/ctheory/article/view/14743/5613
6 Feilder, K. 'The Y2K disease' (17 February 2000), cited in McKinney and Mulvin (December 2019).
7 Wilding, E., 'Popp goes the weasel', *Virus Bulletin* (January 1992). Available at www.virusbulletin.com/uploads/pdf/magazine/1992/199201.pdf
8 McKinney and Mulvin (December 2019).
9 Wilding (January 1992).

10 Clough, B. and Mungo, P., *Approaching Zero: Data Crime and the Computer Underworld* (Faber & Faber, London, 1992).
11 From the letter accompanying the AIDS Diskette printed in Grimes, Roger, *Ransomware Protection Playbook* (Wiley, London, 2021), p. xxiv.
12 Bates, J., 'Technical Analysis. Trojan Horse: AIDS Information Introductory Diskette Version 2.0', *Virus Bulletin* (1 January 1990). Available at www.virusbulletin.com/uploads/pdf/magazine/1990/199001.pdf p.7
13 Wilding (January 1992).
14 Clough and Mungo (1992), p. 139.
15 Wilding (January 1992).
16 Bates (1 January 1990).
17 Bates (1 January 1990), p. 6.
18 Wilding, E., 'Editorial', *Virus Bulletin* (January 1990). Available at www.virusbulletin.com/uploads/pdf/magazine/1990/199001.pdf
19 Simone, Alina, 'The Strange History of Ransomware', *Medium* (26 March 2015). Available at https://medium.com/@alinasimone/the-bizarre-pre-internet-history-of-ransomware-bb480a652b4b
20 Wilding (January 1992).
21 Ibid.
22 www.facebook.com/p/Joseph-L-Popp-Jr-Butterfly-Conservatory-100063816556971/

3: Idealists vs Mischief-makers

1 Interview with Roland Rosner and Robert Clark (15 May 2024).
2 Rosner, R., 'From Copernicus to computer networking', *Interfaces in Computing*, 1(2) (May 1983), pp. 95–104.
3 Rosner, R., 'Protocols for computer networks', *Nature*, 272 (1978), pp. 128–9.
4 Rosner, R., 'Information systems strategy – a university perspective', paper presented at the International Conference on Information Technology in the Workplace (1991). Available at https://www.studocu.com/my/document/universiti-utara-malaysia/business-accounting/information-systems-strategy-a-university-perspective/45934953

NOTES

5 Bailey, S., 'Janet: Securing UK research and education's e-infrastructure for the decade to come', Efficiency Exchange (2013). Available at http://www.efficiencyexchange.ac.uk/wp-content/uploads/Janet-case-study-21.pdf

6 JvNC Network Information Center, 'The U.S. Connection to JANET' in LaQuey, T. (ed.), *The User's Directory of Computer Networks* (Digital Press, 1990), pp. 382–83.

7 'Bloomsbury computing consortium of college centres seeks project funding from industry', Tech Monitor (24 May 1991). Available at https://techmonitor.ai/technology/bloomsbury_computing_consortium_of_college_centres_seeks_project_funding_from_industry

8 Computer History Museum, Protocol wars. Available at www.computerhistory.org/revolution/networking/19/376

9 Cooper, C., *JANET: The First 25 Years* (The JNT Association, 2010), chapter 6.

10 Clark, R. I. A., Stockdale, J. E., Wells, A., 'Software Piracy: How is it Perceived?', Paper given to 4th International Congress on Computing and the Law (Rome, 16–21 May 1988).

11 Interview with Roland Rosner and Robert Clark (15 May 2024).

12 Clark, R. I. A., 'Letters: Cybervandals', *New Scientist* (31 August 1996).

13 Times Higher Education, 'Porn students face action' (9 February 1996).

14 The original text of the release of Crack is available here: https://alecmuffett.com/article/7674

15 Clark, R. I. A., 'Letters: SATAN'S offence', *New Scientist* (8 February 1997).

16 Littman, J., *The Fugitive Game: Online with Kevin Mitnick* (Little, Brown and Company, New York, 1996).

17 Greene, T., 'Kevin Mitnick's "lost" bio', Chapter 1, The Register (13 January 2003). Available at www.theregister.com/2003/01/13/chapter_one_kevin_mitnicks_story/

18 Littman (1996).

19 There are multiple videos online where Mitnick recounts the story, for example at Tekzilla, Protect *Yourself from Online Scam & Hacking*

With Kevin Mitnick! Available at www.youtube.com/watch?v=knkBTlbwDmk
20 Mitnick, K., *Ghost in the Wires: My Adventures as the World's Most Wanted Hacker* (Little, Brown and Company, New York, 2011).
21 Ibid.
22 Littman (1996).
23 Johnson, J., 'Computer an "Umbilical Cord to His Soul": "Dark Side" Hacker Seen as "Electronic Terrorist"', *Los Angeles Times* (8 January 1989). Available at www.latimes.com/archives/la-xpm-1989-01-08-mn-285-story.html
24 Ibid.
25 Mitnick (2011).
26 Markoff, J., 'Cyberspace's Most Wanted: Hacker Eludes F.B.I. Pursuit', *The New York Times* (4 July 1994).
27 Mitnick (2011).
28 See the website of Mitnick Security at www.mitnicksecurity.com

4: Operation Flyhook

1 Pompon, R., 'Russian Hackers, Face to Face', J5 Labs (21 June 2017). Available at www.f5.com/labs/articles/threat-intelligence/russian-hackers-face-to-face
2 Varese, F., *The Russian Mafia: Private Protection in a New Market Economy* (Oxford University Press, Oxford, 2001).
3 Chen, L. C., et al., 'The Upsurge of Mortality in Russia: Causes and Policy Implications', *Population and Development Review*, 22(3) (September 1996), pp. 517–30.
4 Pompon (2017).
5 Adams, J. T., *The Epic of America* (Blue Ribbon Books, New York, 1931, reprinted 1941), p. 404.
6 Jahnke, A., 'Alexey Ivanov and Vasiliy Gorshkov: Russian Hacker Roulette' CSOonline (2005). Available at www.csoonline.com/article/515203/malware-cybercrime-alexey-ivanov-and-vasiliy-gorshkov-russian-hacker-roulette.html
7 Winkler, I., *Spies Among Us: How to Stop the Spies, Terrorists, Hackers, and Criminals You Don't Even Know You Encounter Every Day* (Wiley & Sons, 2005), chapter 10.

NOTES

8. Ibid.
9. Jahnke (2005).
10. Attfield, P., 'United States v Gorshkov: Detailed Forensics and Case Study; Expert Witness Perspective', *Proceedings of the First International Workshop on Systematic Approaches to Digital Forensic Engineering (SADFE'05)* (2005). Available at https://ieeexplore.ieee.org/stamp/stamp.jsp?arnumber=1592518
11. United States District Court for the District of Connecticut – 175 F. Supp. 2d 367 (D. Conn. 2001) (6 December 2001). Available at https://law.justia.com/cases/federal/district-courts/FSupp2/175/367/2419190/
12. Winkler (2005).
13. Pompon (2017).
14. US Department of Justice, 'Russian Computer Hacker Convicted by Jury' (2001). Available at www.justice.gov/archive/criminal/cybercrime/press-releases/2001/gorshkovconvict.htm
15. A partial copy of the CV is shown in Pompon (2017).
16. Attfield (2005).
17. Malicious Life Podcast, 'Inside Operation Flyhook, Part 2'. Available at https://www.cybereason.com/blog/malicious-life-podcast-inside-operation-flyhook-part-2
18. Pompon (2017).
19. Ibid.
20. Jahnke (2005).
21. Ibid.
22. Brenner, S. W., 'Law, Dissonance, and Remote Computer Searches', *North Carolina Journal of Law & Technology* (2012). Available at https://scholarship.law.unc.edu/ncjolt/vol14/iss1/4
23. Ibid.
24. Brunker, M., 'FBI agent charged with hacking', NBC News (15 October 2002). Available at www.nbcnews.com/id/wbna3078784
25. Attfield (2005).
26. Jahnke (2005).
27. Moseley, J. A., 'The Fourth Amendment and Remote Searches: Balancing the Protection of the People with the Remote Investigation of Internet Crimes', *Notre Dame Journal of Law, Ethics & Public Policy*, 19 (2005).

28 Jahnke (2005).
29 US Department of Justice, 'Russian Computer Hacker Convicted by Jury' (2001). Available at www.justice.gov/archive/criminal/cybercrime/press-releases/2001/gorshkovconvict.htm
30 US Department of Justice, 'Russian Man Sentenced for Hacking into Computers in the United States' (2003). Available at https://www.justice.gov/archive/criminal/cybercrime/press-releases/2003/ivanovSent.htm
31 Brunker (15 October 2002).
32 Schroeder, S. C., *The Lure: The True Story of how the Department of Justice Brought Down Two of the World's Most Dangerous Cyber Criminals* (Cengage Learning, 2011).
33 Jahnke (2005).
34 Winkler (2005).
35 Brunker (15 October 2002).
36 Seitz, N., 'Transborder Search: A New Perspective In Law Enforcement?', *Yale Journal of Law and Technology* (2004). Available at https://yjolt.org/sites/default/files/seitz-7-yjolt-23.pdf
37 Newsweek, 'Hacking for Dollars' (21 December 2003). Available at www.newsweek.com/hacking-dollars-131683
38 Sullivan, B., 'Inside a Net Extortion Ring', NBC News (21 June 2002). Available at www.nbcnews.com/id/wbna3078571

5: The Missing Puzzle Pieces

1 www.torproject.org
2 Lusthaus, J., *Industry of Anonymity: Inside the Business of Cybercrime* (Harvard University Press, Cambridge, MA, 2018).
3 Ibid, p. 84.
4 Poulsen, K., *Kingpin: How one hacker took over the billion dollar cybercrime underground* (Crown Publishing, New York, 2011), p. 38.
5 Lusthaus (2018).
6 Verini, J., 'The Great Cyberheist', *The New York Times* (10 November 2010). Available at www.nytimes.com/2010/11/14/magazine/14Hacker-t.html
7 Lusthaus (2018).

NOTES

8   Glenny, M., *Dark Market: Cyberthieves, Cybercops and You* (Bodley Head, London, 2011).
9   https://archives.fbi.gov/archives/news/stories/2008/october/darkmarket_102008
10 Bruce, M., et al. 'Mapping the global geography of cybercrime with the World Cybercrime Index', *PLoS One*, 19(4) (10 April 2024). Available at doi: 10.1371/journal.pone.0297312
11 Young, A. and Yung, M. 'Cryptovirology: Extortion-based Security Threats and Countermeasures', *Proceedings of the IEEE Symposium on Security and Privacy* (1996), pp. 129–140.
12 Young, A. L. and Yung, M., 'Cryptovirology: The Birth, Neglect, and Explosion of Ransomware', *Communications of the ACM*, 60(7) (July 2017), pp. 24–26.
13 Young and Yung (1996).
14 Ibid.
15 Young and Yung (July 2017).
16 Levy, S., 'E-money (That's What I Want)', *Wired* (1 December 1994). Available at www.wired.com/1994/12/emoney/
17 Editors of the Encyclopaedia Britannica, 'PayPal: American Company', *Encyclopaedia Britannica* (updated 31 January 2024). Available at www.britannica.com/topic/PayPal
18 Levy (1 December 1994).
19 Young, A. and Yung, M., *Malicious Cryptography: Exposing Cryptovirology* (Wiley & Sons, 2004).
20 Young and Yung (July 2017).
21 Young, A. and Yung, M., 'On Ransomware and Envisioning the Enemy of Tomorrow', *Computer*, 50 (2017), pp. 82–5.
22 Young M., '"Yes we can't!" On Kleptography and Cryptovirology', research presented at the 26th Chaos Communication Congress (26C3) in Berlin (2009). Available at https://privacy-pc.com/articles/yes-we-cant-on-kleptography-and-cryptovirology.html
23 Nakamoto, S., 'Bitcoin: a peer-to-peer electronic cash system' (2018). Available at www.ussc.gov/sites/default/files/pdf/training/annual-national-training-seminar/2018/Emerging_Tech_Bitcoin_Crypto.pdf
24 Harper, C., 'The Man Behind Bitcoin Pizza Day Is More Than a Meme: He's a Mining Pioneer', *Bitcoin Magazine* (22 May 2019).

Available at https://bitcoinmagazine.com/culture/the-man-behind-bitcoin-pizza-day-is-more-than-a-meme-hes-a-mining-pioneer
25 Bitcoin.com, 'What is Bitcoin?'. Available at www.bitcoin.com/get-started/what-is-bitcoin/
26 Smith, A., *Wealth of Nations* (1776), Book I, chapter 5.
27 Harper (22 May 2019).
28 Foley, S. et al., 'Sex, Drugs, and Bitcoin: How Much Illegal Activity Is Financed through Cryptocurrencies?', *Review of Financial Studies*, 32(5) (2019), pp. 1798–1853.
29 McMillan, R., 'Take a Tour of Robocoin, the World's First Bitcoin ATM', *Wired* (29 October 2013). Available at www.wired.com/2013/10/bitcoin-atm-gallery/

6: CryptoLocker

1 Krebs, B., 'Inside the 100mn Business Club crime gang', KrebsonSecurity (5 August 2015). Available at https://krebsonsecurity.com/2015/08/inside-the-100m-business-club-crime-gang/
2 'The Life and Death of the Zeus Trojan', Threat Intelligence (21 July 2021). Available at www.malwarebytes.com/blog/news/2021/07/the-life-and-death-of-the-zeus-trojan
3 Krebs, B., 'Top Zeus botnet suspect tank arrested in Geneva', KrebsonSecurity (15 November 2022). Available at https://krebsonsecurity.com/2022/11/top-zeus-botnet-suspect-tank-arrested-in-geneva/
4 Krebs (5 August 2015).
5 United District Court of Pennsylvania, Complaint against members of the Business Club (May 2014). Available at www.justice.gov/sites/default/files/opa/legacy/2014/05/30/complaint.pdf
6 Krebs (5 August 2015).
7 Krebs (15 November 2022).
8 O'Neill, P. H., 'Inside the FBI, Russia, and Ukraine's failed cybercrime investigation', *MIT Technology Review* (8 July 2021). Available at: www.technologyreview.com/2021/07/08/1027999/fbi-russia-ukraine-cybercrime-investigation-ransomware/
9 US Department of Justice, 'Foreign national pleads guilty to role in cybercrime schemes involving tens of millions of dollars in losses' (15

February 2024). Available at: www.justice.gov/opa/pr/foreign-national-pleads-guilty-role-cybercrime-schemes-involving-tens-millions-dollars

10 Zetter, K., 'Microsoft Seizes ZeuS Servers in Anti-Botnet Rampage', *Wired* (26 March 2012). Available at www.wired.com/2012/03/microsoft-botnet-takedown/

11 US Department of Justice, 'U.S. Leads Multinational Action Against "Gameover Zeus" Botnet and "Cryptolocker" Ransomware, Charges Botnet Administrator' (2 June 2014). Available at www.justice.gov/opa/pr/us-leads-multi-national-action-against-gameover-zeus-botnet-and-cryptolocker-ransomware

12 Levy, R., 'Hell to Pay: Ransomware Pt. 2', *Malicious Life Podcast* (7 August 2017). Available at www.cybereason.com/blog/malicious-life-podcast-hell-to-pay-ransomware-part-2

13 US Department of Justice (2 June 2014).

14 Krebs, B., 'DDoS Attack on Bank Hid $900,000 Cyberheist', KrebsonSecurity (19 February 2013). Available at https://krebsonsecurity.com/2013/02/ddos-attack-on-bank-hid-900000-cyberheist/

15 Krebs, B., 'I'll Take Two Mastercards and a Visa Please', KrebsonSecurity (22 September 2010). Available at https://krebsonsecurity.com/2010/09/ill-take-2-mastercards-and-a-visa-please/

16 Image of CryptoLocker screen shown to customers with antivirus software. Available at https://www.avast.com/c-cryptolocker

17 United District Court of Pennsylvania. Complaint against members of the Business Club (May 2014). Available at www.justice.gov/sites/default/files/opa/legacy/2014/05/30/complaint.pdf

18 Stahl, L., 'The growing partnership between Russia's government and cybercriminals', CBS News (21 April 2019). Available at www.cbsnews.com/news/evgeniy-mikhailovich-bogachev-the-growing-partnership-between-russia-government-and-cybercriminals-60-minutes/

19 US Department of Justice (2 June 2014).

20 Schwirtz, M. and Goldstein, J., 'Russian espionage piggybacks on a cybercriminal's hacking', *The New York Times* (12 March 2017).

Available at www.nytimes.com/2017/03/12/world/europe/russia-hacker-evgeniy-bogachev.html
21. FBI Most Wanted, 'Evgeniy Mikhailovich Bogachev'. Available at www.fbi.gov/wanted/cyber/evgeniy-mikhailovich-bogachev
22. United District Court of Pennsylvania (May 2014).
23. Schwirtz and Goldstein (12 March 2017).
24. Yeborov, O., 'Fantomas. Why did a French comedy villain inspire real crime in the USSR?', Russia Beyond (28 May 2019). Available at www.rbth.com/history/330414-fantômas-ussr-crime
25. Stewart, W., 27 Febaruary 2015. 'Fantomas', the FBI's Most Wanted, *Daily Mail*, available at www.dailymail.co.uk/news/article-2970223/Fantomas-FBI-s-Wanted-Russian-100m-cyber-crime-boss-nicknamed-movie-villain-largest-bounty-head-flees-mysterious-tip-amid-fears-Kremlin-protecting-hero.html
26. Mirovalev, M. and Freeman, C., 'FBI's Most Wanted: The Man Who Could Take Down Banks', *Irish Independent* (15 June 2014). Available at www.independent.ie/life/fbis-most-wanted-the-man-who-could-take-down-banks/30352207.html
27. Krebs, B., 'FBI $3mn bounty for Zeus Trojan author', KrebsonSecurity (25 February 2015). Available at https://krebsonsecurity.com/2015/02/fbi-3m-bounty-for-zeus-trojan-author/
28. US Department of Justice (15 February 2024).

7: A Masterpiece of Criminality

1. The Hollywood Presbyterian Hospital Facebook page is available at www.facebook.com/CHAHPMedCenter/?locale=en_GB
2. Vanian, J., 'Hollywood Hospital Pays off Hackers to Restore computer System', Fortune (18 February 2016). Available at https://fortune.com/2016/02/18/hollywood-hospital-hackers-computer-system/
3. Brewster, T., 'As Ransomware Crisis Explodes Hollywood Hospital Coughs up $17,000 in Bitcoin', *Forbes* (18 February 2016). Available at www.forbes.com/sites/thomasbrewster/2016/02/18/ransomware-hollywood-payment-locky-menace/
4. Kandel, J. and Kovacik, R., 'Hollywood Hospital "Victim of Cyberattack"', NBC (11 February 2016). Available at www.

nbclosangeles.com/news/local/hollywood-hospital-victim-of-cyber-attack/2021148/

5   Ragan, S., 'Ransomware takes Hollywood hospital offline. $3.6mn demanded by attackers', CSOonline (14 February 2016). Available at www.csoonline.com/article/554745/ransomware-takes-hollywood-hospital-offline-36m-demanded-by-attackers.html

6   Krebs, B., 'Hospital declares "Internal State of Emergency" after Ransomware Infection', KrebsonSecurity (22 May 2016). Available at https://krebsonsecurity.com/2016/03/hospital-declares-internet-state-of-emergency-after-ransomware-infection/

7   Beaumont, K., 'You, your Endpoints and Locky', *Medium* (17 February 2017). Available at https://doublepulsar.com/you-your-endpoints-and-the-locky-virus-b49ef8241bea#.fo805k8qy

8   Loedby, J., 'Locky Ransomware 101. Everything you need to know', Heimdahl Security (updated 14 June 2024). Available at https://heimdalsecurity.com/blog/locky-ransomware-101/

9   'Locky Ransomware Information, Help Guide, and FAQ', *Bleeping Computer* (9 May 2016). Available at www.bleepingcomputer.com/virus-removal/locky-ransomware-information-help

10 FBI Cyber Bulletin, 'Identification of Locky Ransomware' (26 July 2016). Available at https://publicintelligence.net/fbi-locky-ransomware/

11 Locky maintained a network of hundreds of thousands of secretly hijacked personal and business computers called Necurs: Schwartz, M., 'Locky Returns via Spam and Dropbox-Themed Phishing Attacks', Bank Info Security (1 September 2017). Available at www.bankinfosecurity.com/locky-returns-via-spam-dropbox-themed-phishing-attacks-a-10250

12 Oosthoek, K., Cable, J. and Smaragdakis, G., 'A Tale of Two Markets: Investigating the Ransomware Payments Economy', *Computer Science* (10 May 2022). Available at https://arxiv.org/abs/2205.05028

13 Schwartz, M., 'Locky Ransomware Returns With Two New Variants', Euro Security Watch (18 August 2017). Available at www.databreachtoday.com/blogs/locky-ransomware-returns-two-new-variants-p-2528

14 Ponemon Institute, *Cyber Security in Healthcare: The Cost and Impact on Patient Safety and Care* (2023). Available at www.proofpoint.com/sites/default/files/threat-reports/pfpt-us-tr-cyber-insecurity-healthcare-ponemon-report.pdf
15 Krebs, B., 'Is REvil the New GandCrab ransomware?' KrebsonSecurity (15 July 2019). Available at https://krebsonsecurity.com/2019/07/is-revil-the-new-gandcrab-ransomware/
16 Greenberg, A., 'Hackers Behind the Change Healthcare Ransomware Attack Just Received a $22 Million Payment', *Wired* (4 March 2024). Available at www.wired.com/story/alphv-change-healthcare-ransomware-payment/
17 Full statement: Salvio, J., 'GandGrab Threat Actors Retire … Maybe', Fortinet (24 June 2019). Available at www.fortinet.com/blog/threat-research/gandcrab-threat-actors-retire
18 Klovig Skelton, S., 'BlackMatter goes on record about DarkSide and REvil links', *Computer Weekly* (2 August 2021). Available at www.computerweekly.com/news/252504921/BlackMatter-goes-on-the-record-about-DarkSide-and-REvil-links
19 'A successor to BlackMatter and Revil gangs, BlackCat targets corporate environments with highly effective and customizable ransomware', Kapersky blog (7 April 2022). Available at www.kaspersky.com/about/press-releases/a-successor-to-blackmatter-and-revil-gangs-blackcat-targets-corporate-environments-with-highly-effective-and-customizable-ransomware

8: The Ransomeware Ecosystem

1 Palassis, A., Speelman, C. P. and Pooley, J. A., 'An Exploration of the Psychological Impact of Hacking Victimization', *Sage Open* 11(4) (29 November 2021). Available at https://doi.org/10.1177/21582440211061556
2 Cross, C., '(Mis)Understanding the Impact of Online Fraud: Implications for Victim Assistance Schemes', *Victims & Offenders*, 13(6) (22 May 2018), pp. 757–76. Available at https://doi.org/10.1080/15564886.2018.1474154
3 American Guarantee & Liability Insurance Company v. Ingram Micro Inc., 2000 WL 1094761.

NOTES

4   Baker, T. and Shortland, A., 'Insurance and enterprise: cyber insurance for ransomware', *The Geneva Papers on Risk and Insurance – Issues and Practice*, 48 (December 2022), pp. 275–99.
5   Interview with Ross Anderson (14 February 2023).
6   Love, J. and Ketchen, A., 'Emerging Law on Electronic Data insurance', *For the Defense*, 18 (May 2010). Available at www.robinskaplan.com/-/media/pdfs/emerging-law-on-electronic-data-insurance.pdf
7   Ericson, R. and Doyle, A., *Insurance as Governance* (University of Toronto Press, Toronto, 2003).
8   Woods, D. W. and Böhme, R., 'Incident Response as a Lawyers' Service', *IEEE Security & Privacy*, 20(2) (2021).
9   Shortland, A., *Kidnap: Inside the Ransom Business* (Oxford University Press, Oxford, 2019).
10 Baker and Shortland (December 2022).
11 Dudley, R., 'The Extortion Economy', ProPublica (27 August 2019). Available at www.propublica.org/article/the-extortion-economy-how-insurance-companies-are-fueling-a-rise-in-ransomware-attacks
12 Dudley, R. and Kao, J., 'The Secret Trade', ProPublica (15 May 2019). Available at https://features.propublica.org/ransomware/ransomware-attack-data-recovery-firms-paying-hackers/
13 'Beware of Dishonest Ransomware Recovery Firms', Coveware blog (11 December 2018). Available at www.coveware.com/blog/2018/12/11/beware-of-dishonest-ransomware-recovery-firms
14 Ibid.
15 Sheriff Scott Cass, Lamar County, Texas, Testimonial provided for MonsterCloud Security. Available at https://monstercloud.com/testimonials/
16 Sergeant Alex Foster, Mexico Beach, Florida, Testimonial provided for MonsterCloud Security. Available at https://monstercloud.com/testimonials/
17 Ward Calhoun, Deputy Chief Sheriff of Lauderdale County Sheriff's Department in Mississippi. Testimonial provided for MonsterCloud Security. Available at https://monstercloud.com/testimonials/
18 Chadwick Henson, Chief of Police, Trumann Police Department,

Testimonial provided for MonsterCloud Security. Available at https://monstercloud.com/testimonials/
19   Charles Jones, IT manager, Trumann Police Department, Testimonial provided for MonsterCloud Security. Available at https://monstercloud.com/testimonials/
20   Kevin Ward, IT Manager, Franklin County Sherriff's office, Testimonial provided for MonsterCloud Security. Available at https://monstercloud.com/testimonials/
21   Robert Wilson, IT manager at Lauderdale County Sheriff's Department in Mississippi, Testimonial provided for MonsterCloud Security. Available at https://monstercloud.com/testimonials/
22   Brandon Watson, IT manager, West City Police Department, Testimonial provided for MonsterCloud Security. Available at https://monstercloud.com/testimonials/
23   Joel Witherspoon, Network Administrator at Lamar County, Testimonial provided for MonsterCloud Security. Available at https://monstercloud.com/testimonials/
24   Cedric Crawford, Network Administrator at Lamar County, Testimonial provided for MonsterCloud Security. Available at https://monstercloud.com/testimonials/
25   Calhoun, Testimonial for MonsterCloud.
26   MonsterCloud Website. Available at https://monstercloud.com/ransomware-removal/
27   Ibid.
28   Dudley and Kao (15 May 2019).
29   Ibid.
30   Ibid.

9: Ransomwar

1   Campbell, C., 'The world can expect more cybercrime for North Korea', *Time Magazine* (20 February 2017). Available at https://time.com/4676204/north-korea-cyber-crime-hacking-china-coal/
2   Yoon, S., 'North Korea recruits hackers at school', Al Jazeera (20 June 2011). Available at www.aljazeera.com/features/2011/6/20/north-korea-recruits-hackers-at-school
3   NBC News, 'In North Korea, hackers are a handpicked, pampered

NOTES

elite' (5 December 2014). Available at www.nbcnews.com/tech/security/north-korea-hackers-are-handpicked-pampered-elite-reuters-n262396

4 Groll, E., 'Gold-smuggling North Korean Diplomat Provides Glimpse at Criminal Empire', *Foreign Policy* (6 March 2015). Available at https://foreignpolicy.com/2015/03/06/gold-smuggling-north-korean-diplomat-provides-glimpse-at-criminal-empire/

5 US Department of Justice, 'North Korean Regime-Backed Programmer Charged With Conspiracy to Conduct Multiple Cyber Attacks and Intrusions', (6 September 2018). Available at www.justice.gov/opa/pr/north-korean-regime-backed-programmer-charged-conspiracy-conduct-multiple-cyber-attacks-and

6 Stengel, R., 'The Untold Story of the Sony Hack', *Vanity Fair* (6 October 2019). Available at www.vanityfair.com/news/2019/10/the-untold-story-of-the-sony-hack

7 BBC News, 'The Lazarus Heist' (21 June 2021). Available at www.bbc.co.uk/news/stories-57520169

8 Caesar, Ed, 'The Incredible Rise of North Korea's Hacking Army', *The New Yorker* (19 April 2021). Available at www.newyorker.com/magazine/2021/04/26/the-incredible-rise-of-north-koreas-hacking-army

9 Cybernews, 'Unravelling EternalBlue: Inside the WannaCry's enabler' (updated 15 November 2023). Available at https://cybernews.com/security/eternalblue-vulnerability-exploit-explained/

10 Al Jazeera News, 'Global hacking attack infects 57,000 computers' (13 May 2017). Available at www.aljazeera.com/news/2017/5/13/global-hacking-attack-infects-57000-computers

11 National Audit Office (UK), *Investigation: WannaCry cyber attack and the NHS* (25 April 2018). Available at www.nao.org.uk/wp-content/uploads/2017/10/Investigation-WannaCry-cyber-attack-and-the-NHS.pdf

12 BBC News, 'Ransomware cyber-attack: Who has been hardest hit?' (15 May 2017). Available at www.bbc.co.uk/news/world-39919249

13 Screenshot available here: https://news.sky.com/story/us-blames-wannacry-ransomware-attack-on-north-korea-11177034

14 Kan, M., 'Paying the WannaCry ransom will probably get you

nothing. Here's why', PCWorld News (15 May 2017). Available at www.pcworld.com/article/406793/paying-the-wannacry-ransom-will-probably-get-you-nothing-heres-why.html

15 Greenberg, A., 'The Confessions of Marcus Hutchins, the Hacker Who Saved the Internet', *Wired* (12 May 2020). Available at www.wired.com/story/confessions-marcus-hutchins-hacker-who-saved-the-internet/

16 Ibid.

17 Ibid.

18 United States Attorney's Office, 'Marcus Hutchins Pleads Guilty to Creating and Distributing the Kronos Banking Trojan and UPAS Kit Malware' (3 May 2019). Available at www.justice.gov/usao-edwi/pr/marcus-hutchins-pleads-guilty-creating-and-distributing-kronos-banking-trojan-and-upas

19 Greenberg (2020).

20 Marcus Hutchins' own blog post on the events of the afternoon can be found on the website of the UK's National Cyber Security Centre (undated): 'Finding the Kill Switch that stopped the Spread of Ransomware'. Available at www.ncsc.gov.uk/blog-post/finding-kill-switch-stop-spread-ransomware-0

21 Greenberg (2020).

22 Ibid.

23 Ibid.

24 United States' Attorney's Office (3 May 2019).

25 BBC News, 'Marcus Hutchins spared US jail sentence over malware charges' (26 July 2019). Available at www.bbc.co.uk/news/technology-49127569

26 Khasru, S. M., 'WannaCry shows that businesses and government must cooperate', World Economic Forum (1 June 2017). Available at www.weforum.org/agenda/2017/06/wannacry-exposes-need-for-better-public-private-cooperation-in-the-cyber-space/

27 Greenberg, A., 'The Untold Story of NotPetya, the Most Devastating Cyberattack in History', *Wired* (22 August 2018). Available at www.wired.com/story/notpetya-cyberattack-ukraine-russia-code-crashed-the-world/

28 Stone, L., 'hack-petya mission accomplished!!!' (13 April 2016). Available at https://github.com/leo-stone/hack-petya
29 Vijayan, J., '3 Years after NotPetya Many Organizations Still in Danger of Similar Attacks', Dark Reading (30 June 2020). Available at www.darkreading.com/threat-intelligence/3-years-after-notpetya-many-organizations-still-in-danger-of-similar-attacks
30 Kimhy, E., 'NotPetya intrusion vectors and propagation', Cybereason blog (2017). Available at www.cybereason.com/blog/notpetya-intrusion-vectors-and-propagation
31 US Department of Justice, 'Six Russian GRU Officers Charged in Connection with Worldwide Deployment of Destructive Malware and Other Disruptive Actions in Cyberspace' (19 October 2020). Available at www.justice.gov/opa/pr/six-russian-gru-officers-charged-connection-worldwide-deployment-destructive-malware-and
32 Greenberg (2018).
33 Swinhoe, D., 'Rebuilding after NotPetya: How Maersk moved forward', CSOonline (9 October 2019). Available at www.csoonline.com/article/567845/rebuilding-after-notpetya-how-maersk-moved-forward.html
34 Quotes from an interview with Amit Serper on the Malicious Life Podcast, 'Inside NotPetya: Part 1'. Available at www.cybereason.com/blog/malicious-life-podcast-inside-notpetya-ransomware-part-1
35 Asher-Dotan, L., 'NotPetya Vaccine Discovered by Cybereason', Cybereason blog (2017). Available at www.cybereason.com/blog/cybereason-discovers-notpetya-kill-switch
36 Cimpanu, C., 'Surprise! NotPetya is a Cyber-Weapon. It's not Ransomware', *Bleeping Computer* (28 June 2017). Available at www.bleepingcomputer.com/news/security/surprise-notpetya-is-a-cyber-weapon-its-not-ransomware/
37 The White House, Statement from the Press Secretary (15 February 2018) https://trumpwhitehouse.archives.gov/briefings-statements/statement-press-secretary-25/

10: No More Ransoms?

1 BBC News, 'Petya ransomware encryption system cracked' (11 April 2016). Available at www.bbc.co.uk/news/technology-36014810

2. Simonite, T., 'Companies Are Stockpiling Bitcoin to Pay Off Cybercriminals', *MIT Technology Review* (7 June 2016). Available at www.technologyreview.com/2016/06/07/159783/companies-are-stockpiling-bitcoin-to-pay-off-cybercriminals/
3. Paquet-Clouston, M., Haslhofer, B., Dupont, B., 'Ransomware payments in the Bitcoin ecosystem', *Journal of Cybersecurity*, 5(1) (2019). Available at https://doi.org/10.1093/cybsec/tyz003
4. Kharraz, A. et al., 'Cutting the Gordian Knot: A look Under the Hood of Ransomware Attacks', 12th Conference on Detection of Intrusions and Malware, and Vulnerability Assessment (July 9–10, 2015, Milan, Italy). Available at http://dx.doi.org/10.1007/978-3-319-20550-2_1
5. Drozhzhin, A., 'How to remove CoinVault ransomware and restore your files', Kaspersky Lab (14 April 2015). Available at www.kaspersky.com/blog/coinvault-ransomware-removal-instruction/8363/
6. No More Ransom Project website: www.nomoreransom.org/en/about-the-project.html
7. No More Ransom Project website: www.nomoreransom.org/crypto-sheriff.php?lang=en
8. No More Ransom Project website: www.nomoreransom.org/en/decryption-tools.html
9. No More Ransom Project website: www.nomoreransom.org/en/index.html
10. 'INTRODUCING COVEWARE!', Coveware bog (7 May 2018). Available at www.coveware.com/blog/2018/5/7/hello-world
11. Tidy, J., 'Hated and Hunted', BBC (March 2019). Available at www.bbc.co.uk/news/resources/idt-sh/hated_and_hunted_the_computer_virus_malware_ransomware_cracker
12. Dudley, R. and Kao, J., 'The Secret Trade', ProPublica (15 May 2019). Available at https://features.propublica.org/ransomware/ransomware-attack-data-recovery-firms-paying-hackers/
13. 'We hear this story. OFTEN', Coveware blog (7 May 2018). Available at www.coveware.com/blog/2018/5/8/we-hear-this-story-often-wp4ne
14. O'Flaherty, K., 'Meet the Firm That Pays Bitcoin Ransoms on Behalf of its Customers', *Forbes* (updated 18 September 2018). Available at

NOTES

www.forbes.com/sites/kateoflahertyuk/2018/09/17/meet-the-firm-paying-ransoms-in-bitcoin-on-behalf-of-its-customers/#55decd973bb9

15 Meurs, T., Hoheisel, R., Junger, M., Abhishta, A. and McCoy, D., 'What to Do Against Ransomware? Evaluating Law Enforcement Interventions,' 2024 APWG Symposium on Electronic Crime Research (eCrime), Boston, MA, USA, 2024, pp. 76–93, doi: 10.1109/eCrime66200.2024.00012

16 Fidler, D., 'President Trump's Legacy on Cyberspace Policy', Council on Foreign Relations (2 December 2020). Available at www.cfr.org/blog/president-trumps-legacy-cyberspace-policy

17 CISA, 'CISA Insights: Ransomware Outbreak' (21 August 2019). Available at www.cisa.gov/sites/default/files/2019-08/CISA_Insights-Ransomware_Outbreak_S508C.pdf

18 Baker, T. and Shortland, A., 'The government behind insurance governance: Lessons for ransomware', *Regulation & Governance*, 17, (2023), pp. 1000–20. Available at https://doi.org/10.1111/rego.12505

19 OECD 2005, 'Terrorism Risk Insurance in OECD Countries' (OECD Paris). Available at www.oecd.org/content/dam/oecd/en/publications/reports/2005/07/terrorism-risk-insurance-in-oecd-countries_g1gh5785/9789264008748-en.pdf

20 Ralph, O., and Armstrong, R., 'Mondelez sues Zurich in test for cyber hack insurance', *Financial Times* (10 January 2019). Available at www.ft.com/content/8db7251c-1411-11e9-a581-4ff78404524e

21 Greenberg, A., 'The Untold Story of NotPetya, the Most Devastating Cyberattack in History', *Wired* (22 August 2018). Available at www.wired.com/story/notpetya-cyberattack-ukraine-russia-code-crashed-the-world/

22 Henriquez, M., 'Merck wins $1.4B lawsuit over NotPetya attack', *Security* (26 January 2022). Available at www.securitymagazine.com/articles/96972-merck-wins-14b-lawsuit-over-notpetya-attack

23 Mondelez v. Zurich. 2018. *Complaint in Mondelez International, Inc. v. Zurich American Insurance Company* WL 4941760 (Circuit Court of Illinois).

24 Mondelez v. Zurich. 2018. *Complaint in Mondelez International, Inc.*

v. *Zurich American Insurance Company* WL 4941760 (Circuit Court of Illinois) (Trial Pleading), p. 3.
25   Mondelez v. Zurich. 2018.
26   Merck & Co. v. ACE Am. Ins. Co. N.J., No. A-62/63-22.
27   US Department of Justice, 'Six Russian GRU Officers Charged in Connection with Worldwide Deployment of Destructive Malware and Other Disruptive Actions in Cyberspace' (19 October 2020). Available at www.justice.gov/opa/pr/six-russian-gru-officers-charged-connection-worldwide-deployment-destructive-malware-and
28   Mondelez v. Zurich. 2018 (Trial Pleading).
29   Von Clausewitz, C. (1832), *Vom Kriege* (English translation: *On War*). Available at Project Gutenberg, www.gutenberg.org/files/1946/1946-h/1946-h.htm
30   Woods, D. and Weinkle, J., Insurance definitions of cyber war. *Geneva Pap Risk Insur Issues Pract* 45, 639–656 (2020). https://doi.org/10.1057/s41288-020-00168-5
31   Supreme Court of New Jersey, Brief of Amici Curiae Insurance Law Scholars in Support of Merck & Co., Inc. and Affirming the Decision of the Appellate Division (2 October 2023).
32   Supreme Court of New Jersey (October 2023), p. 7.

11: Big Game Hunting

1   FBI Public Service Announcement, 'High-Impact Ransomware Attacks Threaten U.S. Businesses And Organizations' (2 October 2019). Available at www.ic3.gov/PSA/2019/psa191002
2   Centre for Internet Security, 'Security Primer – Ryuk' (10 January 2020). Available at www.cisecurity.org/insights/white-papers/security-primer-ryuk
3   'Decrypt Ryuk Ransomware. How to Recover Ryuk Encrypted Files', Coveware blog (11 April 2019). Available at www.coveware.com/blog/decrypt-ryuk-ransomware-guide-to-recovery-encrypted-files
4   Baker, T. and Shortland, A., 'Insurance and enterprise: cyber insurance for ransomware', *The Geneva Papers on Risk and Insurance – Issues and Practice*, 48 (December 2022), pp. 275–99.
5   Ibid.

NOTES

6   Tidy, J., 'Hated and Hunted', BBC (March 2019). Available at www.bbc.co.uk/news/resources/idt-sh/hated_and_hunted_the_computer_virus_malware_ransomware_cracker
7   Coveware Ransomware Recovery Blog. Available at www.coveware.com/ransomware-blog
8   Shortland, A., *Kidnap: Inside the Ransom Business* (Oxford University Press, Oxford, 2019).
9   Interview with Bill Siegel (1 May 2024).
10 Centre for Internet Security, 'Security Primer – Ryuk'.
11 Interview with Lizzie Cookson (9 May 2024).
12 Coveware blog (11 April 2019).
13 Logue, K. and Shniderman, A., 'The Case for Banning (and Mandating) Ransomware', *Connecticut Insurance Law Journal*, 28(1) (2022). Available at https://repository.law.umich.edu/cgi/viewcontent.cgi?article=3485&context=articles
14 Cimpanu, C., 'Ryuk gang estimated to have made more than $150 million from ransomware attacks', ZDNet (7 January 2021). Available at www.zdnet.com/article/ryuk-gang-estimated-to-have-made-more-than-150-million-from-ransomware-attacks/
15 'The Marriage of Data Exfiltration and Ransomware', Coveware blog (10 January 2020). Available at www.coveware.com/blog/marriage-ransomware-data-breach
16 Krebs, B. 16 December 2019. Ransomware Gangs now outing businesses that don't pay up. https://krebsonsecurity.com/2019/12/ransomware-gangs-now-outing-victim-businesses-that-dont-pay-up/
17 Abrams, L. 12 December 2019. Another ransomware will now publish victims' data if not paid. Bleeping Computer. https://www.bleepingcomputer.com/news/security/another-ransomware-will-now-publish-victims-data-if-not-paid/
18 'Ransomware Demands continue to rise as Data Exfiltration becomes common, and Maze subdues', Coveware blog (4 November 2020). Available at www.coveware.com/blog/q3-2020-ransomware-marketplace-report
19 Cybersecurity and Infrastructure Security Agency, *Protecting Sensitive and Personal Information from Ransomware-Caused Data Breaches* (undated). Available at www.cisa.gov/sites/default/files/

publications/CISA_Fact_Sheet-Protecting_Sensitive_and_Personal_Information_from_Ransomware-Caused_Data_Breaches-508C.pdf
20 McMahon, W., 'Ransomware "extortion" under GDPR?' *UK Finance* (31 May 2018). Available at www.ukfinance.org.uk/Blogs/ransomware-%25E2%2580%2598extortion-under-gdpr
21 'Ransomware as a Service Innovation Curve', Coveware blog (27 January 2022). Available at www.coveware.com/blog/2022/1/26/ransomware-as-a-service-innovation-curve
22 'Q2 Ransom Payment Amounts Decline as Ransomware becomes a National Security Priority', Coveware blog (23 July 2021). Available at www.coveware.com/blog/2021/7/23/q2-ransom-payment-amounts-decline-as-ransomware-becomes-a-national-security-priority
23 Alder, S., '400,000 Patients Potentially Affected by Planned Parenthood Ransomware Attack', *The HIPAA Journal* (3 December 2021). Available at www.hipaajournal.com/400000-patients-potentially-affected-by-planned-parenthood-ransomware-attack/
24 Planned Parenthood Los Angeles, Notice of Patient Privacy Incident (November 2021). Available at www.plannedparenthood.org/planned-parenthood-los-angeles/notice
25 Bradley, T., 'Lives at Risk from Planned Parenthood Ransomware Attack', Cybereason blog (November 2021). Available at www.cybereason.com/blog/planned-parenthood-ransomware-attack-puts-lives-at-risk
26 United States District Court Central District of California, Class Action Complaint: Demand For Jury Trial. Case number 21-CV-09563 (9 December 2021). Available at www.classaction.org/media/ko-v-planned-parenthood-los-angeles.pdf
27 United States District Court Central District of California, Final Rulings. Case 21-STCV-44106 (2 January 2024). Available at https://docs.simpluris.com/websites/d6a43116-50ec-4d70-a1e9-161c21117a33/documents/47052700-9375-449a-91f6-50a8426320a1/PlannedParenthood_Orellana%20-%20Unconditional%20PAO.pdf
28 PPLA Settlement, Planned Parenthood Los Angeles Data Incident Litigation, Frequently Asked Questions (November 2021). Available at www.pplasettlement.com/faq/

NOTES

29 Alder, S., 'The Biggest Healthcare Data Breaches of 2024', *The HIPAA Journal* (19 March 2025). Available at www.hipaajournal.com/biggest-healthcare-data-breaches-2024/
30 Martin, A., 'Data on nearly 1 million NHS patients leaked online following ransomware attack', *The Record* (16 September 2024). Available at https://therecord.media/data-on-nearly-1-million-nhs-patients-leaked-hospital-ransomware
31 Ignatovski, M., 'Healthcare Breaches During COVID-19: The Effect of the Healthcare Entity Type on the Number of Impacted Individuals', *Perspectives in Health Information Management*, 19(4) (1 October 2022). Available at https://pmc.ncbi.nlm.nih.gov/articles/PMC9635044/
32 Mishra, V., 'Cyberattacks on healthcare: A global threat that can't be ignored', United Nations (8 November 2024). Available at https://news.un.org/en/story/2024/11/1156751
33 Riggi, J., 'Ransomware Attacks on Hospitals Have Changed', American Hospital Association, Cybersecurity and Risk Advisory Services (May 2020). Available at www.aha.org/center/cybersecurity-and-risk-advisory-services/ransomware-attacks-hospitals-have-changed

12: A Matter of National Security

1 Lallie, H. S., et al., 'Cyber security in the age of COVID-19: A timeline and analysis of cyber-crime and cyber-attacks during the pandemic', *Computers & Security*, 105, 102248 (June 2021). Available at www.sciencedirect.com/science/article/pii/S0167404821000729
2 Valeriano, B., 'Assessing President Trump's Legacy of Cyber Confusion', Council on Foreign Relations (21 December 2020). Available at www.cfr.org/blog/assessing-president-trumps-legacy-cyber-confusion
3 Interview with Megan Stifel, Phil Reyner, Chris Painter and Michael Daniel (22 August 2024).
4 Ibid.
5 Interview with Jen Ellis (14 August 2024).

6   Interview with Megan Stifel, Phil Reyner, Chris Painter and Michael Daniel (22 August 2024).
7   Institute for Security and Technology, *RTF Report: Combating Ransomware: A Comprehensive Framework for Action* (21 April 2021). Available at https://securityandtechnology.org/ransomwaretaskforce/report/
8   Interview with Jen Ellis (14 August 2024).
9   ID Agent, Kaseya, 'RockYou2021 Password Leak Supercharges Dark Web Danger' (11 June 2021). Available at www.idagent.com/blog/rockyou2021-password-leak-supercharges-dark-web-danger/
10 Russon, M. A., 'US fuel pipeline hackers "didn't mean to create problems"', BBC News (10 May 2021). Available at www.bbc.co.uk/news/business-57050690
11 'Colonial Pipeline: Don't put Gas in plastic bags, feds warn', AL.com News (13 May 2021). Available at www.al.com/news/2021/05/colonial-pipeline-dont-put-gas-in-plastic-bags-feds-warn.html
12 Eaton, C. and Volz, D., 'Colonial Pipeline CEO tells why he paid hackers a $4.4 million ransom', *Wall Street Journal* (19 May 2021). Available at www.wsj.com/tech/cybersecurity/colonial-pipeline-ceo-tells-why-he-paid-hackers-a-4-4-million-ransom-11621435636
13 The White House, 'Fact Sheet: The Biden–Harris administration has launched an all government effort to address Colonial Pipeline incident' (11 May 2021). Available at https://bidenwhitehouse.archives.gov/briefing-room/statements-releases/2021/05/11/fact-sheet-the-biden-harris-administration-has-launched-an-all-of-government-effort-to-address-colonial-pipeline-incident/
14 The White House. 11 May 2022. Executive order on improving the natio9n's cybersecurity. Available at www.whitehouse.gov/briefing-room/presidential-actions/2021/05/12/executive-order-on-improving-the-nations-cybersecurity/
15 Wray, C., 'Working with Our Private Sector Partners to Combat the Cyber Threat', *FBI News* (28 October 2021). Available at www.fbi.gov/news/speeches/working-with-our-private-sector-partners-to-combat-the-cyber-threat-wray-ecny-102821
16 Radio Free Europe, 'Biden says Russia has "some responsibility" in pipeline ransomware attack' (10 May 2021). Available at www.rferl.

org/a/fbi-confirms-darkside-hacker-group-pipeline-cyberattack-russia/31248174.html
17. Russon (10 May 2021).
18. 'The Moral Underground? Ransomware operators retreat after Colonial Pipeline hack', Intel 471 blog (14 May 2021). Available at https://intel471.com/blog/darkside-ransomware-shut-down-revil-avaddon-cybercrime
19. Ibid.
20. PSBE Cybernews Group, 'Dark Side Ransomware Creates "Oh, Dear!" Server Shutdowns!' (16 May 2021). Available at www.cybernewsgroup.co.uk/2021/05/16/dark-side-ransomware-creates-oh-dear-server-shutdowns/
21. BBC News, 'Irish cyber-attack: Hackers bail out Irish health service for free' (21 May 2021). Available at www.bbc.co.uk/news/world-europe-57197688
22. Fung, B., 'CNN JBS says it paid $11 million ransom after cyberattack' (9 June 2021). Available at https://edition.cnn.com/2021/06/09/business/jbs-cyberattack-11-million/index.html
23. SecurityScorecard, 'JBS Ransomware Attack Started in March and Much Larger in Scope than Previously Identified' (8 June 2021). Available at https://securityscorecard.com/blog/jbs-ransomware-attack-started-in-march/
24. BBC News, 'JBS: Cyber-attack hits world's largest meat supplier' (2 June 2021). Available at www.bbc.co.uk/news/world-us-canada-57318965
25. SecurityScorecard (8 June 2021).
26. Sonicwall, *2022 Sonicwall Cyber Threat Report*. Available at www.sonicwall.com/medialibrary/en/infographic/infographic-2022-sonicwall-cyber-threat-report.pdf
27. 'Senate Homeland Security Hearing on Colonial Pipeline Cyber Attack', C-Span (8 June 2021). Available at www.c-span.org/video/?512247-1/senate-homeland-security-hearing-colonial-pipeline-cyber-attack
28. Cohen, Z., et al., 'Biden administration officials privately frustrated with Colonial Pipeline's weak security ahead of crippling cyberattack', CNN (11 May 2021). Available at https://edition.cnn.

29. com/2021/05/11/politics/biden-administration-ransomware-frustration/index.html
29. C-Span (8 June 2021).
30. US Department of Justice, 'Department of Justice Seizes $2.3 Million in Cryptocurrency Paid to the Ransomware Extortionists', Darkside Press Release (7 June 2021). Available at www.justice.gov/opa/pr/department-justice-seizes-23-million-cryptocurrency-paid-ransomware-extortionists-darkside
31. The Joint Ransomware Task Force website. Available at www.cisa.gov/joint-ransomware-task-force
32. Bing, C., 'Exclusive: U.S. to give ransomware hacks similar priority as terrorism', Reuters (21 June 2021). Available at www.reuters.com/technology/exclusive-us-give-ransomware-hacks-similar-priority-terrorism-official-says-2021-06-03/
33. Council on Foreign Relations, 'Countering the Ransomware Threat with Anne Neuberger' (24 October 2023). Available at www.cfr.org/event/countering-ransomware-threat-anne-neuberger
34. Singh, J., 'Ransomware Groups on Notice: U.S. Cyber Operation Against REvil is Permissible Under International Law', *American University International Law Review*, 38(1) (2023), pp. 271–314.
35. Soldatkyn, V. and Pamuk, H., 'Biden tells Putin certain cyberattacks should be "off-limits"', Reuters (17 June 2022). Available at www.reuters.com/technology/biden-tells-putin-certain-cyber-attacks-should-be-off-limits-2021-06-16/

13: In One Fell Swoop

1. Alspach, K., 'Kaseya Ransomware Victim Speaks Out: From "The Abyss" To Recovery With Aid From MSP Community', CRN (12 July 2023). Available at www.crn.com/events/kaseya-ransomware-victim-speaks-out-from-the-abyss-to-recovery-with-aid-from-msp-community
2. Barrett, B., 'A new kind of Tsunami hits hundreds of companies', *Wired* (2 July 2021). Available at www.wired.com/story/kaseya-supply-chain-ransomware-attack-msps/
3. Andersson, A., 'How the Kaseya VSA zero-day exploit worked',

Truesec Insight (6 July 2021). Available at www.truesec.com/hub/blog/kaseya-vsa-zero-day-exploit

4 Kaseya Helpdesk. Incident overview and technical details. Available at https://helpdesk.kaseya.com/hc/en-gb/articles/4403584098961-Incident-Overview-Technical-Details

5 UK Foreign and Commonwealth Office Press release, 'Russia: UK and US expose global campaign of malign activity by Russian intelligence services' (15 April 2021). Available at www.gov.uk/government/news/russia-uk-and-us-expose-global-campaigns-of-malign-activity-by-russian-intelligence-services

6 Temple-Raston, D., 'A "Worst Nightmare" Cyberattack: the untold story of the SolarWinds hack', NPR (16 April 2021). Available at www.npr.org/2021/04/16/985439655/a-worst-nightmare-cyberattack-the-untold-story-of-the-solarwinds-hack

7 Barrett (2 July 2021).

8 Cybereason 2021, 'Organizations at Risk. Ransomware attackers don't take holidays'. Ebook available at www.cybereason.com/ebook-ransomware-attackers-dont-take-holidays

9 Kaseya Press Release, 'Kaseya responds swiftly to sophisticated cyberattack' (5 July 2021). Available at www.kaseya.com/press-release/kaseya-responds-swiftly-to-sophisticated-cyberattack-mitigating-global-disruption-to-customers/#:~:text='Our%20global%20teams%20are%20working,feverishly%20to%20get%20this%20resolved.

10 Kaseya Helpdesk. Important Notice 4 August 2021. Available at https://helpdesk.kaseya.com/hc/en-gb/articles/4403440684689-Important-Notice-August-4th-2021

11 Kaseya Press Release (5 July 2021).

12 BBC News, 'Swedish Coop supermarkets shut due to US ransomware cyber-attack' (3 July 2021) Available at www.bbc.co.uk/news/technology-57707530

13 Truesec, 'Back in Business After the Largest Ransomware Attack of All Time'. Available at www.truesec.com/cases/back-in-business-after-the-largest-ransomware-attack-of-all-time

14 Osborne, C., 'Updated Kaseya ransomware attack FAQ: What we know

15 now', ZDNet (23 July 2021). Available at www.zdnet.com/article/updated-kaseya-ransomware-attack-faq-what-we-know-now/
15 Ibid.
16 Alspach (12 July 2023).
17 Greig, J., 'Should Kaseya pay REvil ransom? Experts are torn', ZDNet (7 July 2021). Available at www.zdnet.com/article/should-kaseya-pay-revil-ransom-experts-are-torn/
18 BBC News, 'Revil: Ransomware websites disappear from the internet' (13 July 2021). Available at www.bbc.co.uk/news/technology-57826851
19 Kaseya Helpdesk. Important Notice 4 August 2021.
20 Ibid.
21 Novinson, M., 'FBI Delayed Helping Kaseya Ransomware Victims For Weeks: Report', CRN (21 September 2021). Available at www.crn.com/news/security/fbi-delayed-helping-kaseya-ransomware-victims-for-weeks-report?itc=refresh
22 Novinson, M., 'REvil: We Accidentally Leaked Kaseya Universal Decryptor Key', CRN (21 September 2021). Available at www.crn.com/news/security/revil-we-accidentally-leaked-kaseya-universal-decryptor-key
23 Ibid.
24 BBC News, 'Meat giant JBS pays $11m in ransom to resolve cyber-attack' (10 June 2021). Available at www.bbc.co.uk/news/business-57423008
25 Singh, J., 'Ransomware Groups on Notice: US Cyber Operation against REvil is Permissible Under International Law', *American University International Law Review*, 38(1) (2023), p. 281.
26 Bailey, C., 'Offensive Cyberspace Operations: A Gray Area in Congressional Oversight. *International Law Review*, 38(2) (2020), pp. 240–85.
27 Klovig Skelton, S., 'Multi-Government Operation Targets Revil Ransomware Group', *Computer Weekly* (22 October 2021). Available at www.computerweekly.com/news/252508564/Multi-government-operation-targets-REvil-ransomware-group
28 Menn, J. and Bing, C., 'EXCLUSIVE: Governments turn tables on ransomware gang REvil by pushing it offline', Reuters (21 October

2021). Available at www.reuters.com/technology/exclusive-governments-turn-tables-ransomware-gang-revil-by-pushing-it-offline-2021-10-21/

29 US Department of Justice, 'Sodinokibi/REvil Affiliate Sentenced for Role in $700m Ransomware Scheme' (1 May 2024). Available at www.justice.gov/opa/pr/sodinokibirevil-affiliate-sentenced-role-700m-ransomware-scheme

30 US Department of Justice, 'Ukrainian Arrested and Charged with Ransomware Attack on Kaseya' (8 November 2021). Available at www.justice.gov/opa/pr/ukrainian-arrested-and-charged-ransomware-attack-kaseya

31 Europol News, 'Five affiliates to Sodinokibi/REvil unplugged' (8 November 2021). Available at www.europol.europa.eu/media-press/newsroom/news/five-affiliates-to-sodinokibi/revil-unplugged

32 Balmforth, T. and Tsvetkova, M., 'Russia takes down REvil hacking group at U.S. request – FSB', Reuters (14 January 2022). Available at www.reuters.com/technology/russia-arrests-dismantles-revil-hacking-group-us-request-report-2022-01-14/

33 Ibid.

34 Sayegh, E., 'The REvil Gang Story: The "Good Guys" Can Still Prevail', Forbes (22 March 2023). Available at www.forbes.com/sites/emilsayegh/2023/03/22/the-revil-gang-story-the-good-guys-can-still-prevail/

35 Kovacs, E., 'Four REvil Ransomware Group Members Sentenced to Prison in Russia', Security Week (28 October 2024). Available at www.securityweek.com/four-revil-ransomware-group-members-sentenced-to-prison-in-russia/

36 Greig, J., 'Researchers warn of REvil return after January arrests in Russia', The Record (16 May 2022). Available at https://therecord.media/researchers-warn-of-revil-return-after-january-arrests-in-russia

37 Santos, D. and Martineau, J., 'Understanding REvil: REvil Threat Actors May Have Returned (Updated)' (3 June 2022). Available at https://unit42.paloaltonetworks.com/revil-threat-actors/

38 Casas, P., Blancas, J. and Villanueva, A., 'Ransomware Report 2023: targets, motives, and trends', Outpost24 Blog (updated 21 May 2025).

Available at https://outpost24.com/blog/ransomware-report-2023-targets-motives-and-trends/

14: Conti 'at War' with Costa Rica

1. Stuenkel, O., 'Costa Rica's New Populist President Could Be a Lesson in Democracy – or a Worrying Trend', Carnegie Fund (4 May 2022). Available at https://carnegieendowment.org/posts/2022/05/costa-ricas-new-populist-president-could-be-a-lesson-in-democracyor-a-worrying-trend?lang=en
2. Bruno, M., 'Cyberattacks on Costa Rica prompt action from carriers', Port Technology International (18 May 2022). Available at www.porttechnology.org/news/cyber-attacks-on-costa-rica-prompt-action-from-carriers/
3. Joint Committee on National Security, 'A hostage to fortune: ransomware and UK national security', UK Parliament (4 December 2023). Available at https://publications.parliament.uk/pa/jt5804/jtselect/jtnatsec/194/report.html
4. BBC News, 'President Rodrigo Chaves says Costa Rica is at war with Conti hackers' (18 May 2022). Available at www.bbc.co.uk/news/technology-61323402
5. Conti's messages to Costa Ricans. Available at https://x.com/BrettCallow/status/1525512920968310786/photo/1
6. BBC News (18 May 2022).
7. Krebs, B., 'Costa Rica May Be Pawn in Conti Ransomware Group's Bid to Rebrand, Evade Sanctions', KrebsonSecurity (30 May 2022). Available at https://krebsonsecurity.com/2022/05/costa-rica-may-be-pawn-in-conti-ransomware-groups-bid-to-rebrand-evade-sanctions/
8. Rosch, C., 'A massive cyberattack in Costa Rica leaves citizens hurting', Rest of World (1 June 2022). Available at https://restofworld.org/2022/cyberattack-costa-rica-citizens-hurting/
9. Purtill, J., 'Costa Rica is "at war" with Russian hackers and other countries will be next, experts warn', ABC News (3 June 2022). Available at www.abc.net.au/news/science/2022-06-04/costa-rica-at-war-with-russian-hackers-cyber-criminals/101116930
10. Krebs, B., 'Conti's Ransomware Toll on the Healthcare Industry',

NOTES

KrebsonSecurity (18 April 2022). Available at https://krebsonsecurity.com/2022/04/contis-ransomware-toll-on-the-healthcare-industry/

11 Cited in Krebs, B., 'Conti Ransomware Group Diaries, Part I: Evasion', KrebsonSecurity (1 March 2022). Available at https://krebsonsecurity.com/2022/03/conti-ransomware-group-diaries-part-i-evasion/

12 Chainanalysis, 'As Ransomware Payments Continue to Grow, So Too Does Ransomware's Role in Geopolitical Conflict', Chainanalysis blog (10 February 2022). Available at www.chainalysis.com/blog/2022-crypto-crime-report-preview-ransomware

13 Gibson, S., 'Dis-CONTI-nued: The End of Conti?', Security Now Podcast No 872 (24 May 2022). Transcript available at www.grc.com/sn/sn-872.pdf

14 Burgess, M., 'The Workaday Life of the World's Most Dangerous Ransomware Gang', *Wired* (16 March 2022). Available at www.wired.com/story/conti-leaks-ransomware-work-life/?_sp=dd11288d-5232-41d1-aa9d-2f6b50debfe7.1724167174762

15 Krebs, B., 'Conti Ransomware Group Diaries, Part II: The Office', KrebsonSecurity (2 March 2022). Available at https://krebsonsecurity.com/2022/03/conti-ransomware-group-diaries-part-ii-the-office/

16 Flashpoint Intel Team, 'Conti Ransomware: Inside One of the World's Most Aggressive Ransomware Groups' (4 October 2022). Available at https://flashpoint.io/blog/history-of-conti-ransomware/

17 Burgess (16 March 2022).

18 Bing, C., 'Russia-based ransomware group Conti issues warning to Kremlin foes', Reuters News (25 February 2022). Available at www.reuters.com/technology/russia-based-ransomware-group-conti-issues-warning-kremlin-foes-2022-02-25/

19 Krebs, B. (30 May 2022).

20 Conti leaks @ContiLeaks, X. Available at https://x.com/contileaks

21 Krebs (2 March 2022).

22 Burgess (16 March 2022).

23 Krebs (2 March 2022).

24 Ibid.

25 Ibid.

26 Krebs, B., 'Conti Ransomware Group Diaries, Part III: Weaponry',

KrebsonSecurity (4 March 2022). Available at https://krebsonsecurity.com/2022/03/conti-ransomware-group-diaries-part-iii-weaponry/

27 Conti leaks @ContiLeaks, X. Available at https://x.com/contileaks
28 Burgess, M., 'Leaked Ransomware Docs Show Conti Helping Putin from the Shadows', *Wired* (18 March 2022). Available at www.wired.com/story/conti-ransomware-russia/
29 Enders, W. and Su, X., 'Rational Terrorists and Optimal Network Structure', *The Journal of Conflict Resolution*, 51(1) (February 2007), pp. 33–57.
30 Burgess, M., 'Conti's Attack Against Costa Rica Sparks a New Ransomware Era', *Wired* (12 June 2022). Available at www.wired.com/story/costa-rica-ransomware-conti/
31 Newman, L. H., 'Black Basta: The Fallen Ransomware Gang That Lives On', *Wired* (14 April 2025). Available at www.wired.com/story/black-basta-ransomware-gang/
32 Joint Cybersecurity Advisory, 'Indicators of Compromise Associated with Blackbyte Ransomware' (11 February 2022). Available at www.ic3.gov/Media/News/2022/220211.pdf
33 CISA Cybersecurity Advisory 'Karakurt Data Extortion Group' (revised 12 December 2023). Available at www.cisa.gov/news-events/cybersecurity-advisories/aa22-152a
34 Chainanalysis, 'Ransomware Revenue Down As More Victims Refuse to Pay' (19 January 2023). Available at www.chainalysis.com/blog/crypto-ransomware-revenue-down-as-victims-refuse-to-pay/
35 US Department of Justice, 'Multiple Foreign Nationals Charged in Connection with Trickbot Malware and Conti Ransomware Conspiracies' (7 September 2023). Available at www.justice.gov/opa/pr/multiple-foreign-nationals-charged-connection-trickbot-malware-and-conti-ransomware
36 US Department of Justice, 'Russian National Sentenced for Involvement in Development and Deployment of Trickbot Malware' (25 January 2024). Available at www.justice.gov/opa/pr/russian-national-sentenced-involvement-development-and-deployment-trickbot-malware#:~:text=In%202021%2C%20Dunaev%20was%20extradited,wire%20fraud%20and%20bank%20fraud

37 Sentsova, A., 'Women In Russian-Speaking Cybercrime: Mythical Creatures or Significant Members of Underground?' Sans blog (18 November 2024). Available at https://www.sans.org/blog/women-in-russian-speaking-cybercrime-mythical-creatures-or-significant-members-of-underground/
38 Chainanalysis (19 January 2023).

15: The Lockbit Takedown

1 Wosar, F., 'Hitting the BlackMatter gang where it hurts: in the wallet', Emisoft blog (15 October 2021). Available at www.emsisoft.com/en/blog/39181/on-the-matter-of-blackmatter/
2 Meurs, T., et al., 'What To Do Against Ransomware? Evaluating Law Enforcement Interventions', *2024 APWG Symposium on Electronic Crime Research (eCrime)*, Boston, MA, USA, 2024, pp. 76-93, doi: 10.1109/eCrime66200.2024.00012.
3 Interview with Will Lyne (10 July 2024).
4 The Global Initiative Podcast, 'LockBit: Is this the end? Deep Dive. Exploring Organized Crime' (26 March 2024). Available at www.youtube.com/watch?v=036T0IMODE0
5 Redsentry blog, 'LockBit: The Rise, The Fall, and Law Enforcement's Take Down of The LockBit Empire' (2024). Available at https://www.redsentry.com/blog/lockbit-the-rise-the-fall-and-law-enforcements-take-down-of-the-lockbit-empire-2
6 Burgess, M., 'A Global Police Operation Just Took Down the Notorious LockBit Ransomware Gang' *Wired* (20 February 2024). Available at www.wired.com/story/lockbit-ransomware-takedown-website-nca-fbi
7 Abrams, L., 'LockBit 3.0 introduces the first ransomware bug bounty program' (27 June 2022). Available at www.bleepingcomputer.com/news/security/lockbit-30-introduces-the-first-ransomware-bug-bounty-program/
8 Krebs, B., 'Feds Seize LockBit Ransomware Websites, Offer Decryption Tools, Troll Affiliates', KrebsonSecurity (20 February 2024). Available at https://krebsonsecurity.com/2024/02/feds-seize-lockbit-ransomware-websites-offer-decryption-tools-troll-affiliates/
9 DiMaggio, J., 'Ransomware Diaries, Volume 5: Unmasking LockBit',

Analyst1 blog (7 May 2024). Available at https://analyst1.com/ransomware-diaries-volume-5-unmasking-lockbit-2/

10 DiMaggio, J., 'Ransomware Diaries: Volume 1', Analyst1 blog (16 January 2023). Available at https://analyst1.com/ransomware-diaries-volume-1/

11 Trend Micro, 'LockBit Attempts to Stay Afloat With a New Version' (22 February 2024). Available at www.trendmicro.com/en_gb/research/24/b/lockbit-attempts-to-stay-afloat-with-a-new-version.html

12 MalWare News, 'An interview with LockBit: The risk of being hacked ourselves is always present' (October 2021). Available at https://malware.news/t/an-interview-with-lockbit-the-risk-of-being-hacked-ourselves-is-always-present/53960

13 United States District Court, District of New Jersey, Indictment of Dmitry Yurevich Khoroshev (2 May 2024). Available at www.justice.gov/opa/media/1350921/dl?inline

14 DiMaggio (16 January 2023).

15 Ibid.

16 DiMaggio (7 May 2024).

17 National Crime Agency (UK), 'International investigation disrupts the world's most harmful cyber crime group' (20 February 2024). Available at www.nationalcrimeagency.gov.uk/news/nca-leads-international-investigation-targeting-worlds-most-harmful-ransomware-group

18 Abrams, L., 'Ransomware gang apologizes, gives SickKids hospital free decryptor', *Bleeping Computer* (1 January 2023). Available at www.bleepingcomputer.com/news/security/ransomware-gang-apologizes-gives-sickkids-hospital-free-decryptor/

19 Available at https://x.com/NCA_UK/status/1759842879688655053

20 Krebs (20 February 2024).

21 Image available at www.redsentry.com/blog/lockbit-the-rise-the-fall-and-law-enforcements-take-down-of-the-lockbit-empire-2

22 DiMaggio (7 May 2024).

23 Burgess (20 February 2024).

24 *Click Here Podcast*, '151. Mic Drop: Embattled LockBit leader: "Now I want to create even more noise"' (26 Jul 2024). Available at https://

NOTES

podcasts.apple.com/gb/podcast/151-mic-drop-embattled-lockbitleader-now-i-want-to/id1225077306?i=1000663404389

25 Temple-Raston, D. and Powers, S., 'Exclusive: After LockBit's takedown, its purported leader vows to hack on', *The Record* (15 March 2024). Available at https://therecord.media/after-lockbit-takedown-its-purported-leader-vows-to-hack-on

26 Click Here Podcast, '129. Mic Drop: LockbitSupp tells us: UK and US have got the wrong guy' (10 May 2024). Available at https://podcasts.apple.com/gb/podcast/129-mic-drop-lockbitsupp-tells-us-uk-and-us-have-got/id1225077306?i=1000655143257

27 Redsentry blog (2024).

28 Temple-Raston and Powers (15 March 2024).

29 DiMaggio (7 May 2024).

30 Ibid.

31 Deslandes, N., 'Ransomware gangs of 2024: The rise of the affiliates', Tech Informed blog (30 August 2024). Available at https://techinformed.com/ransomware-gangs-of-2024-the-rise-of-the-affiliates/

32 DiMaggio (7 May 2024).

33 Image available at https://x.com/NCA_UK/status/1787845496574222782

34 United States District Court, District of New Jersey (2 May 2024).

35 Franceschi-Bicchierai, L., 'How a cybersecurity researcher befriended, then doxed, the leader of LockBit ransomware gang', TechCrunch blog (9 August 2024). Available at https://techcrunch.com/2024/08/09/how-a-cybersecurity-researcher-befriended-then-doxed-the-leader-of-lockbit-ransomware-gang/

36 Krebs, B., 'How Did Authorities Identify the Alleged Lockbit Boss?', KrebsonSecurity (13 May 2024). Available at https://krebsonsecurity.com/2024/05/how-did-authorities-identify-the-alleged-lockbit-boss/

37 DiMaggio (7 May 2024).

38 Martin, A. and Matishak, M., 'LockbitSupp identified as Dmitry Khoroshev and indicted for ransomware crimes', *The Record* (7 May 2024). Available at https://therecord.media/lockbitsupp-suspect-accused-lockbit-ransomware-gang

39 Alan, J., 'LockBitSupp Denies Identification of Group "Admin", Opens

Contest to Find Named Dmitry Yuryevich', *Cyber Express* (10 May 2024). Available at https://thecyberexpress.com/lockbitsupp-denies-being-dmitry-khoroshev/

40 US Department of Justice, 'Two Foreign Nationals Plead Guilty to Participating in LockBit Ransomware Group' (18 July 2024). Available at www.justice.gov/opa/pr/two-foreign-nationals-plead-guilty-participating-lockbit-ransomware-group

41 US Department of Justice, 'United States Charges Dual Russian and Israeli National as Developer of LockBit Ransomware Group' (20 December 2024). Available at www.justice.gov/opa/pr/united-states-charges-dual-russian-and-israeli-national-developer-lockbit-ransomware-group

42 National Crime Agency (UK), 'Evil Corp: Behind the Screens' (October 2024). Available at www.nationalcrimeagency.gov.uk/who-we-are/publications/732-evil-corp-behind-the-screens/file

43 Jones, C., 'Russia arrests one of its own – a cybercrime suspect on FBI's most wanted list', The Register (2 December 2024). Available at www.theregister.com/2024/12/02/russia_ransomware_arrest/

44 Poireault, K., 'LockBit Admins Tease a New Ransomware Version', *Infosecurity Magazine* (20 December 2024). Available at www.infosecurity-magazine.com/news/lockbit-admins-tease-a-new/

45 Jones, C., 'Crimelords at Hunters International tell lackeys ransomware too "risky"', The Register (2 April 2025). Available at www.theregister.com/2025/04/02/hunters_international_rebrand/

46 'The organizational structure of ransomware threat actor groups is evolving before our eyes', Coveware blog (1 May 2025). Available at www.coveware.com/blog/2025/4/29/the-organizational-structure-of-ransomware-threat-actor-groups-is-evolving-before-our-eyes

47 Beek, C., 'The 2024 Ransomware Landscape', Rapid7 blog (27 January 2025). Available at www.rapid7.com/blog/post/2025/01/27/the-2024-ransomware-landscape-looking-back-on-another-painful-year/

48 Bleih, A., 'RansomHub: The New Kid on the Block You Should Know About', CyberInt blog (20 February 2025). Available at https://cyberint.com/blog/research/ransomhub-the-new-kid-on-the-block-to-know/

49. Poireault, K., 'The Top Ten Most Active Ransomware Groups of 2024', *Infosecurity Magazine* (27 December 2024). Available at www.infosecurity-magazine.com/news-features/top-10-most-active-ransomware/
50. Click Here Podcast, '151. Mic Drop: Embattled LockBit leader: "Now I want to create even more noise"' (26 Jul 2024). Available at https://podcasts.apple.com/gb/podcast/151-mic-drop-embattled-lockbit-leader-now-i-want-to/id1225077306?i=1000663404389

Conclusion

1. Biggar, G., *UK Joint Committee on the National Security Strategy. Oral evidence: Ransomware.* (19 June 2023). Available at https://committees.parliament.uk/oralevidence/13376/html/
2. Greig, J., 'Top White House cyber official urges Trump to focus on ransomware, China', *The Record* (13 November 2024). Available at https://therecord.media/neuberger-urges-trump-admin-focus-china-ransomware
3. Neuberger, A., 'The ransomware battle is shifting – so should our response', *Financial Times* (4 October 2024). Available at www.ft.com/content/3b172a2a-4be5-4ef4-87cb-7fdcdee2ad99
4. Interpol, *Interpol African Cyberthreat Assessment Report 2024* (April 2024).
5. IT News Asia, 'Bulk of Indonesia data hit by cyberattack not backed up' (1 July 2024). Available at www.itnews.asia/news/bulk-of-indonesia-data-hit-by-cyberattack-not-backed-up-609303
6. Harding, L., et al., '"Vulkan Files" leak reveals Putin's global and domestic cyberwarfare tactics' *Guardian* (30 March 2023). Available at www.theguardian.com/technology/2023/mar/30/vulkan-files-leak-reveals-putins-global-and-domestic-cyberwarfare-tactics
7. UK Joint Committee on the National Security Strategy, *A Hostage to Fortune: ransomware and UK national security* (4 December 2023). Available at https://committees.parliament.uk/publications/42493/documents/211438/default/
8. Coveware, 'Will Law Enforcement success against ransomware continue in 2025?' (4 February 2025). Available at www.coveware.com/blog/2025/1/31/q4-report

9. Meurs, T., Hoheisel R., Junger, M., Abhishta, A. and McCoy, D., 'What to Do Against Ransomware? Evaluating Law Enforcement Interventions,' 2024 *APWG Symposium on Electronic Crime Research (eCrime)*, Boston, MA, USA, 2024, pp. 76-93, doi: 10.1109/eCrime66200.2024.00012.
10. A term coined by Max Smeets in his book, *Ransom War: How Cyber Crime Became a Threat to National Security* (Hurst Publishers, London, 2025).
11. Doffman, Z., 'Ashley Madison hack returns to haunt its victims', *Forbes* (1 February 2020). Available at www.forbes.com/sites/zakdoffman/2020/02/01/ashley-madison-hack-returns-to-haunt-its-victims-32-million-users-now-have-to-watch-and-wait/
12. Smeets (2025).
13. Hernandes, R., Aratani, L. and Craft, W., 'Revealed: the tech bosses who poured $394.1m into US Election', *Guardian* (7 December 2024). Available at www.theguardian.com/us-news/2024/dec/07/campaign-spending-crypto-tech-influence

INDEX

Page references in *italics* indicate images.

A

Advanced Research Projects Agency Network (ARPANET) 18–19, 38
AdvIntel 207
affiliates 227, 228
    Change Healthcare exit scam and 234
    Conti and 202, 204–6, 222
    DarkSide and 174–8
    GandCrab and 104
    LockBit and 210–17, 220–23
    Locky and 99–100, 103
    model of 99–104
    re-establishing trust of 228–9
    REvil and 187, 194–6
    second-generation ransomware and 151–2, 154–6, 158–9, 162
    spray-and-pray approach and 233
African Medical and Research Foundation 23
AI (artificial intelligence) 226
AIDS 23–4, 25–6, 27, 28, 29, 30, 31, 32, 225
AIDS Information – Introductory Diskette 26–9, 28
AIDS Trojan 21, 23–33, 28
Akira 10
Alliance for Immediate Payment 200
ALPHV 103, 104, 196, 222
Alvarado Quesada, Carlos 197
Amazon (online retailer) 73, 129
American Hospital Association (AHA) 166
Apple Computer Company 15–19
    Apple I 16, 19
    Apple II 16
Ashley Madison 232
authentication procedures 159, 186, 230
AvosLocker 208

B

back doors 4, 153, 188
Baker, Kenneth 39, *39*
Bangladeshi National Bank 122
bank account data 67, 70, 82, 220
Bates, Jim 31
Biden, Joe/Biden-Harris administration 168, 176, 182, 224
big game hunting 151, 202, 207, 221

biometric identification 159
Bitcoin 102, 117, 139
  ALPHV and 103
  Conti and 200, 205
  CryptoLocker and 87, 88, 89
  DarkSide and 180
  LockBitSupp and 212
  Locky and 96, 97, 99–100
  origins 76–80, 85
  Ryuk and 155
  stockpiling in preparation for cyberattacks 137
  WannaCry and 124, 125, 126
Black Basta 207
BlackCat 104, 208, 222
Black-Matter 104
blockchain 168, 170
  analysts track down and help police snatch ransoms 209, 235
  Bitcoin and 78, 103
Bloomsbury Computing Consortium 40
Blount, Joe 175, 179–81
Bogachev, Evgeniy 91–3
bots 82–3, 85, 86, 90–92, 99
Business Club 81–3, 91–3, 220–21
business interruption 106, 111
  costs 110
  crisis responders and 111
  insurance 89

C
Capo/Capo di Capi 68
CarderPlanet 68–9
cashing out 67–8, 70, 80
central banks 74, 77
Change Healthcare 103, 234
chatrooms 65, 67
Chaves, Rodrigo 197, 199

chief information officers 159
China 70, 83, 120–21, 124
Chingiz911 (aka Chingiz) 92
Cioffi, Robert 185, 189–91
Cisco 188
Clark, Robert 41–3
Clausewitz, Carl von 146–7
Colonial Pipeline 174–82, 185, 191, 195–6, 201, 226
common protocol 38–40
compensation payments
  customers for faulty software or inadequate services 109, 110
  insurance and 107
  NotPetya and 145
  Planned Parenthood and 163, 164
  Ransomware Task Force and 172
  Royal Mail and 8
  Ryuk and 152
Compulink Information eXchange (CIX) 29
Conti ransomware group 178, 196, 197–210, 213, 222, 226
ContiLeaks 203–8
Cookson, Lizzie 155–6
Coop 190
copyright infringements 106, 109
Costa Rica 197–208
  Social Security Fund 199–200
counter-ransomware
  dashboard 228–35
    openness 228, 230–31
    penalties 228–30
    ransom payments 228, 232–5
    resilience 228, 231–2
  police force cooperation, international and 209–22, 219
  policy, proactive 167–83, 173

INDEX

Coveware 141–2, 154, 155–7, 208
Covid-19 pandemic 197, 231
  ransomware attacks during 2, 165–6, 167, 174, 175, 200
  ransomware compared with 235–6
  Ransomware Task Force and 173
Crack 43
credit card details 17, 53, 54, 59, 61, 67, 68, 70, 73–4, 220
crisis responders 108–11, 140, 153–8, 162, 172, 181, 191, 233
critical national infrastructure 5, 176
Cronos, Operation 209–10, 213–18, 220, 221
cryptocurrencies 105, 206
  Bitcoin *see* Bitcoin
  Conti and 203
  DarkSide and 177, 180
  lifeblood of ransomware ecosystem 234–5
  LockBit and 214, 216
  Locky and 100
  origins 77–80, 223
  Ransomware Task Force and 170
  REvil and 191
  WannaCry and NotPetya and 138
cryptography 70, 75, 140
CryptoLocker 86–92, 87, 110
cyber-hygiene 71, 142, 171, 178, 179, 180, 228, 230, 231
cybersecurity, outsourcing to specialists 10, 105–17, 155–7 *see also individual area of cybersecurity and individual company name*
cyberstalkers 41
cybervandals 41, 43, 132

cyberwar 144–8, 226, 235

D

DarkMarket 69
DarkSide 174–7, 180, 201
Dark Web 65, 66, 79, 86, 178–9
data exfiltration 227, 232, 234
  Conti and 198
  double extortion and 159–63, 165, 211
  KaraKurt/fourth-generation ransomware model focused on 207–8
  LockBit 211, 213, 216
  Planned Parenthood 164
data privacy
  counter-ransomware dashboard and 230, 234
  insurers and *see* insurance
  penalties for breaching data privacy regulation 6–7, 60, 106, 108, 110, 153, 158, 161, 228–30, 234
  Ryuk and 152, 153, 159
  tightening regulations 64, 66
data recovery/restoration 2, 4, 6, 8
  asymmetric encryption technology and 86
  calmness and 156
  Coveware publishes DIY recovery guide 157
  decryption key and *see* decryption key
  demand for data recovery services outstrips capacity of ethical responders 158
  discounts and 156
  free recovery options 139, 140, 154, 233

Kaseya attack and 188–92
No More Ransom initiative and 233–4
outsourcing process to specialists 105–17
patience and 156
resilience to ransomware attacks and 231
reverse-engineering encryption programs 153–4
second-generation ransomware and 153–8
usurious and predatory firms 141–2
data transfer 37
Davis, Major General John 169
decryption process/keys 64, 71, 162, 214, 225, 229, 234
  Conti attack and 199, 200, 208
  cooperation between international police forces and 209
  CryptoLocker and 86–8, 91
  Kaseya and 190–94
  LockBit Black and 4, 6, 7, 8, 216
  Locky and 96, 98, 99, 101–2
  MonsterCloud and 115, 116
  No More Ransom initiative and 139–40
  NotPetya and 134, 137
  private key 72
  ransomware-settlement-as-a-service and 111–13, 141, 143, 151–4, 157, 159–60
  REvil and 177–8, 180–81, 190–94
  Ryuk and 151–4, 157, 159–60
  WannaCry and 124–5, 137
Ded 92
Deep Web 65, 86, 89, 98, 100, 122

DEF CON (hacker convention), Las Vegas 129–30
Dharma 151
digital forensics 152
DiMaggio, Jon 214, 220
DoppelPaymer 160
double extortion 159–63, 165, 211
Draper, John 15

E
e-money 72–6, 79. *See also* cryptocurrencies
eBay 53, 54, 55, 73
Ellis, Jen 169
email
  Covid-19 and 166
  GameOver Zeus and 83, 91
  Ivanov and 53, 54, 55
  Kaseya and 189
  Locky and 96, 97, 98
  No More Ransom initiative and 139
  origins 18, 73
  PayPal and 53
  phishing 83, 89, 152, 166, 199, 202
  Popp and 35
  Ryuk 155
  spam 82, 85–6, 97, 98, 99
  UK's first citizen's arrest of a suspected cybercriminal and 42
  WannaCry and 121
  Zeus and 81–2
emerging markets 225
encryption 64, 66, 223, 227, 231, 232
  AIDS Trojan 26–7, 31, 32
  asymmetric 70–72, 75, 77, 80, 86, 87, 88, 98–9, 101, 102, 110, 113–14, 139, 140

INDEX

Conti 198, 199, 208
DarkSide 176
LockBit 3, 4, 6, 210
NotPetya 131, 133, 134, 137
Revil 177, 190, 193
Ryuk 151, 152, 153, 157, 158, 160
WannaCry 123, 124, 128, 129, 137
Eneo 225
Engressia, Josef (aka Joybubbles) 14
EternalBlue 122–4, 131–2
ethernets 37, 38
Europol 70, 90
Evil Corp 220–21
exit scam 103, 192, 222, 234

F
FBI 20, 102
   American Hospital Association (AHA) and 166
   Blackbyte and 207
   Blount and 180, 181
   Computer Fraud and Abuse Act (1986) and 20
   Conti and 206
   DarkMarket and 69–70
   decline in indiscriminate (spray-and-pray)/increase in 'big game hunting', observes 151
   Hutchins and 130
   Internet Crime Complaint Centre 158
   JabberZeus network and 83–4
   Kaseya/REvil and 191, 192, 193, 195, 196

   'laser-focused' on the ransomware threat 176
   LockBitSupp and 217, 220, 221
   Locky ransomware and 98, 99
   Mitnick and 47
   MonsterCloud and 114, 116
   most wanted list 47, 64, 84, 221
   Operation Flyhook and 54–61
   Operation Tovar and 90, 92–3, 95–6
   Penchukov and 84
   Popp and 31
   REvil 190
Federal Reserve 74, 122
Federal Security Service (FSB) 52
FedEx 132
Feilder, Karl 24
filesharing applications/sites 65
Flyhook, Operation 54–61
Fourth International AIDS Conference, Stockholm (1988) 25
Frankenware 209–10
free-rider problem 101–2
Fulton County 217–18

G
GameOver Zeus 85–6
GandCrab ransomware group 104
GDPR 161
Global Cyber Alliance 168
Global Ghost Team 48
Gorshkov, Vasily 53, 55, 57, 58, 59, 61, 63

H

hackers 10
  AIDS Trojan/first attempt to hijack data for ransom 21, 22–33
  cybercriminal forums, late 1990s/early 2000s and 67–70
  DEF CON (hacker convention), Las Vegas 129–30
  little blue boxes and 14–19, 17
  origins and 12, 13–21, 17
  phreaks 14–18, 45, 46, 210
  ransomware and see ransomware and individual attack name
  script kiddie (hackers with limited coding skills) 44
  social engineering 44, 47, 48, 49, 202
  term 13
  unsettling feeling of being hacked 105
  WarGames and 20
  white-hat 125, 127, 130, 139, 168, 170
ham radio 14–15, 45
'handle' (nickname) 15, 65–6, 91, 92, 103
healthcare sector 174, 182, 200, 224, 225
  American Hospital Association (AHA) 166
  'big game hunting' and 151
  Change Healthcare 103, 234
  Conti and 200
  Irish Health Service, attack on (2020) 2, 177–8
  Locky and 96–7, 100
  Planned Parenthood 163–6
  REvil and 177

US Department of Health and Human Services 166
WannaCry and 124
HelloKitty 208
helpline numbers 95, 109
herders 70
Hive ransomware gang 196, 200, 208, 222
Holdman, Alex 140–41, 154
Hollywood Presbyterian Medical Center, Los Angeles 95–7
Homebrew Computer Club 19
hostage crises/recovery protocols 6, 73, 109, 153, 154, 156, 161
Hunters International 221–2
Hutchins, Marcus 125–31, *128*

I

Indonesia national data centre breach (2024) 225
Institute for Security and Technology (IST) 168–9, 174, 182
insurance 89, 102, 155, 163, 164, 169, 171, 224, 227, 233
  'all risk' property insurance 145, 148
  claims adjusters 108, 109
  NotPetya attack and 138–9, 143–9
  origins of cyberinsurance 106–9, 111, 112, 138–9, 143–9
  Ryuk and 157–9
Intel 188
intellectual property rights 106
intelligence services 52, 60–61, 92, 93, 110, 113, 125. See also *individual intelligence service name*

INDEX

internal divisions, cybergang 102–4
internet
   Dark Web 65, 66, 79, 86, 178–9
   Deep Web 65, 86, 89, 98, 100, 122
   InterNet protocol 39–41, 230
   Internet Provider (IP) 63
   Onion Router (TOR) protocol 65–6, 69, 80, 89, 98, 113
   origins 18, 20, 23–4, 25, 35–6, 39–41, 48
   VPN (virtual private network) and *see* VPN (virtual private network)
Interpol 70, 98
Interview, The 121
Invita 55–7
Iran 70
Irish Health Service, attack on (2020) 2, 177–8
IT security companies 127, 130, 137, 139, 140, 142–4, 157, 185, 189–90, 222. See also *individual company name*
IT staff/specialists 3, 4, 39, 41, 49, 51, 52, 54, 95, 97, 100, 105, 108, 109, 110, 111, 112, 115, 125
Ivanov, Alexey 51–61, 63

J
JabberZeus 82, 83
JANET (Joint Academic Network, UK) 39–41
JBS S.A 178, 185, 194–6
Jobs, Steve 15–19, 17, 21
Joint Ransomware Task Force (JRTF) 182

K
KaraKurt 196, 207–8
Kaseya supply chain attack 185–95, *187*
Khoroshev, Dmitry Yuryevich 218–20, *219*
Kim Jong-Il 119, *120*
Kim Jong-Un 121, 124
K.O., patient 164–5
Krebs, Brian 83, 205
Kronos 127, 130

L
Lake City Police Department, Florida 111
law
   class action lawsuits 108, 110, 164
   enforcement *see* police *and individual agency name*
   firms 21, 46, 109, 110, 153, 164, 165, 168
   international law 58, 139, 168, 182, 194–5, 223
   privacy lawyers 109, 153, 168
Lazarus Group 121–4, 130–31
leo-stone 131, 135, 137
little blue boxes 14–19, *17*
Lloyd's of London 147, 148
LockBit 226, 234
   Royal Mail attack 2–8, *5*, 210
   StealBit and 211
   takedown of 209–22, 234
   3.0 leak site 5–8, *5*, 216
LockBitSupp 4–5, 210–22, *219*
lockscreens 89, 113, 124, 133, 139, 160
Locky ransomware 96–100, 103
lucky12345 91

M

M.E.Doc 132
Maersk 132–3, 145
MalwareTech 127
Managed Service Provider (MSP) 185, 186, 188–91
Mango 204, 208
Matveev, Mikhail 221
Maze 160–61
McDonald's 45
Medicare in-hospital mortality rates during ransomware attacks 2
Merck 132, 145, 146, 147, 148
Methodist Hospital, Kentucky 96
Microsoft 85, 169, 188
  operating code 122–3, 124
  VPN (virtual private network) 64
  Windows 86
Military College 119
Ministerio de Hacienda 197–8
MIT 13, 123n
Mitnick, Kevin 43–8, 63
Mitnick Security Consulting 48
modems 37, 38
Mondelez 132, 145, 146, 147, 148
money mules 70, 81–4, 93
MonsterCloud 114–16
Mr Kykypyky 92
Muffett, Alec 43, 43n
Mularski, Keith 69
multi-factor authentication 159

N

Nakamoto, Satoshi 76
naming and shaming 154, 160, 209
Napster 65
National Crime Agency (NCA), UK 209–10, 215, 218, 219, 223

National Health Service (NHS), UK 124, 129, 165
negotiators, professional ransom 6, 109, 110, 155, 156, 158, 168
Neuberger, Anne 182, 223–4
neurodiversity 10, 13, 21
No More Ransom initiative (2016) 139–40, 142, 154, 233
Noriega, General 30
North Korea 70, 119–31, 120
notchy 103
NotPetya 131–4, 137, 138, 144–8, 175, 185, 226
NTC Vulkan 226

O

Odessa, CarderPlanet convention in (2001) 68
O_neday 193, 195
Onion Router (TOR) protocol 65–6, 69, 80, 89, 98, 113
openness, security and 229, 230–31
organised crime 9, 18, 51, 57, 59, 119, 193, 223

P

Pacific Bell 45
Panama, shell companies in 24–5, 30–31
passwords 159, 230
  Colonial Pipeline and 174, 178, 185
  Deep Web and 65
  Hutchins and 126
  Ivanov and 53, 57–9
  Kaseya and 186, 230
  NotPetya and 131–2
  security of 42–4, 47
PayPal 53–4, 74

INDEX

PC *Business World* 26, 28
PC Cyborg Corporation 24–5, 27, 30
peer-to-peer digital payments 75
pen-and-paper mode 97, 111, 154, 232
Penchukov, Vyacheslav 84, 91, 93
penetration testers 202
Pentagon 18, 38–9, 188
Petya 131–2
Philips, Michael 169
phishing and spear-phishing techniques 81, 166
   Conti and 199, 202
   GameOver Zeus and 82, 89
   Mitnick and 48
   Ryuk and 152
   WannaCry and 123, 126
Phobos 151
phreaks 14–18, 45, 46, 210
Pinhasi, Zohar 116
Pistole, John 116
Planned Parenthood 163–5
police 11, 18, 24, 30, 42, 46, 56, 58, 73, 84–6, 89, 95, 126–7, 183, 191, 235
   ContiLeaks and 206, 208, 209
   cooperation between international forces 209
   hackers and 63, 66, 68–9
   LockBitSupp 212, 214–16
   MonsterCloud 110–17
Polyanin, Yevgeniy 195
Pompon, Ray 56–7
Popp, Jr, Joseph L. 21, 23–33, 35, 63
pornography 41
Poulsen, Kevin 68
prepaid chip-cards 74

Presidential Executive order on improving cybersecurity (2022) 176
privacy lawyers 109, 153, 168
private key 72, 77, 78, 99, 113
Progressive Computing 185, 191
proof of deletion 161, 162
property rights 49, 106
Protocol Wars 40–41, 230
Proven Data Recovery 111
public key 72, 77, 79
Putin, Vladimir 176, 179, 182–3, 196, 203

R
RadioShack 46
ransoms
   AIDS Trojan (world's first attempt to hijack data for ransom) 21, 22–33
   ALPHV and 103–4
   bans on paying 167, 172–3, 181, 227–8, 233
   Change Healthcare and 234
   closing a deal, best way to 154
   Conti and 198, 201
   counter-ransomware dashboard and 228, 232–5
   Coveware facilitates payments 141–2, 154–5
   CryptoLocker and 86–8
   DarkSide and 175, 176, 178, 180, 181
   'discounts' on ransom payments 113, 141, 154, 155, 156, 234
   double extortion tactic and 161–3
   extortive crime, encourages 114

freezing 170
inflation 137–8, 154–5, 158
insurers *see* insurance
Kaseya and 192
Lockbit and 6–8, 211, 213, 214, 221, 222
Locky and 96–100
median payment 2
MonsterCloud and 114
negotiators, professional 6, 109, 110, 155, 156, 158, 168
No More Ransom initiative (2016) 139–40, 142, 154, 233
normalising negotiations and payments 9, 111, 134
notes 73, 86, 88, 123, 139, 155, 175
NotPetya and 133, 134
paying 4, 111–17, 137–40, 142, 161, 162, 163, 166, 170–72, 180, 191, 195, 211, 227, 230–35
payments database 154
Planned Parenthood and 163
police snatch from criminals' crypto accounts 209
prices 7, 86, 88, 96, 111, 112, 113, 124, 138, 141, 147, 151, 153, 154–9, 190, 198, 199, 212
refusing to pay 4, 7–8, 76, 140, 152, 161, 165, 172, 190, 198
reporting of 142, 166, 170–71, 172, 178, 191, 233, 235
Revil and 161, 190, 191, 194, 195
Ryuk and 151, 152–4
US payments of (2021–24) 224
WannaCry and 123, 124, 125

RansomHub 222
ransomwar 131, 137, 138, 144, 146, 229
ransomware
-as-a-service 98–104, 111, 112, 177, 213
'clean finish' to ransomware incident 161–2
cost of stopping, prohibitive 235–6
cost to global economy 2
counter-ransomware *see* counter-ransomware
Covid-19 and *see* Covid-19 pandemic
development/origins of 8–9, 11–12, 13–61
fades from public consciousness and political agenda 224
first attempt to use malware to extract a ransom (1989) 9, 21, 23–33, 35
first-generation 158–9
fourth-generation 207–8
Frankenware 209–10
frequency of attacks 1–2, 113, 233
Joint Ransomware Task Force (JRTF) *see* Joint Ransomware Task Force (JRTF) 182
law enforcement and *see* police *and individual agency name*
losses from attacks 8, 90, 107–8, 110, 135, 138, 144–9, 151, 165, 225–6
national security, recognised as serious threat to 9, 135, 167–83, 196, 223–4, 227
payment mills 113

INDEX

ransom payments *see* ransom payments
Ransomware Task Force *see* Ransomware Task Force
rise of since 2013 11, 12, 63, 81–93, 110
second-generation 151–2, 154–6, 158–9, 162
-settlement-as-a-service 105–117
supply chain attacks 185–95, *187*
third-generation 160–66
See also individual attack, malware and victim name
Ransomware Task Force 11, 168–73, *173*
   Deterrence group 169–71
   Prepare working group 169, 171
   Response group 169, 171–2
   report 172–3, 173–4, 182
re-extortion 162
Reiner, Phil 168
Reshaev 201, 205
resilience 85, 134, 159, 180, 205, 228, 230, 231–3, 235–6
restoring encrypted data. *See* date recovery
reverse-engineering 127, 139, 202
REvil 104, 161, 177–9, 186–96, *187*, 208, 226
Rosneft 132
Rosner, Roland 36–7, 39–41
Royal Mail 2–8, 5, 210
Russia 64, 70, 201
   Biden meeting with Putin, Geneva 182–3
   Conti and 201–8, 212
   DarkSide and 176–7
   Foreign Intelligence Service (SVR) 188

government, ransomware and 58, 92, 146, 176–8, 182–3, 206, 226
LockBit and 4, 219–21
Locky and 100
Microsoft and 123
Military Intelligence Services (GRU) 52
NotPetya and 132, 145–7
Operation Flyhook and 51–61
Operation Tovar and 90–93
ransomwar and 229
REvil and 177–9, 186, 193–6
Royal Mail and 5
SolarWinds and 188, 193–6
Ukraine War 93, 196, 203–4, 206
WannaCry and 131
Zeus and 81, 83, 90
See also individual ransomware attack and victim name
Rutherford Laboratories 36–7, 39
Ryuk 151–9, 201

S

Saint-Gobain 132
SamSam 111, 151
scam websites 53
scareware 102
Scotland Yard Computer Crime Unit 30, 31, 42
secrecy around data breaches 110–11
security consulting 43, 48, 53, 54
Serper, Amit 133
Shadow Brokers 122
SickKids hospital, Toronto 214
Siegel, Bill 140–41, 154, 208
Skippy 204
Slavik 81, 83, 85, 92

Smeets, Max 234
Smith, Adam 77
social engineering 44, 47, 48, 49, 202
software
   antivirus 71, 88, 99, 101, 152, 201
   -as-a-service 98–104
   updates 1, 100, 104, 122–3, 131, 132, 186, 187, 187, 188, 189, 217, 230
SolarWinds 188
SONY 121
South African National Health Laboratory Services 225
spray-and-pray campaigns 97, 151, 233
Stanford University 123*n*
   Linear Accelerator Center 15
StealBit 211
Stifel, Megan 168
subbsta 54–6
supply chain attacks 185–95, 187
Synnovis 165

T
Tank 84
tech.net.ru 54–5, 57–9
Telecom Namibia 225
Telefonica 124
telephone systems 10, 13–18, 25, 37, 45, 47, 124, 189
Temp Special 92
Tovar, Operation 90–92
Trickbot 202, 208
trust paradox 234

U
UK
   Computer Misuse Act (1990) 33
   critical national infrastructure 5, 124, 129, 165
   internet development in 38–41
   law enforcement and ransomware attacks in 27, 28, 30–33, 42, 209–10, 215, 218, 219, 223
   National Cyber Security Centre 129
   See also individual ransomware attack and victim name
Ukraine 69, 84, 92, 100, 131–2, 145, 196, 216
   Russian War in (2014–) 196, 203–4, 206
United Nations Security Council 166
UnitedHealth Group 103
University of Automation 119–20
University of California 46
Unknown (aka UNKN) 193
URLs 40
USA
   Biden-Harris administration 168, 176, 182, 224
   Computer Fraud and Abuse Act (1986) 20
   Cybersecurity and Infrastructure Security Agency (CISA) 144, 181, 188
   cybersecurity policy, governmental 20, 27–8, 30, 55, 59–61, 93, 114, 117, 121, 144, 153, 166–83, 188, 194–6, 216–20, 224, 226, 229, 235
   Department of Energy 188

Department of Health and
  Human Services 166
Department of Justice 55, 60, 61,
  146, 180, 182, 216, 219, 220
  FBI *see* FBI
  Insurance Services Office 107–8
  Intelligence Community 65–6
  military 64, 70, 194
  National Security Agency (NSA)
    122
  Ransomware Task Force *see*
    Ransomware Task Force
  Treasury 188
  Trump administration, first
    (2017–2021) 168
  White House 134, 170, 174, 176,
    178, 181, 182
*See also individual ransomware
attack and victim name*

V

Vasinskyi, Yaroslav 195
virtual discussion groups 18
virus, computer
  antivirus software 71, 88, 99,
    101, 152, 201
  GameOver Zeus botnet 91
  Locky 97, 98
  NotPetya 131
  term 24, 29, 31
  'vaccinating' computers against
    71
  Young and Yung's doomsday
    scenario 70–73

Virus Bulletin 31
VPN (virtual private network)
  64–5

W

Walden, Kemba 169
'wall of shame' intimidation tactic
  160–61
WannaCry ransomware attack
  (2017) 121–5, 127–32, 137, 138,
  144, 175, 185, 226
war clause 145–8
WarGames 20
Washington Post 83, 192
whistle-blowers 171, 209
Witte, Alla (Klimova) 208
World Health Organization
  (WHO) 23, 26, 29–30, 166
World Wide Web 37, 41
Wosar, Fabian 141
Wozniak, Steve 15–19, 17, 21

Y

Yanukovych, Viktor 84
Young, Adam 70–76; *Malicious
  Cryptography – Exposing
  Cryptovirology* 75–6
Yung, Moti 70–76; *Malicious
  Cryptography – Exposing
  Cryptovirology* 75–6

Z

Zeus Trojan 81–6, 88–91, 127, 220
Zurich Insurance Group 146